Cannon County, Tennessee
MARRIAGES
1838-1873

BY

BYRON & BARBARA SISTLER

Janaway Publishing, Inc.
Santa Maria, California

Originally Published:
Nashville, Tennessee
1985

Reprinted by

Janaway Publishing, Inc.
732 Kelsey Ct.
Santa Maria, California 93454
(805) 925-1038
www.JanawayGenealogy.com

2006, 2012

ISBN: 978-1-59641-044-2

Made in the United States of America

CANNON COUNTY, TN MARRIAGES

1838-1873

Where two dates appear on an entry, the first one is the date license was issued, the second (in parentheses) the date marriage was solemnized. If only one date, it can mean (1) the date of execution was the same as the date of license issuance, or (2) execution of the marriage was not reported to the courthouse, or (3) the clerk failed to note in the marriage book that the license was returned.

Ordinarily, if there was any evidence the license was not returned we would so indicate in the entry. Sometimes the book would reveal definitely that a certain marriage did not take place, and in such instances we would make note of that in our entry.

We transcribed these marriage records directly from a microfilmed copy of the original county marriage books, so error, where it occurs, will usually be ours. However, it should be remembered that entries in the books themselves were copied from the licenses by clerks, and it is obvious from examining the pages that many of them were not prepared with great care. Sometimes, for example, the date of execution will appear in the book as a date prior to license issuance. In such cases, as well as where we had to guess in deciphering the handwriting, a question mark or "sic" is inserted on the entry.

Byron Sistler
Barbara Sistler
Nashville, Tennessee
June 1985

-----, E. J. TO JOSEPH STACY
ACRES, MEREDITH TO ELIZABETH POLLETT 12-25-1841
ADAMS, ALEXANDER TO MISS MARTHA TURNER 12-21-1867
ADAMS, JOHN TO MISS ANN ELIZA DANIEL 10-16-1841 (10-18-1841)
ADAMS, MARY TO JOSEPH HANCOCK
ADAMS, NANCY TO A. F. JAMES
ADAMS, PETER TO MISS RACHEL ESTES 12-30-1868 (12-31-1868)
ADAMS, TEMPY TO JAMES HANCOCK
ADAMS, W. P. TO SARAH SMITH 7-8-1873 (7-9-1873)
ADAMS, WM. J. TO MISS E. N. SMITH 3-2-1854
ADAMSON, ALSE TO SAMUEL SNOW
ADAMSON, MALISSA TO S. E. H. OWEN
ADAMSON, NANCY M. TO LEONARD WALKER
ADAMSON, PRESLEY A. TO MISS NANCY C. HALE 1-25-1867 (1-31-1867)
ADAMSON, PRESTLY L. TO MISS MARY FRANCES WARREN 7-28-1845 (7-29-1845)
ADCOCK, AMERICA ANN TO WM. B. MCCABE
ADCOCK, KATHARINE TO ADAM PARKER
ADCOCK, LEONARD TO MISS SARAH WOOD 10-30-1841
ADONIS, PEGGEY G. TO SIMON BARRETT
AKEN, B. H. TO MISS MAY FLETCHER 11-13-1847 (11-14-1847)
AKERS, N. J. TO JACOB MOORE
AKERS, T. P. TO R. C. LORANCE
ALDEN, MANERVA ANN TO WILLIAM CUMMINGS
ALDRIDGE, MILLIA TO JOHN A. THOMAS
ALEXANDER, A. O. TO MISS MARTHA FRANCES SAND? 10-5-1847
ALEXANDER, ABNER D. TO NANCY SAULS 5-25-1842
ALEXANDER, B. C. TO N. E. DEVENPORT 10-22-1872
ALEXANDER, BENJAMIN T. TO MISS MARY ISABELLA BARKLEY 9-12-1851 (9-18-1851)
ALEXANDER, E. TO T. M. KEEL
ALEXANDER, ELISABETH TO THOMAS J. MEARS
ALEXANDER, GEO. TO N. C. MCADOO 12-31-1872
ALEXANDER, HELAN TO ROBERT D. MOORE
ALEXANDER, J. G. TO MISS CAROLINE WARD 12-21-1852 (12-30-1852)
ALEXANDER, J. M. TO MISS BETTIE JANE TASSEY 8-12-1868 (8-13-1868)
ALEXANDER, JAMES A. TO MISS ANLIZA HAY 1-1-1860 (1-3-1860)
ALEXANDER, JOHN D. TO MISS MARGARET S. DAVENPORT 8-23-1870 (8-25-1870)
ALEXANDER, JOHN MC. TO MISS MARY N. BRAGG 7-15-1867 (7-16-1867)
ALEXANDER, JOHN TO MISS C. YOUNG 12-28-1870 (12-29-1871?)
ALEXANDER, M. P. TO JOHN TENPENNY
ALEXANDER, M. P. TO JOHN TURNHEN?
ALEXANDER, MARGARETT A. TO JOHN K. WITHERSPOON
ALEXANDER, MARTHA L. TO THOS. O. WOOD
ALEXANDER, MARY A. TO C. C. READY
ALEXANDER, MARY ADALINE TO JOHN W. CRANE
ALEXANDER, N. J. T. TO DANIEL TENPENNY
ALEXANDER, NANCY TO DANIEL BRYSON
ALEXANDER, NANCY TO JOHN A. GEORGE
ALEXANDER, NEOMI TO JOHN A. TRAVIS
ALEXANDER, OSIN TO MARIAN FISHER 10-4-1864 (10-7-1864)
ALEXANDER, RACHEL TO MORGAN BARKLEY
ALEXANDER, ROXANNA TO JOHN MCBROOM
ALEXANDER, SARAH E. TO STEPHEN COOK
ALEXANDER, SARAH JANE TO JAMES C. CRIESON
ALEXANDER, W. T. TO EMLEY T. CONLEY 2-1-1872
ALFORD, ELIZABETH TO JAMES ROGERS
ALFORD, JOHN TO DRUCILLA SULLIVAN 3-6-1865
ALFORD, MALINDA TO ANDERSON MORGAN
ALFORD, MARY TO W. D. MOSS
ALFORD, WM. C. TO MISS SARAH ANN DUNCAN 4-30-1855 (5-16-1855)

ALLEN, BENJAMIN F. TO MISS YOUFFEY YOUNG 4-13-1841
ALLEN, G. R. TO M. H. LOWRANCE 2-13-1873
ALLEN, JAMES L. TO SARAH E. CARRICK 11-16-1865
ALLEN, JAMES TO EMELINE SMITH 12-13-1872
ALLEN, JOHN M. TO A. T. HANCOCK 2-14-1855 (NO RETURN)
ALLEN, NANCY V. TO TILFORD M. YONG
ALLEN, REBECA TO ROBERT W. CLENDENNEN
ALLEN, SAMUEL B. TO MISS MANERVA ANN WEST 12-10-1841
ALLEN, SAMUEL TO MISS MARY ANN BURCH 9-2-1869
ALLISON, H. E. TO A. BARRETT
ALLMON, E. H. TO P. T. MCGILL 7-13-1864
ALMON, ANN TO ALEXANDER DUKE
ALMON, SARAH E. TO TAYLOR THOMPSON
AMUS, SARAH TO ROBT. GANN
ANDERSON, ASA TO MARY ANN ELLIS 12-30-1841
ANDERSON, ELIGAH TO MISS ELIZABETH TAYLOR 4-6-1841
ANDERSON, J. G. TO MISS MARTHA MCGILL 8-22-1866 (8-26-1866)
ANDERSON, J. M. TO N. C. GOOD 8-14-1872 (NO RETURN)
ANDERSON, JAMES TO ANN ELIZA ASHFORD 12-22-1842
ANDERSON, JANE TO GEORGE L. TAYLOR
ANDERSON, JOHN TO MISS JERUSHA HARGUS 7-13-1843 (7-14-1843)
ANDERSON, LUCINDA TO W. S. ENSEY
ANDERSON, MARTHA TO LENY PEALER
ANDERSON, MARY TO KING PEALER
ANDERSON, STEPHEN A. TO NANCY A. EVANS 8-13-1863 (NO RETURN)
ANDERSON, WILLIAM W. TO MISS MARTHA L. TAYLOR 4-6-1867 (4-7-1867)
ANDREW, MARY F TO S. H. A. MCKNIGHT
ANDREWS, ELEANOR F. TO G. D. A. MCKNIGHT
ANDREWS, ELIZABETH TO G. O. SMITH
ANDREWS, J. M. TO MISS SARAH J. MCKNIGHT 10-31-1846 (11-24-1846)
ANGLES, MILISA JANE TO JESSE SISSOM
ARMSTRONG, ALLEN TO ETTA WRIGHT 8-3-1870 (NO RETURN)
ARMSTRONG, JOHN TO MISS CAROLINE RAMSEY 12-5-1868 (12-6-1868)
ARMSTRONG, JOHN TO MISS MAHALY CAMPBELL 9-3-1857 (8?-3-1857)
ARMSTRONG, MAHALA TO THOMAS VANCE
ARMSTRONG, MISS N. TO S. F. HAYS
ARMSTRONG, PERNINA S. TO THOMAS CAMPBELL
ARMSTRONG, RICHARD TO ELIZABETH DENNIS 6-15-1844 (6-25-1844)
ARNET, JAMES TO SARAH HENDRIX 3-20-1865 (NO RETURN)
ARNETT, JAS. E. TO IZZAN GRIZZELL 9-11-1860 (NO RETURN)
ARNETT, PINKNEY TO MARTHA VAUGHN 6-1-1872 (6-2-1872)
ARNOLD, AMERICA TO MISS ISSABELLA HEROLD 1-12-1849 (1-13-1849)
ARNOLD, ELIZABETH TO ROBERT BEECHBOARD
ARNOLD, HARVY TO MISS M. E. BUSH 7-3-1869 (7-4-1869)
ARNOLD, HOWEY? TO MISS JENETTA HERALD 12-26-1851 (12-28-1851)
ARNOLD, MARIAH TO WM. VASSER
ARNOLD, N. C. TO S. A. COTHREN 9-15-1860 (NO RETURN)
ARNOLD, W. J. TO MISS P. J. TOLBERT 9-15-1870 (9-18-1870)
ARNOLD, WILLIAM JEFFERSON TO MISS MARIAH ELVINA SAGELY 12-25-1847
ARNOLD, WILLIAM TO MISS LUCINDA CANTRELL 8-30-1856
ARRINGTON, F. M. TO MISS MARTHA BYNUM 2-5-1866 (2-6-1866)
ARVIN, WILLIAM TO MARTHA MULLINS 8-3-1855 (8-10-1855)
ASE, SARAH ANN TO JAMES KNIGHT
ASHFORD, ANN ELIZA TO JAMES ANDERSON
ASHFORD, ANTALIZA TO WALTER MATHEWS
ASHFORD, BAZEL TO MISS JANE RIGSBY 9-17-1858 (9-27-1858)
ASHFORD, COMPTON TO MISS MARGARETT E. MCPHEARSON 11-24-1841 (11-25-1841)
ASHFORD, ELIZABETH TO RUSSEL GANN
ASHFORD, GEORGE TO MISS SARAH P. HAMMONS 12-31-1867
ASHFORD, GEORGE TO NANCY MULLENS 2-3-1852

ASHFORD, MALLISSA TO RICHARD MELTON
ASHFORD, MARY TO ALEXANDER YOUNG
ASHFORD, NANCY JANE TO CREED W. HALE
ASHFORD, NANCY TO JOSEPH MULLENS
ASHFORD, POLK TO SARAH COLLINS 10-19-1865 (10-20-1865)
ASHFORD, POLLY TO ELI LEDBETTER
ASHFORD, RICHARD TO MISS RUTHY MILLIGAN 5-7-1859 (NO RETURN)
ASHLEY, JOHN R. TO MISS CLARISSA DUNCAN 8-11-1849 (8-16-1849)
ASHLEY, MARY TO BENJAMIN WEBBER
ASHLY, WILLIAM C. TO MISS MARY M. SPRY 3-9-1850
ASHWORTH, THOMAS C. TO JANE SMITH 11-4-1842
ATCHLEY, MARGARET E. TO HOUSTON BARRETT
ATCHLEY, NANNIE? A. TO R. F. EASON
AUSMENT, MARY TO WILLIAM P. BURCH
AUSTIN, J. W. TO MISS M. J. BARRETT 7-24-1858 (NO RETURN)
AUSTON, ELISABETH TO NATHAN EARLS
AUSTON, SARAH TO WM. M. PHINS
BABBETT, S. F. TO W. G. O. GARIS
BABBITT, S. F. TO W. G. D. GARIS
BABET, S. F. TO WILLIAM G. D. GARRIS
BAILEY, ANDREW J. TO MISS LAURA ANN SULLIVAN 4-21-1851 (NO RETURN)
BAILEY, DILLARD TO RUTH A. STONE 1-13-1872 (1-14-1872)
BAILEY, JACOB TO MISS CALAFORNIA MARKUM 8-25-1870 (8-24?-1870)
BAILEY, JOSEPH A. TO MISS SALLIE L. EVANS 8-31-1870
BAILEY, JOSEPH TO MISS SALLIE PRESTON 11-25-1867 (12-8-1867)
BAILEY, JOSEPHINE TO WARREN CUMMINS
BAILEY, L. A. TO A. R. HIPP
BAILEY, M. J. TO W. H. TURNER
BAILEY, MALISSA TO ABRAHAM OWEN
BAILEY, MANERVA TO SAMUEL C. SULLIVAN
BAILEY, MARTHA E. TO J. D. CAMPBELL
BAILEY, MARY J. TO A. J. CONLEY
BAILEY, R. A. TO ELIAS R. MELTON
BAILEY, ROBERT TO MISS ISSABELLA STONE 7-18-1843 (7-20-1843)
BAILEY, ROBERT TO MISS RHODA RAINS 12-14-1849 (12-19-1849)
BAILEY, ROBERT TO MISS T. P. CUMINGS 12-8-1855 (12-9-1855)
BAILEY, SARAH N. TO ALFRED SHIRLEY
BAILEY, WILLIAM M. TO MISS ELIZABETH NEELY 3-22-1850 (EXECUTED--NO DATE)
BAILEY, WM. TO MISS MARTHA E. MELTON 9-30-1859 (NO RETURN)
BAILY, BETTIE TO BENJ. DAVIS
BAILY, HUGH L. TO PARASADE CUMMINGS 10-19-1863 (NO RETURN)
BAILY, JOHN N. TO MARY STONE 5-23-1838 (6-3-1838)
BAILY, MARGARETT E. TO JOHN W. SHIRLY
BAILY, MARY A. TO B. F. WOOD
BAILY, NANCY TO ELIJAH MEARS
BAILY, ROBERT TO MISS CAROLINE NEELY 6-5-1857 (6-7-1857)
BAILY, VINSON TO PARALEE CAMPBELL 10-19-1872 (10-20-1872)
BAIN, FRANCES ANN TO W. L. COVINGTON
BAINE, ISAIAH TO MISS REBECCA STANTON 1-16-1844 (1-18-1844)
BAIRD, HENRY TO MARY CLARK 2-22-1867
BAIRD, J. A. TO MISS FRANCES ANN WILEY 8-30-1844 (9-1-1844)
BAIRD, MARY TO N. T. WHEELER
BAKER, JOHN W. TO SARAH PRIOR? 11-11-1851 (11-13-1851)
BALEY, JAMES TO CENNINE FERRELL 10-31-1872
BALEY, MARTHA A. TO JAMES SEALS
BALEY, S. F. TO N. J. LENING
BALTIMORE, JOSEPH TO MISS JANE SIMPSON 12-19-1853 (12-20-1853)
BALTIMORE, P. J. TO MISS R. S. MCCULLER 9-28-1870 (9-29-1870)
BALTIMORE, PHILIP J. TO MISS MARY ELIZABETH SIMPSON 11-7-1848)
BALY, JOHN S. TO MISS MELVINA J. MARCUM 11-25-1859 (NO RETURN)

BALY, MARTHA H. TO P. P. MAXEY
BALY, MARY TO T. B. SMITH
BALY, RUTHA A. TO ELYSIS R. MELTON
BANK, LUCY P. TO JOSHUA C. SMITHSON
BANKS, ARRENEA TO JOHN PARKER
BANKS, DENNIS TO MISS MARANDA M. HAYS 8-11-1856 (8-12-1856)
BANKS, ELIZABETH TO JESSEE STROUD
BANKS, LETHIE J. TO SAMUL SPANGLER
BANKSTON, JAMES M. TO MISS JULIAN J. WISER 6-15-1866 (6-17-1866)
BANKSTON, JOHN TO MISS MARGARETT MOTEN 3-26-1853 (3-27-1853)
BARETT, ABRAHAM TO MISS MARTHA E. ELKINS 3-19-1853 (3-20-1853)
BARETT, MARTHA TO W. A. WILLSON
BARHAM, JOHN TO MARY HIET 12-7-1842 (12-13-1842)
BARKER, DONALSON TO MISS MARY NEELEY 2-27-1866 (3-1-1866)
BARKLEY, FRANKLIN TO AIMEY MCKNIGHT 8-21-1865 (8-26-1865)
BARKLEY, MARY ISABELLA TO BENJAMIN T. ALEXANDER
BARKLEY, MORGAN TO RACHEL ALEXANDER 8-21-1865 (NO RETURN)
BARKLEY, NANCY ANN TO ALEXANDER WARREN
BARNES, ALEX TO TENNIE TRIBBABLE 6-14-1873 (6-15-1873)
BARNES, DOSIA TO FRANK RUSHING
BARNES, HARRETT TO JAMES SULLENS
BARNES, HENRY TO EMILY RUSHING 8-15-1868 (8-18-1868)
BARNES, J. A. TO S. BURGER 11-27-1855 (NO RETURN)
BARNES, JESSEE TO SUSAN J. BURGNER 11-27-1855
BARNES, LUTISIA TO ZEKE MCFERRIN
BARNES, MARY J. TO WILSON TODD
BARRATT, A. B. TO CATHARINE MORGAN 9-15-1860 (NO RETURN)
BARRATT, ELI B. TO MISS ISABELLA MOON 9-23-1844
BARRATT, J. W. TO PERLINE ESCUE 1-11-1873 (1-12-1873)
BARRATT, JESSE TO MISS NANCY C. EVANS 11-22-1845 (11-27-1845)
BARRATT, MARTHA J. TO JOSEPH O. WILLIAMS
BARRATT, MARY J. TO A. W. CATES
BARRATT, POLLY TO GREENBERRY SMITH
BARRATT, RICHARD TO ELIZABETH PHILIPS 12-18-1841 (12-19-1841)
BARRATT, SARAH TO FRANCIS FANN
BARRATT, WARD JR. TO MISS ELIZABETH PRESTON 9-18-1844
BARRET, B. F. TO M. E. WELCH 10-4-1865 (4-11-1865)
BARRET, JAMES P. TO REBECCA ANN KENSER 5-5-1865 (5-7-1865)
BARRETT, A. B. TO SALLIE B. HIPP 7-17-1872 (NO RETURN)
BARRETT, A. TO D. E. MANES
BARRETT, A. TO MISS H. E. ALLISON 12-5-1867 (12-9-1867)
BARRETT, ANNIS TO WILLIAM MORGAN
BARRETT, BABE TO ED MCNKNIGHT
BARRETT, CHARITY M. TO WILLIAM C. HIBDON
BARRETT, E. C. TO G. W. P. MITCHEL
BARRETT, ELENDER TO WILLIAM MOODY
BARRETT, ELI B. TO MARY ANN GANNON 9-7-1872
BARRETT, ELIZA TENNESSEE GOWEN TO WILLIAM A. SMITH
BARRETT, ELIZABETH TO BENNETT WHEELING
BARRETT, ELIZABETH TO WILLIS F. COUCH
BARRETT, FRANCES L. TO ROBERT VINSON
BARRETT, HAMES TO MISS MARGARETT JONSEN 12-22-1855 (12-23-1855)
BARRETT, HOUSTON TO MARGARET E. ATCHLEY 10-3-1865 (10-8-1865)
BARRETT, J. M. TO E. L. BOGLE 2-3-1873 (2-4-1873)
BARRETT, J. M. TO MISS ELVIRA BLAIRE 12-2-1867 (12-5-1867)
BARRETT, J. M. TO MISS SARAH BERRYHILL 4-12-1871
BARRETT, J. W. TO MISS MARY VALENTINE 9-20-1869
BARRETT, JAMES P. TO MISS NANCY P. JONES 9-18-1866
BARRETT, JAMES TO MARGARETT LANG 3-1-1858
BARRETT, JOHN TO JANE SAPP 8-10-1839 (8-11-1839)

BARRETT, JOHN W. TO MISS MANERVA LANCE 3-14-1850
BARRETT, JOHN W. TO SARAH VINSON 2-20-1849
BARRETT, JOSEPH TO MISS NANCY A. WARD 12-23-1852
BARRETT, LEVI TO MARY C. JACO 7-12-1872 (7-14-1872)
BARRETT, M. J. TO J. W. AUSTIN
BARRETT, M. TO T. P. LEMAY
BARRETT, MARGARET AN TO R. L. BARRETT
BARRETT, MARY TO N. HOLLANDSWORTH
BARRETT, NATHAN TO MISS MARY VINSON 3-4-1851
BARRETT, R. L. TO MARGARET AN BARRETT 11-15-1865 (11-16-1865)
BARRETT, RUTHA TO TELFORD MILES
BARRETT, S. A. TO M. G. HENDERSON
BARRETT, SIMON TO MISS PEGGEY G. ADONIS 5-22-1853
BARRETT, THOS. TO MARY HOLLANDSWORTH 6-25-1872 (6-26-1872)
BARRETT, TISBY A. TO JOHN L. GUNTER
BARRETT, WARD JR. TO MISS JOICE V. HAMMONDS 11-9-1848
BARRETT, WILLIAM C. TO MISS FRANCES DENTON 12-23-1867 (12-24-1867)
BARRETT, WILLIAM TO MISS PARLIE FITCH 1-4-1849
BARRETT, WM. TO SUSAN HOLLANDSWORTH 5-23-1872 (5-24-1872)
BARRUTT, HENRY TO SARAH FUSTON 1-1-1864 (1-3-1864)
BARRY, JOHN TO MISS MATILDA B. COWEN 9-24-1850 (NO RETURN)
BARRY, MATILDA B. TO T. G. SULLIVAN
BARTHEN?, SARAH TO G. W. WILLSON
BARTON, ALF TO FLORENCE MOORE 3-13-1873
BARTON, DANIEL TO RACHEL MCBROOM 12-24-1866 (3-4-1867)
BARTON, EDMUND TO NANCY ANN STONE 1-9-1840
BARTON, EZEKIEL TO MISS LAURA FERRELL 6-7-1871 (NO RETURN)
BARTON, JAMES S. TO MISS BETTIE K. FARR 12-6-1855
BARTON, JANE TO JOHN TENPENNY
BARTON, MARY TO WESLEY TAYLOR
BARTON, ROBERT TO MARGARET DANIEL 12-14-1867 (12-15-1867)
BARTON, SOPHA TO SANDY MILTON
BARTON, WILLIAM JR. TO SARAH J. MCBROOM 11-1-1838
BASHAM, ELIZABETH TO JAMES N. GANN
BASHAM, JAMES M. TO MARY A. STAFFORD 6-30-1859 (NO RETURN)
BASHAM, WM. TO MISS H. D. OWEN 8-15-1858
BASHHAM, WILLIAM TO MISS M. E. PRATOR 6-24-1858 (HANDED IN WITHOUT RETURN)
BASSHAM, ALVIS TO S. A. WILSON 12-31-1873
BASSHAM, M. E. TO J. W. COUCH
BASSHAM, T. G. TO MISS M. E. GAITHER 11-18-1870 (NO RETURN)
BATES, ABAGAIL TO FRANCIS M. SEAWELL
BATES, ALVIN TO MISS MARRY C. ST. JOHNS 8-14-1854
BATES, LOU TO JOHN L. SHACKLETT
BATES, LUCY TO SAMUEL R. JAMES
BATES, MARTHA JANE TO HARMAN ST. JOHN
BATSON, ELIZABETH M. TO RICHARD MAXEY
BATSON, JANE TO JOSHUA WILLIAMS
BATSON, MERANDA JANE TO DAVID BRYANT
BATTON, ANGIE TO WILLIAM H. TYREE
BATTON, P. D. TO M. A. WOOD 8-30-1873 (9-2-1873)
BAXTER, MARY TO R. F. BAXTER
BAXTER, R. F. TO MISS MARY BAXTER 1-31-1866 (2-1-1866)
BAXTER, RICHARD TO CHARLOTT COOK 10-5-1865
BEADON, S. E. TO J. D. SAWLES?
BEARGIN, THOMAS TO MISS AMANDA GORDON 8-26-1867 (8-27-1867)
BEASON, J. H. TO MISS S. H. DUKE 3-9-1871 (3-15-1871)
BEATY, A. J. TO RADID? GOODING 8-3-1839 (8-4-1839)
BEATY, ALLEN TO MISS MARGARET DAVIS 7-26-1844
BEATY, GRISSY TO ELEAZOR REED
BEATY, JAMES TO MISS NANCY BIVINS 11-20-1866

BEATY, JANE TO RICHARD BROWN
BEATY, MARY TO NORRIS KUYKENDALL
BEATY, PHILIP D. TO MISS POLLY ANN GREEAR 12-4-1841 (12-5-1841)
BEATY, THOMAS K. TO SUSANAH GOODIN 1-14-1840 (SOLEMNIZED, NO DATE)
BEECHBOARD, ROBERT TO MISS ELIZABETH ARNOLD 11-30-1850 (12-1-1850)
BEESON, MARGARETT J. TO JOHN A. MULLINS
BELK, JOHN TO POLLY BURNETT 5-8-1839
BELL, EMALINE TO WILLIAM JAMISON
BELL, J. T. TO MISS R. A. YOUNG 11-24-1858 (11-25-1858)
BELL, JAMES H. TO MISS SARAH E. FISHER 1-1-1855
BELL, JAMES TO NANCY MOORE 8-27-1839 (8-29-1839)
BELL, JANE ANN TO CHARLES GILEY
BELL, M. E. TO J. H. TODD
BELL, REBECCA C. TO JAMES STAMPER
BELL, S. J. TO N. F. MASON
BELL, W. W. TO REBECA C. KELL 8-16-1854
BELL, WILLIAM C. TO MISS SUSAN J. BRYSON 10-6-1866 (10-7-1866)
BENJAMIN WILSON TO MARY ANN SCOTT 8-6-1842 (8-7-1842)
BENNET, J. D.? TO MATTIE L. JONES 11-16-1871
BENNETT, C. O. TO LEVINA COLEMAN 9-12-1872
BENNETT, ELIZABETH M. TO JOHN H? GAM
BENSON, MARY E. TO JOHN WARREN
BERKS, MARY TO SAMUEL A. MOORE
BERRETT, E. M. TO R. R. MOSES
BERRETT, JOHN TO MISS MILLY CATHY 5-10-1856
BERRETT, SAMUEL TO MISS PHEBA J. NICHOLS 4-29-1857 (4-30-1857)
BERRY, JOHN W. TO NANCY STONE 10-25-1851 (10-26-1851)
BERRYHILL, M. J. TO R. L. VICKERS
BERRYHILL, SARAH TO J. M. BARRETT
BESHERS, ELIJAH TO MISS SARAH E. KEATH 5-24-1871 (5-25-1871)
BESS, A. M. TO MISS PARLEE MILLIKIN 11-13-1869
BETHEL, B. J. TO MISS JANE EASON 1-21-1857 (NO RETURN)
BETHEL, CAROLINE TO ISAAC BETHEL
BETHEL, GREEN W. TO MISS ELIZA MARCUM 3-22-1851 (NO RETURN)
BETHEL, HENRY TO SALLY BETHEL 8-28-1865 (8-29-1865)
BETHEL, IDIE TO J. T. QUARLES
BETHEL, ISAAC TO CAROLINE BETHEL 8-28-1865 (8-29-1865)
BETHEL, SALLY TO HENRY BETHEL
BETHELL, C. F. TO MRS. S. C. SMITH 10-2-1868
BETHELL, INDIA C. TO JOHN A. COVINGTON
BETHELL, LAFAYETT TO MISS TENNESSEE GANN 11-26-1859 (NO RETURN)
BETHELL, LYDIA H. TO J. W. KENNEDY
BETHELL, M. E. TO R. F. TATUM
BETHELL, MARK TO MISS ISABELLA DONNELL 12-15-1869 (NO RETURN)
BETHELL, T. N. TO W. M. MCKNIGHT
BETHELL, TENNIE L. TO JOHN R. RUSHING
BEVERLY, JANE TO ROBERT TODD
BEVINS, CYNTHIA A. TO GEO. HEATHERLY
BEWREY, ELIZABETH TO GEORGE W. CONLEY
BINEM, MARTHA TO JONATHAN WIMBERLY
BIVENS, ALFORD TO MARY LASETER 10-5-1871 (NO RETURN)
BIVINS, L. M. S. TO ELIZABETH S. ZUMBRO 12-27-1862 (12-28-1862)
BIVINS, NANCY TO JAMES BEATY
BIVVANS, A. J. TO MISS M. A. BRYANT 3-2-1858
BLACK, SARAH TO DANIEL THOMPSON
BLACKBURN, JOHN TO SARAH A. BROWN 6-29-1860 (NO RETURN)
BLAIN, JONATHAN T. TO ELIZA YORK 11-19-1860 (NO RETURN)
BLAIR, ISAAC P. TO MISS ELVIRA WARREN 9-7-1844 (9-8-1844)
BLAIR, JAMES TO JANE CAROLINE MELTON 11-25-1842 (NO RETURN)
BLAIR, MILLIA TO ANTNEY YORK

BLAIR, POLLY TO BALDY H. SUMMAR
BLAIR, SARAH C. TO CHARLES MARCUM
BLAIRE, ELVIRA TO J. M. BARRETT
BLAIRE, OLLEY TO G. W. GATES
BLAIRE, W. B. TO MISS MARTHA C. FORD 7-27-1868 (7-28-1868)
BLANCET, CALVIN TO MISS ISSABELLA CANTRELL 12-13-1845 (12-14-1845)
BLANCET, ELIZA TO THOMAS OWEN
BLANCET, M. J. TO M. L. EDWARDS
BLANCETT, JORDAN TO MISS AMANDA REED 4-23-1860 (4-26-1860)
BLANK, WILLIAM TO W. A. SUMMER 10-8-1858 (NO RETURN)
BLANKS, JULIA ANN TO JOHN C. LEECH
BLANKS, MARY ANN TO CLAIBORNE OWENS
BLANSETT, LAVISA TO JOHN R. TODD
BLANTON, HANNAH TO WILLIAM GILLY
BLANTON, JANE TO J. H. WALE
BLANTON, M. J. TO E. M. PHILLIPS
BLANTON, VINSON TO MISS MARTHA RIGSBY 4-18-1846 (4-26-1846)
BLANTON, WILLIAM TO MISS FRANCES PATTERSON 5-15-1868 (5-18-1868)
BLEW, JOHN TO SAMANTHA WEBB 4-1-1869
BLUE, JOHN TO MARY A. HUNTER 8-28-1858 (8-30-1858)
BLUE, N. J. TO MISS DORETHA MOSEY 10-28-1858
BLUE, SARAH C. TO CHARLES MARCUM
BODKINS, RACHAEL C. TO MILTON TODD
BOGLE, A. C. TO E. M. YOUNG
BOGLE, ALLEN TO CAROLINE YOUNG 3-1-1865
BOGLE, CAROLINE TO J. B. PARRIS
BOGLE, DANIEL TO MISS POLLY ANN SMITH 2-27-1841 (2-28-1841)
BOGLE, E. E. TO J. S. WAMACK
BOGLE, E. L. TO J. M. BARRETT
BOGLE, ELIZA E. TO M. F. HERNDEN
BOGLE, ELIZA J. TO ARMSTED J. ODOM
BOGLE, G. W. TO MISS SARAH E. MULLINGAX 2-9-1857 (NO RETURN)
BOGLE, GEORGE R. TO MISS LOCKY JANE TODD 4-7-1848 (NO RETURN)
BOGLE, GEORGE TO MISS PELINA DAVENPORT 12-23-1869 (12-28-1869)
BOGLE, H. M. TO MISS MALINDA J. PEARCE 2-6-1868 (2-9-1868)
BOGLE, J. M. TO MISS E. WILLSON 10-20-1858
BOGLE, J. Q. TO MISS M. E. DEVENPORT 10-14-1870
BOGLE, JAMES TO MISS CHARITY E. SAULS 10-18-1866
BOGLE, JOHN E. TO MISS DELILA E. WILCHER 7-4-1870 (NO RETURN)
BOGLE, JOHN F. TO MISS LUCY WILLSON 1-3-1859 (1-5-1859)
BOGLE, JOHN TO MISS CHARLOTTE KEATON 12-21-1848 (12-22-1848)
BOGLE, JOSEPH Y. TO MISS A. M. P. SNELLING 3-29-1858
BOGLE, JOSEPHINE E. TO SAMUEL C. ODOM
BOGLE, JOSIAH F. TO LUSEY WILLSON 1-3-1859 (NO RETURN)
BOGLE, L. F. TO MISS M. T. JONES 3-1-1855 (NO RETURN)
BOGLE, LAYFAYETTE TO MISS JULY A. JONES 10-1-1851 (10-9-1851)
BOGLE, MARGARETT TO CALVIN NIGHT
BOGLE, MARGRET TO ABRAM COOPER
BOGLE, MARTHA E. TO WILLIAM J. KING
BOGLE, MARTHA TO WILLIAM SAULS
BOGLE, MICHAEL TO SUSAN J. FERRELL 1-5-1865
BOGLE, N. C. TO B. H. MOORE
BOGLE, N. S. TO M. E. KING 10-11-1873 (10-19-1873)
BOGLE, NANCY M. TO ANDREW SEE
BOGLE, NANCY M. TO THOS. D. STONE
BOGLE, NANCY TO SAM SCOTT
BOGLE, R. M. TO JOSEPH ROBINSON
BOGLE, ROBERT TO ELIZA GANN 9-22-1840
BOGLE, ROBERT TO MISS NANCY CRABTREE 10-18-1855 (10-21-1855)
BOGLE, S. C. TO ISAAC G. GILLEY

BOGLE, SARAH A. TO R. A. KEENY ?
BOGLE, T. L. TO MISS A. T. SPURLOCK 12-?-1870 (12-7-1870)
BOGLE, W. R. TO NANCY M. WAMACK 9-23-1871 (9-27-1871)
BOGLE, WILLIAM TO SARAH SUMERS1-12-1839 (11-14-1839)
BOGLES, MATHEW S. TO MISS MARY E. CLEVELAND 10-11-1851 (10-12-1851)
BOLEN, MARTHA TO GABRIEL MEERS
BOLEY, CLAY J. TO WM. FERRELL
BOLIN, JOHN TO MISS NANCY FRY 2-26-1852
BOMER, WM. TO MISS LUCY BROGON 5-29-1852 (NO RETURN)
BOND, BARTHENA TO STEPHEN WILSON
BOND, JAMES A. TO MISS MATILDA J. GARNER 1-15-1866 (1-17-1866)
BOND, LEWIS TO ELIZABETH HOLLIS 7-?-1839 (7-29-1839)
BOND, R. J. TO MISS SARAH C. MATHEWS 11-18-1850 (11-19-1850)
BOND, WILLIAM TO SARAH L. COOPER 11-19-1842 (12-10-1842)
BONDS, RICHARD J. TO ALAMINTA COOPER 10-13-1842 (10-14-1842)
BONDS, WILLIAM TO MARGARETT REYNOLDS 9-18-1839 (NO RETURN)
BONERS, GILES S. TO VISA E. NORTHCUT 12-31-1863
BONN, A. TO R. E. WALDON 3-5-1860 (NO RETURN)
BOREN, BARTHENA TO M. W. RUSSEL
BOREN, SARAH E. TO JOHN M. F. SMITHSON
BORREN, BRAZELL TO ANNEY VASSER 9-27-1855 (RETURNS MISSING)
BOTKINS, ISSABELLA B. TO JAMES DUNCAN
BOTTEN, GEORGE J. TO MISS MARY D. HALE 9-3-1859 (NO RETURN)
BOUNDS, WESLEY TO MALISA COVINGTON 12-25-1872 (12-26-1872)
BOWEN, ABNER B. TO MISS MARTHA GAITHER 9-12-1843
BOWEN, D. C. TO HYRAM PARRETT
BOWEN, EMALIZA TO THOMAS S. MARTIN
BOWEN, JOHN TO ARY URSULA ROGERS 10-28-1842
BOWEN, MARY FRANCES TO PEYTON LASETER
BOWEN, MARY TO GEORGE HALEY
BOWEN, MARY TO JAMES Y. BRADFORD
BOWEN, R. J. TO J. C. BRADFORD
BOWEN, S. T. TO J. A. THOMASON
BOWEN, SAMUEL TO MISS MANDY M. PITTS 12-7-1854
BOWEN, SAMUEL TO MISS URSULA ANN VINSON 10-26-1847 (10-28-1847)
BOWEN, WM. TO MANDY RICHARDS 8-20-1873 (8-21-1873)
BOWERS, FRANCIS TO MISS SARY LAFEVERS 3-8-1859 (NO RETURN)
BOWERS, FRANCIS TO SARAH PENDLETON 11-14-1860 (NO RETURN)
BOWERS, FRANCIS TO SARY LEFEVEERS 4-8-1859 (4-10-1859)
BOWERS, H. S. TO MISS RACHEL PENDLETON 11-27-1868 (NO RETURN)
BOWERS, WILLIAM TO MISS ELIZABETH WINAHAM 5-28-1845
BOWLIN, JOHN TO MISS AGNESS RICHARDSON 1-30-1850 (2-6-1850)
BOWLIN, RICHARD TO SARAH GOWENS 10-15-1864 (NO RETURN)
BOWLIN, Z. TO L. KEATH 7-17-1873 (7-20-1873)
BOWMAN, JOHN T. W. TO MISS SARAH JANE CAFFEY 10-28-1841
BOWREN, JOSEPH TO DELPHA YONG 9-22-1852
BOWREN, ZEB TO MISS A. GUNTER 11-12-1870 (11-13-1870)
BOXLEY, WESTLEY TO MISS DORCAS HARRIS 11-30-1848 (12-1-1848)
BOYD, ELIZABETH TO SAUNDERS LITTERAL
BOYD, JOHN B. TO MISS SOPHIA ANN SMITH 2-2-1854
BOYLE, REIA M. TO JOSEPH W. ROBINSON
BRADBURY, CULLEN TO NANCY KINCAID 3-23-1839 (3-24-1839)
BRADFORD, J. C. TO MISS R. J. BOWEN 5-21-1857
BRADFORD, JAMES TO KATHARINE PATTON 2-20-1839
BRADFORD, JEMERY TO MISS MARY BOWEN 11-20-1858 (11-21-1858)
BRAGG LAVICA TO JESSE CARTER
BRAGG, D. F. TO MISS SARAH JANE PITARD 2-24-1857 (NO RETURN)
BRAGG, ELIZABETH TO JESSE DENTON
BRAGG, FRANCES TO ANDREW SULLIVAN
BRAGG, JAMES TO LAHAMA E. ROBERSON 7-20-1870 (7-21-1870)

BRAGG, JULIAN TO WILLIAM F. TODD
BRAGG, LIZY TO JACKSON TUCKER
BRAGG, LIZZIE TO WM. POWELL
BRAGG, LORENA TO AMOS CAMPBELL
BRAGG, MARGARET TO JAMES FAULKENBERG
BRAGG, MARGARETT TO THOMAS G. SULLIVAN
BRAGG, MARGART TO WM. B. HAYS
BRAGG, MARY N. TO JOHN MC. ALEXANDER
BRAGG, NANCY J. TO MONFORD PATEN
BRAGG, NANCY TO JAMES B. DAVENPORT
BRAGG, NANCY TO JOHN DENTON
BRAGG, REBECCA J. TO SILAS GAITHER
BRAGG, S. E. TO ISAAC GAITHER
BRAGG, S. E. TO MISS ELIZABETH A. MCBROOM 11-11-1868 (11-12-1868)
BRAGG, SARAH TO H. SMITHSON
BRAGG, SARAH TO JOHN WHITLOCK
BRAGG, SUSAN TO JOSEPH MILLER
BRAGG, THOMAS D. TO MISS MARY P. ROBERSON 2-27-1867 (2-28-1867)
BRAGG, W. M. TO MISS CALLIE MITCHELL 12-2-1871
BRAGG, WILLIAM M. TO MISS LAURENA S. DAVENPORT 12-28-1846
BRAGG, WILLIAM O. TO MISS N. M. BRANDON 2-10-1869 (2-11-1869)
BRALLEY, MARGARETT TO DAVID H. PHILIPS
BRALLEY, NANCY TO WILLIAM C. GIVENS
BRALLEY, SARAH A. TO SAMUEL R. PHILIPS
BRAMATT, MUNRO TO MARTHA WOMACK 1-11-1872 (1-12-1873)
BRAMER, C. P. TO MISS C. J. F. SPURLOCK 1-8-1857 (NO RETURN)
BRANDON, A. G. TO MISS A. B. CATES 5-18-1870 (5-19-1870)
BRANDON, A. J. TO LAURA A. WILSON 2-3-1873 (2-4-1873)
BRANDON, A. T. TO MISS M. J. BRANDON 2-12-1857
BRANDON, A. T. TO MISS R. SIMPSON 9-6-1870
BRANDON, ABRAHAM TO NANCY F. HELTON 11-20-1849
BRANDON, CORNELIUS TO MARY SUMMARS 10-27-1840 (NO RETURN)
BRANDON, CRIDA TO JOHN GANN
BRANDON, DAVID G. TO MISS ELIZABETH PATTON 11-18-1844 (11-19-1844)
BRANDON, E. T. TO SYNTHA MITCHEL 11-14-1863 (11-15-1863)
BRANDON, ELIZABETH TO ZEPHANIAH HARRIS
BRANDON, HIRAM TO AMANDA HARRIS 2-26-1839
BRANDON, J. A. TO MISS M. E. TODD 12-14-1870
BRANDON, J. M. TO MISS O. J. SMITH 7-5-1871 (7-13-1871)
BRANDON, JESSE B. TO MISS MARTHA A. SIMPSON 12-2-1846
BRANDON, JOHN E. TO NANCY MCCRAY 5-16-1839
BRANDON, JOHN F. TO MISS M. A. A. WOMACK 3-14-1857 (3-15-1857)
BRANDON, JOHN TO MISS ROXANNA GANNON 9-7-1848
BRANDON, JONATHAN J. TO MISS HARRIET LOWE 1-3-1851 (NO RETURN)
BRANDON, JONATHAN TO MISS JOANNAH ORRAND 5-24-1866
BRANDON, JONNATHAN TO SARAH REED 10-28-1871 (10-30-1871)
BRANDON, K. T. TO MISS JOSEPHINE ROBERSON 3-28-1868 (3-29-1868)
BRANDON, LAVISA TO GEORGE H. GORDEN
BRANDON, LUCINDA TO JOHN GANN
BRANDON, M. J. TO A. T. BRANDON
BRANDON, M. J. TO H. A. IRVIN
BRANDON, MARGARET E. TO JAMES A. PETTY
BRANDON, MARGARET E. TO R. L. GAITHER
BRANDON, MARY A. TO WM. A. BRANDON
BRANDON, MARY TO CANTRELL B. SUMMAR
BRANDON, MATHEW TO MARY A. VANE 10-26-1854
BRANDON, N. M. TO WILLIAM O. BRAGG
BRANDON, R. TO M. M. BYFORD 6-29-1854
BRANDON, REBECCA TO BENJAMIN A. GODWIN
BRANDON, ROBERT B. TO MISS MALINDA F. BRYSON 8-1-1868 (8-2-1868)

BRANDON, S. S. TO MISS CHRISTENEY JONES 2-15-1867 (2-17-1867)
BRANDON, SABELLA TO WILLIAM GOODIN
BRANDON, WILLIAM TO MISS ELLISABETH BURK 1-12-1856 (NO RETURN)
BRANDON, WM. A. TO MARY A. BRANDON 10-19-1873
BRANDON, WM. TO MISS JANE SHERES 2-27-1855 (NO RETURN)
BRANON, CALVIN C. TO MISS MARY E. SULLIVAN 8-29-1844 (NO RETURN)
BRANTLEY, FRANKLIN TO SYLVA MCKNIGHT 8-21-1865 (8-26-1865)
BRASHEARS, ALEXANDER TO MISS LUCINDA SKURLOCK 7-26-1848
BRASHEARS, ALEXR. TO VINA C. HUTCHENS 3-20-1864
BRASHEARS, NELLY (ALLEY) TO RICHARD TAYLOR
BRASHEARS, REBECCA TO JOHN J. MALONE
BRASHEARS, RUTH TO SAMUEL MOORE
BRASHEARS, WILLIAM TO MISS SALLY HERRIN 11-1-1845 (11-3-1845)
BRASHEARS, WILLIAM TO NANCY NOKES 12-10-1842 (12-13-1842)
BRASHER, J. L. TO AMENA C. KIRLOCK 2-5-1856 (7-6-1856)
BRATON, WM. TO MISS FRANCES KIRSEY 9-13-1854
BRAWLEY, WM. TO MANERVY RAWLINGS 2-13-1872
BRAXTON, J. M. TO MARY PARKER 12-30-1873 (1-1-1874)
BRENTS, SOLOMON TO ELIZABETH BROWNFIELD 5-31-1838
BREVARD, TH. TO MISS M. R. FERRILL 8-24-1853
BREVARD, THOMAS B. TO JANE W. FUGITT 11-2-1847
BREWER, BETTIE TO D. B. VANCE
BREWER, JESSE TO MARTHA E. WEEDON 3-23-1843
BREWER, JOEL TO MARY E. SPANGLER 2-22-1860 (NO RETURN)
BREWER, JOHN L. TO MISS MARTHA F. STEPHENS 12-9-1869
BREWER, MARTHA TO WILLIAM C. MILLER
BREWER, S. A. TO MISS M. E. TURNER 12-19-1870 (12-22-1870)
BREWER, THOMAS J. TO MISS MARY HALL 2-14-1849 (2-15-1849)
BREWER, W. M. TO MISS BETTIE GOWER 11-24-1870
BREWER?, SARAH R. TO WM. GAY
BREWIES, A. E. TO J. H. ODOM
BREWIN?, L. J. TO R. L. ODOM
BRIANT, FRANCES TO F. M. WEBBER
BRIEN, JAMES W. TO M. M. C. TURNER 4-28-1856 (NO RETURN)
BRIGHT, JAMES R. TO MISS PRISCILLA MANEY 11-2-1847 (NO RETURN)
BRIM, OSIAS D. TO JULIAN SPURLOCK 10-28-1869
BRIM, SARAH TO L. P. GOFF
BRISON, B. D. TO MISS E. BRISON 11-11-1858
BRISON, E. TO B. D. BRISON
BROGON, LUCY TO WM. BOMER
BROILES, J. A. TO MISS L. B. LINCH 11-8-1859 (NO RETURN)
BROOKS, ISAAC TO MISS ELIZABETH DUKE 8-5-1848 (8-6-1848)
BROOKS, JOHN R. TO MISS MARTHA WIMBERLEY 1-25-1847 (2-7-1847)
BROOKS, TENNIE W. TO JAMES P. GANNON
BROOKS, WM. TO MISS JULIE A. WILLIAM 9-24-1870 (9-25-1870)
BROWN, A. J. TO MISS NANCY E. BRUCE 2-17-1866 (2-18-1866)
BROWN, ANN TO TOWNSEND FUGITT
BROWN, C. C. TO MISS ANN E. COLEMAN 1-21-1869
BROWN, CALVIN TO MISS LUGY HIGGINS 1-6-1871 (1-8-1871)
BROWN, ELIZABETH H. TO JAMES MARCHBANKS
BROWN, ELIZABETH TO FARMER D. WRATHER
BROWN, FANNIE TO SILAS PARKER
BROWN, JAMES TO MISS R. J. DEBERRY 3-25-1871 (3-28-1871)
BROWN, JAMES W. TO MARGARET A. LEWIS 8-4-1865 (8-6-1865)
BROWN, JANE TO RICHARD PEARSON
BROWN, JANE TO ROBERT C. DANIEL
BROWN, JOHN A. J. TO MISS A. C. WATSON 5-28-1870 (5-29-1870)
BROWN, JOHN TO MISS FERIBA SMITH 12-19-1866 (12-20-1866)
BROWN, JOHN TO MISS SARAH ADALINE STACY 10-7-1870 (10-9-1870)
BROWN, LUCINDA TO WM. N. MOORE

BROWN, M. A. E. TO H. N. GOWEN
BROWN, MANERVA J. TO MARTIN M. WITT
BROWN, MARTIN TO MISS SALINA SELLARS 2-13-1849
BROWN, MARY A. TO DAVID WILLIAMS
BROWN, MARY D. TO ADISON DILL
BROWN, MARY TO HARRISON GROSS
BROWN, NANCY TO JOHN R. SULLIVAN
BROWN, NARCISS TO AARON DUGGAN
BROWN, OMA ANN TO CABELE COX
BROWN, RICHARD TO MISS JANE BEATY 8-20-1841
BROWN, SARAH A. TO JOHN BLACKBURN
BROWN, SARAH P. TO JOHN WELLS
BROWN, SUSAN ANN TO JOHN H. BYFORD
BROWN, T. J. TO MISS M. A. SUMMERS 12-24-1857
BROWN, TEMPA CAROLINE TO WM. P. GRAY
BROWN, W. M. TO MISS MARY E. HALL 6-18-1866 (NO RETURN)
BROWNFIELD, ELIZABETH TO SOLOMON BRENTS
BRUCE, NANCY E. TO A. J. BROWN
BRYANT, B. L. TO BERRY BUSH
BRYANT, DAVID TO MISS MERANDA JANE BATSON 7-31-1848
BRYANT, ELIZABETH TO WILLIAM HOLT
BRYANT, IRA I. TO MISS NANCY E. HOLT 9-1-1853 (NO RETURN)
BRYANT, JAMES W. TO MISS ELIZABETH ANN POLOCK 12-3-1846 (NO RETURN)
BRYANT, M. A. TO A. J. BIVVANS
BRYANT, WESLEY TO TENNESSEE COOPER 12-23-1871 (12-24-1871)
BRYANT, WM. S. TO SUSANNA STACY 8-23-1872 (8-25-1872)
BRYANT, ZACHARIAH T. TO MISS RACHEL P. DODD 12-7-1869 (12-9-1869)
BRYSON, DANIEL TO NANCY ALEXANDER 1-17-1839 (1-23-1839)
BRYSON, DANIEL TO NANCY HUBBARD 10-18-1862 (10-21-1862)
BRYSON, E. D. TO M. L. WILSON 8-4-1865 (8-6-1865)
BRYSON, ELIZABETH TO B. D. SUMMER
BRYSON, EMLEY F. TO W. T. MEARS
BRYSON, FATOMY TO A. D. COOPER
BRYSON, J. A. TO MISS NANCY MOORE 8-30-1859 (NO RETURN)
BRYSON, J. J. TO MISS CINDY L. H. SUMER 8-14-1855 (RETURNS MISSING)
BRYSON, JAMES H. TO MISS SARRAH M. JONES 9-7-1857 (NO RETURN)
BRYSON, LOELY P. TO JOHN M. COOPER
BRYSON, MAHALY T. TO JOHN S. READY
BRYSON, MALINDA F. TO ROBERT B. BRANDON
BRYSON, MARTHA TO A. W. WEST
BRYSON, MARTHA TO MICHAEL WILSON
BRYSON, MARY J. TO JOHN P. MILLIGAN
BRYSON, MARY M. TO M. H. FRANCIS
BRYSON, NANCY TO J. M. GILLAM
BRYSON, PARTHENA TO Z. T. SUMMAR
BRYSON, POLLY TO WILLIAM DAVENPORT
BRYSON, ROBERT TO MISS ---- SUMMERS 8-6-1857 (8-20-1857)
BRYSON, S. S. TO A. M. SMITH
BRYSON, SAMUEL H. TO MISS SARAH M. MCKNIGHT 7-7-1870
BRYSON, SARAH TO JOHN L. HARRIS
BRYSON, SUSAN J. TO WILLIAM C. BELL
BRYSON, WILLIAM TO SALLY WEST 8-15-1838
BRYSON, WM. B. TO MISS M. L. MOORE 12-10-1853 (12-11-1853)
BUCY, GEORGE W. TO MISS SARAH MEARS 1-11-1851 (1-12-1851)
BUCY, SARAH J. TO JESSEE RICHARDS
BULLARD, CHARITY TO F. M. FERGASON
BULLARD, ELIZABETH TO JOHN HENDRICKSON
BULLEN, J. W. TO MISS NANCY A. WATSON 1-15-1859 (NO RETURN)
BULLEN, MAHULDA TO WILBERN ROGERS
BULLEN, SARAH ANN TO WM. MARTIN

BULLING, POLLY TO JOHN ROGERS
BUNCH, MALINDA TO WILLIAM GOAD
BUNCH, NANCY TO JOHN J. SULLINS
BURCH, CLEMENTINE TO THOMAS DENNIS
BURCH, J. M. TO AMANDY A. HOLLAND 7-5-1873 (NO RETURN)
BURCH, JANE TO J. C. WIMBERLY
BURCH, MARY ANN TO SAMUEL ALLEN
BURCH, WILLIAM P. TO MARY AUSMENT 11-22-1865 (EXECUTED--NO DATE)
BURCHETT, THOMAS TO MISS PARTHENA MILLIKIN 1-7-1858 (NO RETURN)
BURGER, CAROLINE TO ROBERT PATTERSON
BURGER, ISAAC TO MISS ADALINE GUNTER 1-26-1867 (NO RETURN)
BURGER, JOSEPHINE TO JAMES L. HODGE
BURGER, M. J. TO A. H. REAVES
BURGER, MARY TO ENOCH JONES
BURGER, PELINA J. TO RICHARD GRIZZLE
BURGER, RUTHA TO JOHN W. MELTON
BURGER, S. P. TO T. J. JETTON
BURGER, S. TO J. A. BARNET
BURGER, W. O. TO H. J. JONES 1-30-1860 (NO RETURN)
BURGETT, MARTHA A. TO J. E. LAMBERT
BURGNER, SUSAN J. TO JESSEE BARNES
BURK, C. TO FRANKLIN RICHERSON
BURK, D. T. W. TO NANCY BURK 1-13-1865
BURK, ELLISABETH TO WILLIAM BRANDON
BURK, ISABELLA TO BASWELL GAITHEN
BURK, JANE TO JOHN C. GREEN
BURK, JOHN TO NANCY PEYDAN 11-18-1852
BURK, N. J. TO MISS S. A. HAILEY 9-2-1858 (HANDED IN--NO RETURN)
BURK, NANCY ANN TO B. HAYS
BURK, NANCY TO D. T. W. BURK
BURK, SARAH TO CAPHUS C. HAILEY
BURKE, DANIEL TO MISS SARAH PEDON 8-3-1856
BURKE, LEMUEL D. TO MISS LAVISA H. FORD 10-19-1850 (10-20-1850)
BURKE, N. J. TO A. E. SULLIVAN 11-10-1866
BURKES, G. C. TO MISS PARLEE TOLBERT 9-30-1868 (NO RETURN)
BURKES, JAMES TO MISS SALLY EADES 11-16-1841 (11-17-1841)
BURKET, JAMES TO MISS MARY A. GILLY 1-17-1856
BURKET, MARTHA TO WILLIAM YOUNG
BURKET, MARY TO JAMES HALL
BURKETT, A. J. TO MISS NANCY JANE DERRYBERRY 10-19-1850 (NO RETURN)
BURKETT, DAVID TO MISS FANNIE FERRELL 11-27-1867 (11-28-1867)
BURKETT, J. M. TO CAROLINE RIGSBY 8-22-1872
BURKETT, JOB TO MISS NANCY A. RICHARDS 9-16-1869
BURKETT, JOHN TO MISS PAULINA MARCUM 3-10-1849 (3-11-1849)
BURKETT, M. C. TO S. J. FORD 11-12-1873 (11-13-1873)
BURKETT, MARGRETT TO SOLOM PORTER
BURKETT, MATILDA TO BERRY MARKUM
BURNETT, MATILDA TO ALBERT M. FLEMMING
BURNETT, MATILDA TO J. W. MEEKS
BURNETT, POLLEY TO JOHN BELK
BURNETT, S. A. TO MISS SARAH S. DAVENPORT 2-1-1870
BURRY?, MARGARET TO JAMES TENPENNY
BURT, SARAH TO J. M. SPRAY
BUSEY, T. J. TO MISS MARY J. FANN 8-9-1871 (8-10-1871)
BUSEY, THOMAS J. TO MISS MALISSA C. REED 1-7-1867 (1-8-1867)
BUSEY, WILLIAM H. TO MISS ELIZABETH A. GIBSON 7-20-1870 (7-21-1870)
BUSH, BERRY TO MISS B. L. BRYANT 8-25-1858 (NO RETURN)
BUSH, ELIZABETH TO JOHN EWELL
BUSH, EMILY MARIAH TO WILLIAM RODGERS
BUSH, H. L TO MISS ELIZABETH F. HOOKER 12-18-1867 (12-19-1867)

BYRN, JOHN TO MIRAM REDDY 6-20-1867 (6-21-1867)
BYRN, W. M. TO MISS D. DOUGHERTY 11-23-1869 (11-24-1869)
BYRNE, JAMES H. TO SARAH E. MCKNIGHT 2-16-1845 (2-20-1845)
BYRNS, TENNESSEE TO H. G. STEPHENS
CAFFEY, SARAH JANE TO JOHN T. W. BOWMAN
CAMBELL, THOMAS TO ANN GAITHER 1-20-1840 (1-21-1840)
CAMPBEL, WILLIAM TO MISS DORA YOUNG 4-6-1857 (RETURNED NOT EXECUTED)
CAMPBELL, A. G. TO MISS N. H. FAIESTAR 8-4-1847
CAMPBELL, AMOS TO LARENA MORGAN 10-21-1868 (10-22-1868)
CAMPBELL, AMOS TO MISS LORENA BRAGG 8-27-1868
CAMPBELL, DOVEY TO WILLIAM GRIZZEL
CAMPBELL, G. R. TO MISS ELISABETH SPURLOCK 9-14-1852
CAMPBELL, HENRY TO MISS CYTHIA AN MELTON 8-29-1857 (RETURNED NOT EXECUTED)
CAMPBELL, ISAAC TO MARTHY BUTCHER 12-27-1856 (RETURNED NOT EXECUTED)
CAMPBELL, J. C. TO AMANDA PEDON 9-13-1872
CAMPBELL, J. D. TO ANN E. HAILY 7-19-1864 (NO RETURN)
CAMPBELL, J. D. TO MARTHA E. BAILEY 11-10-1863 (NO RETURN)
CAMPBELL, J. W. TO ALICE S. WHEELER 2-13-1873
CAMPBELL, J. W. TO MISS SERECIA E. MORGAN 1-30-1867 (1-31-1867)
CAMPBELL, JAMES TO MISS SARAH E. GILLEY 9-18-1859 (NO RETURN)
CAMPBELL, JOHN D. TO ZERUNA MELTON 9-30-1871 (10-1-1871)
CAMPBELL, MAHALY TO JOHN ARMSTRONG
CAMPBELL, MARY TO JOHN DOBBS
CAMPBELL, NANCY TO ALEXANDER TATE
CAMPBELL, PARALEE TO VINSON BAILY
CAMPBELL, RHODA TO W. J. VANDERGRIFF
CAMPBELL, SARAH TO E. R. MELTON
CAMPBELL, SUSAN TO MARION VANDERGRIFF
CAMPBELL, THOMAS TO MRS. NANCY MOON 12-19-1850 (12-20-1850)
CAMPBELL, THOMAS TO MRS. PERNINA S. ARMSTRONG 2-17-1851 (2-18-1851)
CAMPBELL, THOS. TO MISS JENNIE PERRY 10-1-1870 (10-2-1870)
CAMPBELL, VINCENT TO SARAH AN PITMAN 9-26-1863 (SOLEMNIZED, DATE NOT GIVEN)
CAMPBELL, W. D. TO POLLEY WEBBER 11-27-1871
CAMPBELL, W. R. TO MISS JO WEEDON 1-24-1871 (1-25-1871)
CAMPBELL, WM. TO TERISIAN GILLEY 4-14-1860 (NO RETURN)
CAMPBLE, WM. TO MISS SUSAN PATTERSON 12-24-1853 (NO RETURN)
CAMPELL, EMLA TO LAYFAYETT RING
CANES, A. B. TO MISS ELIZABETH DAVIS? 10-19-1858 (10-20-1858)
CANNON, HENRY TO AGNESS TAYLOR 5-15-1838
CANNON, RAYFORD TO MISS ELIZABETH JANE HILLIS 8-17-1843 (8-19-1843)
CANTRELL, EASTER TO THOMAS PARKER
CANTRELL, ELIZABETH TO WILLIAM S. MULLINS
CANTRELL, ISSABELLA TO CALVIN BLANCET
CANTRELL, JAMES TO MISS ELIZABETH HANONS 12-31-1851
CANTRELL, JAMES W. TO MISS MARTHA J. SUMMAR 12-21-1867 (12-28-1867)
CANTRELL, JANETTE TO HENRY B. MULLINS
CANTRELL, LUCINDA TO WILLIAM ARNOLD
CANTRELL, RODA TO THOMAS MERRIMON
CANTRELL, STEPHEN TO MISS LUCINDA MULLINS 3-19-1846
CAPPS, ANN TO ISAEAH NEELY
CAPPS, ELIZABETH TO EZEKIEL MERRIMAN
CAPPS, RUTHY TO GEORGE W. MANESS
CAPSHAW, FREELY TO JOSIAH HERIMAN
CAPSHAW, H. L. W. TO MISS LOUISA FLETCHER 7-17-1856 (7-?-1856)
CAPSHAW, J. J. C. TO MISS MALINDA C. RIGSBY 7-12-1870
CARIC, T. J. TO MISS E. JIMERSON 8-6-1857
CARMICHAEL, ANNA E. TO WM. H. MILLER
CARMICHAEL, MALISSA J. TO JOSEPH SPURLOCK
CARMICHAEL, WILLIAM G. TO MISS MALISSA J. WEST 6-4-1850
CARMON, SAMUEL TO PATIENCE MIDDLETON 3-28-1840

BUSH, HARVY TO MISS EMALINE BYNUM 12-1-1846 (12-3-1846)
BUSH, HENRY L. TO SARAH J. TODD 1?-4-1853 (1-6-1853)
BUSH, JEREMIAH TO MISS ELIZABETH A. DEREBERRY 1-27-1848
BUSH, L. P. TO MISS FRANCES WILLIAMS 12-12-1868 (12-13-1868)
BUSH, LUCINDA TO WM. CAWTHON
BUSH, M. C. TO ALLEN BYNUM
BUSH, M. E. TO HARVY ARNOLD
BUSH, MALINDA TO ROBERT FRASURE
BUSH, MARIAH TO A. THOMAS
BUSH, MARIAH TO ALLEN THOMPSON
BUSH, MARY E. TO WILLIAM S. ROSS
BUSH, MATILDA? TO NEWTON T. WHITTAMORE
BUSH, REBECCA ANNE TO ANDERSON LAMBERTH
BUSH, SARAH JANE TO JAMES IRA BYNUM
BUSH, SARAH TO J. R. Y. GILLEY
BUSH, URIAH TO MARYANN LAMBIRTH 7-22-1839
BUSH, URIAH TO MISS MIARIAH JOHNSON 5-6-1845
BUSH, W. J. TO SUSAN A. STACY 1-1-1866 (NO RETURN)
BUSH, WILLIS TO MISS AMANDA TRIGG 9-18-1844 (9-19-1844)
BUSH, Z. TO MISS E. J. TODD 1-28-1858 (NO RETURN)
BUSY, JENETTA TO JOSHUA DAVIS
BUTCHER, JOSHUA TO MISS ALLAMINTA GAN 9-13-1856 (RETURNED NOT EXECUTED)
BUTCHER, MARTHY TO ISAAC CAMPBELL
BUTCHER, RUTHY TO JAMES F. HOLLANDSWORTH
BUTTER, J. W. TO NANCY A. WATSON 1-15-1859 (NO RETURN)
BYFORD, ELIZABETH TO EVAN A. INGLIS
BYFORD, J. R. TO MISS NANCY E. BYFORD 4-5-1858 (4-7-1858)
BYFORD, JAMES HARDY TO MISS ELIZABETH ANN SOAPE 4-13-1848
BYFORD, JOHN H. TO MISS SUSAN ANN BROWN 6-26-1847 (RETURNED NOT EXECUTED)
BYFORD, JOHN TO MISS SUSANAH COOPER 3-2-1868 (5-8-1868)
BYFORD, L. E. TO A. G. MILLIKIN
BYFORD, LEANDER TO MISS MARY E. SIMMONS 12-28-1867 (12-31-1867)
BYFORD, M. M. TO R. BRANDON
BYFORD, MARY A. TO REUBEN PITT
BYFORD, MARY J. TO J. W. HATFIELD
BYFORD, MATILDA J. TO JAMES SIMMONS
BYFORD, NANCY E. TO J. R. BYFORD
BYFORD, PARTHENY O. TO JOHN MILLIKIN
BYFORD, THOMAS TO NANCY K. LENOX 4-13-1839 (NO RETURN)
BYLER, CAROLINE TO I. F. DICKINS
BYNUM, ALLEN TO MISS M. C. BUSH 9-28-1853 (9-29-1853)
BYNUM, B. I. TO JULY A. TOLBERT 9-3-1873 (9-4-1873)
BYNUM, ELIZABETH JANE TO JOHN A. STACY
BYNUM, ELIZABETH TO L. J. TOLBERT
BYNUM, EMALINE TO HARVY BUSH
BYNUM, JAMES IRA TO MISS SARAH JANE BUSH 12-30-1846 (1-7-1847)
BYNUM, JOHN TO ELIZABETH HOOVER 12-6-1838
BYNUM, LOUISA J. TO THOMAS W. SHELTON
BYNUM, LUCINDA TO C. E. MCCASLIN
BYNUM, LUCINDA TO JESSE N. GILLEY
BYNUM, M. L. TO G. W. EARP
BYNUM, MARTHA TO F. M. ARRINGTON
BYNUM, MARY C. TO J. B. WILLIAMS
BYNUM, NANCY E. TO AUSTIN DONNEL
BYNUM, REDMON TO MISS MARTHA JANE JOYS 11-18-1840 (11-23-1840)
BYNUM, S. W. TO MISS JANE LAW 10-17-1857
BYNUM, SALLIE A. TO L. A. TODD
BYNUM, WILLIAM TO MISS MARY ANN SAGELY 12-30-1846 (12-31-1846)
BYNUM, WM. TO LUCINDA STACY 11-8-1864 (11-11-1864)
BYNUM, WM. TO MISS MARTHA L. WEBBER 11-2-1859 (NO RETURN)

CARNAHAN, J. C. TO M. A. MCGILL 8-28-1865 (8-30-1865)
CARNAHAN, JANE R. TO WM. HOOVER
CARNAHAN, JOHN H. TO MISS SARAH A. TEAGUE 12-2-1868 (12-3-1868)
CARNAHAN, SALLIE E. TO N. T. PASCHAL
CAROLL, CHARLOTTE TO SIMEON D. STEPHENS
CARRACK, T. F. TO A. L. MITCHELL 3-11-1865 (NO RETURN)
CARRELL, MARY TO L. HOUGHS
CARRICK, ESTHER C. TO RICHARD GOODING
CARRICK, JOSEPH N. TO MISS E. J. YOUNG 9-9-1858 (9-8?-1858)
CARRICK, MARY E. TO JAMES CRESON
CARRICK, SARAH E. TO JAMES L. ALLEN
CARRICK, T. A. TO MISS SARAH F. YOUNG 11-13-1868 (11-14-1868
CARRICK, THOMAS TO ELIZA HILL 10-19-1872 (10-20-1872)
CARSON, MARY ANN TO JAMES COOPER
CARTER, AMANDA J. TO JAMES R. HOGWOOD
CARTER, D. R. TO MISS NANNIE A. MCKNIGHT 9-16-1868
CARTER, ELIZABETH TO J. A. WILCHER
CARTER, JAMES R. TO MISS BETTIE MCBROOM 9-12-1867
CARTER, JAMES TO L. C. SULLIVAN 10-4-1864 (10-6-1864)
CARTER, JAMES TO MISS KATHARINE JONES 9-11-1846
CARTER, JESSE TO MISS LAVICA BRAGG 10-15-1847 (10-5?-1847)
CARTER, LUIZA F. TO J. W. EDWARD
CARTER, MAHALY TO AARON F. JONES
CARTER, R. R. TO W. E. YOUREE
CARTER, SARAH E. TO H. B. HAGWOOD
CARTER, THOS. TO LIZZIE SMITH 10-8-1873 (10-9-1873)
CARTER, W. P. TO MISS MARY F. MCNIGHT 3-16-1871
CARUTHERS, JOHN TO MISS JANE REED 11-16-1867 (11-19-1867)
CARUTHERS, MAY E. TO ISAAC L. JARRETT
CARUTHERS, R. J. TO J. H. OGLESBY
CARUTHERS, S. A. E. TO W. P. GAITHER
CATES, A. B. TO A. G. BRANDON
CATES, A. B. TO MISS J. E. CATES 7-17-1869 (7-18-1869)
CATES, A. W. TO MARY J. BARRATT 5-20-1863 (5-28-1863)
CATES, CAROLINE TO J. E. HOLLIS
CATES, J. E. TO A. B. CATES
CATES, JOSEPH M. D. TO MISS MARY JANE TAYLOR 9-5-1848
CATES, M. E. TO W. J. CATES
CATES, MARY TO W. N. TAYLOR
CATES, W. J. TO M. E. CATES 1-19-1873
CATHCART, W. A. TO MISS MARTHA RUSHING 1-11-1871 (NO RETURN)
CATHEY, ALICE TO WILLIAM J. MINGLE
CATHEY, E. N. TO WILLIAM B. OWEN
CATHEY, JANE RUTHERFORD TO JOHN FAULKENBERG
CATHEY, LUCY TO THOMAS FINLEY
CATHEY, MARY TO DOSUNE MULLINS
CATHEY, ROBERT TO ANGALINE STANDLY 1-9-1850
CATHY, MILLY TO JOHN BERRETT
CATHY, SARAH S. TO WM. THOMPSON
CATHY, WILLIAM C. TO MISS NANCY FINLEY 9-26-1847
CAWTHAN, DAVID TO MISS MATILDA C. DECKE 8-29-1856 (NO RETURN)
CAWTHON, HARVEY TO ALSEY A. DAUGHTERY 5-6-1872
CAWTHON, MARY TO SAMUEL MCCULLER
CAWTHON, WM. TO MISS LUCINDA BUSH 10-17-1853 (10-20-1853)
CHAMBERS, MANERVA TO GILBERT HILL
CHAMBERS, SAM TO ELIZABETH HANCOCK 10-16-1872 (10-17-1872)
CHAMBLY, DAVIES TO REBECCA F. HANCOCK 1-23-1865 (1-24-1865)
CHAPELL, T. A. TO GRANVILLE JETTON
CHAPMAN, E. P. TO MISS D. GRAHAM 5-5-1860
CHERRY, ELIZABETH TO JOHN M. COOP

CHERRY, EMALINE TO JOHN A. SHEROD
CHERRY, MARGARETT TO JOHN A. SIMPSON
CHERRY, MARTHA TO JOHN PARKER
CHERRY, MILLEY TO PAGE PEALER
CHILDRESS, STEPHEN P. TO MISS ELIZABETH STANDLY 10-17-1844
CHILDRESS, STEPHEN TO JANE MITCHEL 11-16-1842 (11-17-1842)
CHUMBY, PLEASANT TO CAROLINE OCONNER 3-1-1859 (3-3-1858) (SIC)
CHUMLY, CAROLINE TO RICHARD TALLY
CHUMLY, SARAH TO CHARLES E. EVANS
CHURCH, ELIZABETH TO BENJAMIN H. F. PHILIPS
CHURCH, FRANKLIN TO MISS CAROLINE THOMPSON 3-21-1848
CINLY, DOVY TO DANIEL WALLS
CLARK, JOSEPH M. TO MISS HANAH P. LONG 4-6-1867 (4-7-1867)
CLARK, MARY TO HENRY BAIRD
CLARK, ORTIME TO LABORN GOEN
CLARK, W. J. TO MARY A. PEELER 9-20-1873 (9-21-1873)
CLAY, HENRY TO FRANCES FUGETT 6-12-1868 (6-13-1868)
CLEMENTS, ELIZABETH TO WILLIAM PRICE
CLEMENTS, MARTHA JANE TO SAMUEL GULLETT
CLEMENTS, MEEKY H. TO JOSEPH H. CRAFT
CLEMENTS, PERMELIA ANN TO MITCHEL LORD
CLEMMENTS, SARAH TO HARDY LASETER
CLENDENNEN, ROBERT W. TO MISS REBECA ALLEN 6-4-1849 (6-6-1849)
CLEVELAND, MARY E. TO MATHEW S. BOGLES
CLIFFORD, JOHN H. TO MISS MARY M. HAYES 9-9-1867 (9-13-1867)
CLIFFORD, L. S. TO W. M. HAYES
CLOSE, NANCY J. TO WILLIAM WILSHER
COBERT, VOLENTINE TO LIDIA HARGES 6-1-1839
COCK, JOHN TO MISS NANCY ANN WOOD 12-20-1854 (12-21-1854)
COGWELL, MARTHA TO JAMES WALLACE
COLEMAN, ANN E. TO C. C. BROWN
COLEMAN, BARBARY TO FRANCIS M. HARVEY
COLEMAN, FRANKLIN TO MISS SARAH C. THOMPSON 9-30-1840 (10-1-1840)
COLEMAN, LEVINA TO C. O. BENNETT
COLEMON, MARY TO JOHN W. EARVIN
COLLIN, MARY TO EDMOND PERRY
COLLINS, LAVINA TO M. C. GANN
COLLINS, A. R. TO THOS. J. WOMACK
COLLINS, FRANCES TO GEORGE DAVANPORT
COLLINS, JEREMIAH TO MARY P. KEATON 8-6-1865
COLLINS, M. M. TO ELIM MCKNIGHT
COLLINS, SARAH TO POLK ASHFORD
COLLINS, WILLIAM TO JULIE A. MILLIGAN 12-15-1871 (12-17-1871)
COLVERT, JAMES L. TO MISS JOHANNA E. MATHEWS 4-1-1846
COLVERT, WILLIAM A. TO MISS ELIZABETH M. JOHNSON 7-10-1845
COLWELL, ANDREW J. TO MISS MARTHA ANN WHIT 7-22-1840
COLWELL, NANCY TO JONATHAN WHITT
COMER, JAMES M. TO MISS ELIZABETH HENDRICKSON 8-10-1850 (8-15-1850)
CONLEY, A. J. TO MISS MARY J. BAILEY 7-17-1869 (NO RETURN)
CONLEY, EMLEY T. TO W. T. ALEXANDER
CONLEY, GEORGE W. TO MISS ELIZABETH BEWREY 5-20-1852
CONLEY, ISAH TO MATILDA SULLINS 9-2-1863 (NO RETURN)
CONLEY, JOHN TO MARY J. KERSEY 9-21-1865
CONLEY, N. C. TO MISS V. A. SULLINS 5-21-1869
CONLEY, ZACHARIAH TO MISS MARGARET P. FINLEY 10-18-1869
CONLY, JAMES G. TO MISS CAROLINE WALLS 10-6-1840
CONN, ALLEY TO LEWIS G. MARTIN
CONN, SARAH E. TO GRANVILLE JETTON
CONNELLY, ELIZABETH TO DANIEL WALLS
CONNER, WILLIAM O. TO MRS. LEANAH ROGERS 7-27-1848

CONTY, MARTHA TO BURRELL FOWLER
COO-EN, JAMES W. TO MISS MARY A. C. SISSOM 11-?-1870 (11-20-1870)
COOK, CHARLOTT TO RICHARD BAXTER
COOK, ELIZABETH ANN TO ANDREW WILLSEN
COOK, ELIZABETH TO ISAAC S. MITCHELL
COOK, J. W. TO MISS EMELINE GOODING 11-27-1855 (12-2-1855)
COOK, JOHN W. TO MAT LEA 11-17-1860 (NO RETURN)
COOK, MANERVA TO JOHN JONES
COOK, MARTHA R. TO JAMES H. STEPHENS
COOK, MARY TO C. Y. GUNTER
COOK, NANCEY H. TO RICHARD TENPENNY
COOK, SAMUL TO MISS REBECCA J. WARREN 11-15-1859 (EXECUTED---NO DATE)
COOK, STEPHEN TO MISS SARAH E. ALEXANDER 12-22-1846 (12-23-1846)
COOP, JOHN M. TO MISS ELIZABETH CHERRY 10-27-1858 (10-28-1858)
COOPER, A. D. TO MISS FATOMY BRYSON 10-6-1859 (NO RETURN)
COOPER, ABRAM TO MARGRET BOGLE 11-4-1839 (11-8-1839)
COOPER, ALAMINTA TO RICHARD J. BONDS
COOPER, ANNA TO J. P. FORD
COOPER, BERRY TO MISS CHARITY YOUNG 2-23-1850
COOPER, BETTY TO LOGAN MCCASLIN
COOPER, CHRISTOPHER TO MISS HARRIET M. DAVENPORT 3-10-1847 (3-11-1847)
COOPER, EMELINE TO J. B. GAINS
COOPER, G. W. TO MISS HARIETT FORD 1-13-1853
COOPER, H. J. TO MISS NANCY LAYMAN 9-18-1855
COOPER, HOLLIS TO MISS JEMIMA ESPEY 10-26-1859 (NO RETURN)
COOPER, HONEY TO ELIGIA A. ENSEY
COOPER, ISAIAH TO MISS DELILA C. SISSOM 3-14-1867
COOPER, J. A. TO MISS MARGARET E. KING 8-27-1869
COOPER, JAMES TO MISS MARY ANN CARSON 2-24-1847 (2-28-1847)
COOPER, JEMIMA MALISSA TO JAMES FINLEY
COOPER, JOHN D. TO MISS AZALINE MCADOW 1-7-1870 (1-12-1870)
COOPER, JOHN M. TO MISS LOELY P. BRYSON 10-27-1846
COOPER, JOHN TO MISS MARTHA ANN THOMPSON 7-3-1845
COOPER, M. D. L. TO MISS SARAH SLENDLY 2-3-1858
COOPER, M. E. TO A. A. FRANCIS
COOPER, MARTHA J. TO F. G. THOMPSON
COOPER, MARTHA L. TO HENRY SAULS
COOPER, MARTHA TO BARRY K. TAYLOR
COOPER, MARY C. TO WILLIAM KNOX
COOPER, P. G. TO AMANDA J. SUMMERS 11-25-1867 (11-26-1867)
COOPER, PEYTON L. TO MISS MARY HATFIELD 4-5-1848
COOPER, PHILIP TO MISS MARGARET SULLENS 5-6-1852
COOPER, PHILLIP TO MISS MARGARETT LOLLIN? 5-6-1852
COOPER, RACHIEL TO JOHN A. WEST
COOPER, RUTHA TO WM. J. LANIER
COOPER, S. L. TO S. H. LEWIS 11-18-1873 (11-19-1873)
COOPER, SARAH E. TO H. A. SISSOM
COOPER, SARAH L. TO WILLIAM BOND
COOPER, SUSANAH TO JOHN BYFORD
COOPER, TENNESSEE TO WESLEY BRYANT
COOPER, THOMAS J. TO MISS SARAH E. SISSOM 2-20-1867 (2-21-1867)
COOPER, THOMAS TO SARAH TODD 12-5-1857
COOPER, WILLIAM B. TO MISS DRUCILLA OWEN 3-11-1847 (NO RETURN)
COOPER, WILLIAM TO MISS KATHERIN FORCANA 1-1-1854
COPE, MARY TO J. C. PATTERSON
COPLAND, ARNOLD TO MISS MARTHA PETRILL 9-6-1853 (NO RETURN)
COSBEY, MARY E. TO M. W. LORANCE
COTHRAN, PLESANT TO MISS ANGELINE PARKER 1-12-1853 (1-18-1853)
COTHRAN, W. P. TO LOU G. NEAL 12-18-1873 (12-24-1873)
COTHREN, S. A. TO N. C. ARNOLD

COTTER, T. G. TO MISS S. E. TAYLOR 12-29-1870
COUCH, J. M. TO MISS S. M. ODOM 2-24-1870
COUCH, J. W. TO MISS M. E. BASSHAM 9-2-1871 (9-3-1871)
COUCH, M. M. TO J. M. ELROD
COUCH, WILLIS F. TO MISS ELIZABETH BARRETT 11-11-1840 (11-12-1840)
COUCH, WILLIS F. TO MISS MARTHA WALLS 6-15-1849
COUCH, WM. H. TO KATHARINE LESTER 2-8-1841 (2-10-1841)
COUGHANOUR, E. C. TO WM. C. TODD
COUGHANOUR, J. A. TO MARY RAWLENS 12-25-1863 (12-29-1863)
COULTER, MALINDA TO JAMES TRAVIS
COUSLEY, MARINDA A. TO JAMES HIGGENBOTTOM
COUTHEN, MARTHA J. TO WM. A. JARNEGIN
COVINGTON, EDMOND TO MISS ELIZABETH SILVERTOOTH 12-15-1851 (12-19-1851)
COVINGTON, FRANCES TO J. T. HENDERSON
COVINGTON, HATTIE TO CHARLES MARTIN
COVINGTON, JOHN A. TO INDIA C. BETHELL 3-16-1865
COVINGTON, LEAH TO DAVID MULLINS
COVINGTON, MALISA TO WESLEY BOUNDS
COVINGTON, MARY TO WILLIAM T. WOOD
COVINGTON, W. L. TO FRANCES ANN BAIN 10-6-1856
COVINGTON, WILLIAM L. TO MARIAH GEORGE 10-8-1839
COWEN, MATILDA B. TO JOHN BARRY
COWTHRON, HUGH TO MISS ADLINE? STACY 3-11-1852
COX, C. A. TO GENEVA WATSON 12-27-1871
COX, CABELE TO MISS OMA ANN BROWN 7-16-1849
COX, CAROLINE TO JAMES H. FAGAN
COX, CELIA TO JAMES A. JONES
COX, CHARLES A. TO MISS JULIA ANN EVANS 7-20-1869
COX, CHRISTENA TO ROBERT M. STANLY
COX, D. F. TO J. S. MORGAN
COX, ELEANOR TO WILLIAM RICH
COX, HENRY TO LOUISA MULLINS 2-9-1863 (2-15-1863)
COX, J. S. H. TO JESSEE PATRICK
COX, JEMIMA TO JAMES S. TODD
COX, LAVINA ANN TO WILLIAM MCGEE
COX, MARY A. TO BAZEL GAITHER
COX, MARY M. TO B. F. JONES
COX, MARY N. TO CHARLES M. WILSHER
COX, SALINA JANE TO JAMES B. KNOX
COX, SUSANNAH TO MICAJAH F. TODD
COX, THOMAS TO ELIZA JANE MARSHALL 11-16-1850
COX, WILLIAM TO ALESALA SEATES 3-4-1840 (NO RETURN)
CRABTREE, DORCAS TO JOHN MILLIGAN
CRABTREE, ELIGAH TO MISS ISZA GILLY 1-18-1854
CRABTREE, ELIJAH TO MISS IZZA GILLEY 2-18-1854 (2-19-1854)
CRABTREE, ELIZA J. TO JOHN HOLLANDSWORTH
CRABTREE, NANCY TO ROBERT BOGLE
CRADDOCK, SIMEON TO MARGRETT DENTON 8-8-1872 (9-5-1872)
CRAFT, CHATATA TO JOHN B. GOINS
CRAFT, ELISABETH TO HENRY H. WEST
CRAFT, FRANCES TO WALTER WILSON
CRAFT, HESSIE ANN TO WILLIAM E. PETTY
CRAFT, J. J. TO MISS ASEAH PETTY 6-5-1870
CRAFT, JAMES L. TO MISS REBECCA E. ESSARY 11-29-1845 (11-30-1845)
CRAFT, JONATHAN A. TO NANCY TURNER 5-26-1860 (5-28-1860)
CRAFT, JOSEPH H. TO MISS MEEKY H. CLEMENTS 6-27-1846 (NO RETURN)
CRAFT, MARTHA TO JAMES TRAVIS
CRAIN, HENRY TO MISS MALISA PERRY 3-20-1855
CRAMNER, ROBERT TO MISS MARY KNOX 11-?-1870 (NO RETURN)
CRANE, A. M. TO MISS E. S. SAPP 6-6-1857 (6-7-1857)

CRANE, A. W. TO MISS RODA A. MCDANEL 5-23-1866
CRANE, JOHN W. TO MISS MARY ADALINE ALEXANDER 9-15-1846 (9-17-1846)
CRANE, MARY E. TO WILLIAM M. HENDIX
CRANK, G. W. TO MISS MARRY STEPHENS 2-10-1853
CRAWFORD, JOHN TO MISS RODA GOINGS 9-12-1866 (9-13-1866)
CRESON, H. J. TO ED PERRY
CRESON, JAMES TO MISS MARY E. CARRICK 1-7-1867
CRESON, JOSHUA TO MISS ELIZABETH W. LEIGH 12-17-1846
CRESON, MARY TO J. B. HOLLIS
CRESON, SARAH TO WARE LEIGH
CRESON?, BENJAMIN F. TO MISS SARAH SISSOM 1-3-1846
CRIESON?, JAMES C. TO MISS SARAH JANE ALEXANDER 11-7-1850 (NO RETURN)
CROCKER, EUGENIA TO B. R. GOODLOE
CROSS, ELIZA ISSABELLA TO JOHN TUCKER
CROSS, MARTHA TO FRANKLIN W. TRAVIS
CROUCH, J. B. TO MISS LUCINDA FOSTER 9-7-1871 (9-10-1871)
CROUGHONOUR, MALEDA TO M. F. TODD
CROW, MARTHA JANE TO LORENZO D. SMITH
CUMINGS, T. P. TO ROBERT BAILEY
CUMINS, JULINA TO W. G. STINE
CUMINS, MATILDA TO FLOYD ST. JOHN
CUMMINGS, A. H. TO MISS MARY MELTON 3-30-1853
CUMMINGS, BENJAMIN TO SARAH JANE MELTON 4-28-1842 (4-23-1842) (SIC)
CUMMINGS, CYRENA TO JAMES KEENY
CUMMINGS, MALACHI TO MISS LUCINDA SULLIVAN 12-23-1845
CUMMINGS, MARY E. TO DILLARD S. ELKINS
CUMMINGS, P. D. TO MISS MELVINA MEANS 11-9-1865 (11-12-1865)
CUMMINGS, PARASADE TO HUGH L. BAILY
CUMMINGS, REBECCA J. TO WILLIAM J. LEIGH
CUMMINGS, WARREN TO DOVE SULLIVAN 3-5-1839 (3-6-1839)
CUMMINGS, WILLIAM TO DELPHIA RAINS 3-27-1838
CUMMINGS, WILLIAM TO MISS MANERVA ANN ALDEN 11-6-1845
CUMMINS, ADALINE TO YOUNG FERRELL
CUMMINS, DOVE TO WILLIAM SULLENS
CUMMINS, ELIZABETH TO THOMAS KINCAID
CUMMINS, J. P. TO T. B. ELLEDGE 10-28-1873 (10-29-1873)
CUMMINS, JAMES TO MISS ANN FOSTER 9-20-1849
CUMMINS, JOHN TO ANNE MELTON 5-5-1840 (NO RETURN)
CUMMINS, L. L. C. TO MISS LUCY ANN HOPKINS 10-17-1868 (10-18-1868)
CUMMINS, L. T. TO MISS MATILDA P. WORLEY 10-24-1866 (10-25-1866)
CUMMINS, LUCY E. TO JAMES T. LAWRENCE
CUMMINS, M. TO J. A. MELTON
CUMMINS, MARGARET TO H. P. MELTON
CUMMINS, MARY J. TO G. D. WOODS
CUMMINS, REBECCA A. TO ALFORD MCFERRIN
CUMMINS, W. B. TO MISS FRANCES C. PRESTON 9-8-1869 (9-9-1869)
CUMMINS, WARREN TO MISS JOSEPHINE BAILEY 1-13-1866 (1-14-1866)
CUNINGHAM, J. TO MISS ELIZABETH ROGERS 2-2-1852
CUNNINGHAM, JANE TO CHARLES D. MOSS
CUNNINGHAM, MARY TO MICAGAH PETTY
CURDON, MARRY TO BENJAMIN WARREN
CURLEE, AMANDA R. TO JOHN W. GAITHER
CURLEE, P. B. TO MISS ELIZABETH F. GAITHER 10-10-1855 (10-11-1855)
CURLEE, P. B. TO MISS MARY H. GAITHER 9-26-1853 (9-27-1853)
CURLEE, PEYTON B. TO MISS ROXANAH FERRELL 1-13-1858
CURLEE, T. B. TO BETTIE P. FOSTER 10-24-1872
CURLEE, T. G. TO MISS A. D. THOMAS 11-19-1867 (11-20-1867)
CURNNAY, ADALIN TO JOSEPH YONG
CURTIS, ANN TO WILLIAM MAIES
CURTIS, ELIZA TO JORDAN B. SELLARS

CURTIS, SILAS R. TO MISS EASTER J. KUYKENDALL 12-22-1846
DABBES, JOHN T. TO MISS MARY HATTSON 1-12-1838
DABBS, J. T. TO SARAH TEDDER 8-19-1873 (8-21-1873)
DABBS, L. M. TO J. M. DAVENPORT
DANIEL, ANN ELIZA TO JOHN ADAMS
DANIEL, E. A. TO H. A. JUSTICE
DANIEL, GEO. TO ELIZA SMITH 4-24-1872 (4-25-1872)
DANIEL, GEORGE TO MARY PINKERTON 8-22-1865 (8-27-1865)
DANIEL, MARGARET TO ROBERT BARTON
DANIEL, MARTHA TO LEVI PELHAM
DANIEL, NANCY TO BRICE PARSLEY
DANIEL, R. T. TO MISS MARY A. YOUNG 12-1-1859 (NO RETURN)
DANIEL, ROBERT C. TO MISS JANE BROWN 1-7-1856
DANIEL, SAM TO MISS JENNIE PEOPLES 9-7-1871
DARABERRY, CINDY R. TO ISAAC KIRKLIN
DARBERY, ELIZA TO JOHN PRATER
DARNELL, W. C. TO MISS SARAH ELANDER 12-26-1853 (NO RETURN)
DAUGHTERY, ALSEY A. TO HARVEY CAWITHON
DAULES?, JUDIE TO JERRY WOOD
DAVANPORT, GEORGE TO FRANCES COLLINS 1-21-1864 (1-29-1864)
DAVANPORT, J. B. TO MARGARET MOORE 3-3-1864 (NO RETURN)
DAVENPORT, A. A. TO MARTHA DAVENPORT 8-19-1865 (8-20-1865)
DAVENPORT, B. D. TO MISS D. L. WILLIRD 8-2-1858
DAVENPORT, FANNY E. TO NEIL H. SMITH
DAVENPORT, GEO. TO REBECCA PRESTON 10-3-1873 (11-2-1873)
DAVENPORT, HARDY TO JULIE STRONG 12-5-1872
DAVENPORT, HARRIET M. TO CHRISTOPHER COOPER
DAVENPORT, J. B. TO MARTHA A. DUNCAN 7-11-1863 (NO RETURN)
DAVENPORT, J. B. TO MISS NANCY MERRITT 10-13-1855 (NO RETURN)
DAVENPORT, J. M. TO L. M. DABBS 8-30-1864 (9-4-1864)
DAVENPORT, J. M. TO MISS MELVINA TEDDER 7-5-1869 (7-18-1869)
DAVENPORT, JAMES B. TO MISS NANCY BRAGG 11-14-1848
DAVENPORT, JOHN C. TO SUSAN L. JONES 9-1-1860 (NO RETURN)
DAVENPORT, JOHN F. TO CALIDONIA GAN 12-24-1863 (12-27-1863)
DAVENPORT, JOHN TO MISS SARAH SMITH 11-10-1870
DAVENPORT, LAURENA S. TO WILLIAM M. BRAGG
DAVENPORT, MARGARET S. TO JOHN D. ALEXANDER
DAVENPORT, MARTHA TO A. A. DAVENPORT
DAVENPORT, MARTHA TO FOSTER M. ROBERSON
DAVENPORT, NANCY M. TO THOMAS A. ORRAND
DAVENPORT, NANCY TO HENRY PARTEN
DAVENPORT, PELINA TO GEORGE BOGLE
DAVENPORT, REUBEN TO MISS SARAH MATHEWS 5-4-1847
DAVENPORT, ROBERT TO M. J. LEECH 7-13-1864 (7-14-1864)
DAVENPORT, SAM B. TO MARTHA J. PRESTON 11-1-1873 (11-2-1873)
DAVENPORT, SARAH S. TO S. A. BURNETT
DAVENPORT, THOMAS TO MISS MARY E. JONES 8-20-1850
DAVENPORT, W. R. TO MISS PITSON? SUMMER 9-19-1868 (9-20-1868)
DAVENPORT, W. S. TO MISS BARBARA A. PEYDEN 8-12-1853
DAVENPORT, WARREN TO MISS ANN F. SMITH 7-9-1868
DAVENPORT, WILLIAM TO MISS POLLY BRYSON 7-24-1845
DAVENPORT, WM C. TO ELIZA STANLEY 1-1-1856 (NO RETURN)
DAVENPORT, WM. A. TO SUSAN HIBDON 7-28-1864 (8-2-1864)
DAVIS, ANDERSON TO LUCRETIA TUCKER 8-3-1850 (8-4-1850)
DAVIS, ANDY TO SUSAN C. STANLY 2-17-1873 (NO RETURN)
DAVIS, ANNIE T. TO H. L. KEATON
DAVIS, BENJ. TO BETTIE BAILY 10-24-1872
DAVIS, CINTHIA TO JOHN ROGERS
DAVIS, D. J. TO W. J. FORD
DAVIS, DAVID TO LOTTY MOORE 9-11-1873

DAVIS, J. J. TO MISS MARY H. DOAKE 12-31-1866 (1-1-1867)
DAVIS, JACOB TO MISS CHARLOTTE MOON 7-10-1844 (7-11-1844)
DAVIS, JAMES TO HARRIET HOLLIS 8-23-1868 (NO RETURN)
DAVIS, JOHN TO NANCY EMALINE YOUNG 9-10-1845
DAVIS, JON TO MISS RUTHEY RIGSLY 3-25-1858 (NO RETURN)
DAVIS, JOSHUA TO ELIZABETH DUNCAN 6-28-1865 (6-29-1865)
DAVIS, JOSHUA TO JENETTA BUSY 12-29-1842
DAVIS, LEWIS TO MISS ZILPHA ROGERS 3-14-1848
DAVIS, M. E. TO J. W. THOMAS
DAVIS, MANERVIA TO JAMES PARSLEY
DAVIS, MARGARETT TO ALLEN BEATY
DAVIS, MARY E. TO JOHN W. MATHEWS
DAVIS, PARALEE TO JOURDEN WEST
DAVIS, REBECCA TO MORT STANLY
DAVIS, ROBERT TO MISS JULIAN HIGGINS 5-28-1870 (5-29-1870)
DAVIS, SAMUEL A. TO MARGARET MOON 12-31-1865
DAVIS, SARAH TO JOHN K. RIGSBY
DAVIS, T. J. TO MARY E. WOMACK 10-21-1871
DAVIS, T. Y. TO MISS NANNIE D. PETTY 12-26-1868 (NO RETURN)
DAVIS, WM. H. TO MARIAR F. PETTY 3-1-1865 (3-25-1865)
DAVIS, WM. P. TO JOSIE PRESTON 10-6-1871 (10-11-1871)
DAVIS?, ELIZABETH TO A. B. CANES
DAVIS?, JOSEPH TO MISS KATHARINE E. FINCH 3-2-1848
DEAN, NOAH TO ELIZABETH WILLIAMS 3-22-1839
DEAUBOISE, ELIZABETH TO ROBERT ESPY
DEBERRY, R. J. TO JAMES BROWN
DEBONK?, MINERVY TO J. B. DEVENPORT
DECKE, MATILDA C. TO DAVID CAWTHAN
DELANG, DAVID TO MISS EMILY SHERLEY 3-14-1857 (3-15-1857)
DELANY, WATSON J. TO MISS NORVENA STONE 2-16-1859 (NO RETURN)
DELOACH, LOUSANNA TO SHADERICK W. ELKINS
DELOACH, MARTHA TO WILLIAM C. HOLLIS
DEMENT, VINA TO WESLEY WEEDON
DENBY, HARIETT TO ELISHA HOLLIS
DENBY, WILLIAM TO ANN PATTERSON 6-28-1845 (NO RETURN)
DENIS, EMERLINE TO DAVID HUTCHEANS
DENNES, WILLIAM TO PEGGY HIGGINS 5-8-1839 (5-16?-1839)
DENNIS, CHARLOTTE TO JOHN HOLLINSWORTH
DENNIS, ELIZA TO B. F. MURFREY
DENNIS, ELIZABETH TO RICHARD ARMSTRONG
DENNIS, JOHN N. TO MISS MARTHA N. GRIZZEL 11-11-1869 (11-14-1869)
DENNIS, JOHN TO ELIZA ESQUE 11-21-1843
DENNIS, MARY TO ALFRED MARKUM
DENNIS, MAT TO SUSAN TARLETON? 3-23-1865 (NO RETURN)
DENNIS, THOMAS TO MISS CLEMENTINE BURCH 9-30-1869
DENTON, FRANCES TO WILLIAM C. BARRETT
DENTON, JESSE TO ELIZABETH BRAGG 8-11-1842
DENTON, JOHN TO NANCY BRAGG 2-26-1840 (NO RETURN)
DENTON, MARGARET OT RICHARD MILLER
DENTON, MARGRETT TO SIMEON CRADDOCK
DENTON, WILLIAM TO MARGRET MULLINS 2-4-1840
DERABERRY, PELINA A. TO WILLIAM C. LEWIS
DEREBERRY, ELIZABETH A. TO JEREMIAH BUSH
DERMIS, MATHEW TO SALENA REEVES 2-8-1844
DERRYBERRY, BARBARY TO JOHN R. SMITH
DERRYBERRY, JACOB TO MISS CINDERELLA LASATER 9-29-1848 (10-1-1848)
DERRYBERRY, NANCY JANE TO A. J. BURKETT
DEVANPORT, A.H. TO MISS S. S. WILLSON 10-10-1856 (NO RETURN)
DEVANPORT, JOSEPH TO MISS SARAH GAN 2-16-1853
DEVANPORT, WILLIAM TO MISS M. E. WILLSON 1-15-1858

DEVENPORT, ELIZA TO F. M. JAMES
DEVENPORT, ELIZA TO F. M. JONES
DEVENPORT, GEORGE TO MISS FORDY GIVENS 12-1-1870 (12-6-1870)
DEVENPORT, H. G. TO MISS M. J. PEDON 9-7-1871
DEVENPORT, HENRY TO SARAH PEDIGO 10-3-1838
DEVENPORT, HENRY W. TO SARAH J. MINGLE 12-13-1871
DEVENPORT, J. B. TO MISS MINERVY DEBONK? 10-15-1859 (NO RETURN)
DEVENPORT, J. B. TO MISS NANCY MERRETT 10-13-1852 (10-15-1852)
DEVENPORT, JOHN S. TO SARAH E. WINNETT 10-2-1872 (10-3-1872)
DEVENPORT, M. E. TO J. Q. BOGLE
DEVENPORT, N. E. TO B. C. ALEXANDER
DICKENS, DELEY A. TO PHILIP IVEY
DICKENS, ELISABETH TO JAMES HALEY
DICKENS, FANNY TO W. M. GOTCHER
DICKENS, JOHN TO PARALEE MARTIN 6-13-1873 (6-15-1873)
DICKENS, NANCY M. A. TO G. B. KIPP
DICKINS, I. F. TO CAROLINE BYLER 10-13-1853 (10-16-1853)
DILL, ADISON TO MISS MARY D. BROWN 8-14-1856
DILL, W. C. TO MISS A. L. ODOM 11-27-1866 (11-28-1866)
DILLEN, JOSEPH TO MISS M. J. STEPHENS 9-14-1865
DILLIAN, PHEBE TO WILLIAM VANDERGRIFF
DILLON, CHARLES TO FANNY ODOM 7-19-1866 (7-20-1866)
DILLON, CHARLES TO JUDA ANN ODOM 1-27-1866 (NO RETURN)
DILLON, E. T. TO SALLIE FUGITT 9-18-1871 (9-21-1871)
DILLON, ELIZA TO W. M. MASSIE
DILLON, MISS FRANCES E. TO E. H. PHALON
DILLON, S. J. TO MARY A. ELGIN 12-20-1864 (12-21-1864)
DIRTING?, JOHN TO MISS SALENA TITTLE 3-5-1844 (3-28-1844)
DISTING, CLARISSA TO HENRY KEATON
DOAKE, MARY H. TO J. J. DAVIS
DOBBS, JOHN TO MISS MARY CAMPBELL 5-10-1867 (5-12-1867)
DODD, A. A. TO J. M. WILLIAMS
DODD, ALBERT TO HAMEY SULLIVAN10-5-1865
DODD, DEMARIES E. TO WILLIAM L. SULLIVAN
DODD, JAMES H. TO MISS NANCY E. KING 1-5-1853
DODD, JOHN A. TO MISS ANN E. SULLIVAN 8-25-1869
DODD, MARY E. TO THOMAS HALE
DODD, MARY TO JOHN W. MATHEWS
DODD, RACHEL P. TO ZACHARIAH T. BRYANT
DODD, SMITHY J. TO BLUFORD H. GIVAN
DODD, WILLIAM TO CHARLOTTE MATHEWS 3-12-1842 (3-18-1842)
DOM, JAMES H. TO MISS SUSAN M. OWIN 9-12-1854
DONNEL, AUSTIN TO NANCY E. BYNUM 1-10-1865 (1-11-1865)
DONNELL, ISABELLA TO MARK BETHELL
DONNELL, JAMES TO HARRIETT TULLEY 2-2-1870 (2-5-1870)
DONNELL, SARAH E. TO J. N. SUMMAR
DONNELLE, WILLIAM C. TO MISS SARAH P. LANSDEN 2-8-1847 (2-23-1847)
DONOHO, EDWARD TO MISS VIRGINIA MANEY 6-27-1848
DOOD, SINTHY J. TO BLUFORD H. GEONS
DOUGHERTY, D. TO W. M. BYRN
DOUGHERTY, MARTHA A. TO H. J. MANEY
DOUGLAS, JAMES T. TO MISS MARY F. SPARKS 8-5-1871 (8-6-1871)
DOUGLASS, JAMES I. TO ROSLIN L. MARTIN 2-21-1865 (2-22-1865)
DOZIER, JOHN H. TO MISS MARTHA A. DOZIER 7-26-1849
DOZIER, JONATHAN TO MISS LOUISA CAROLINE HOLLIS 8-12-1847
DOZIER, MARTHA A. TO JOHN H. DOZIER
DOZIER, PETER TO POLLY ELKINS 1-7-1845
DRAKE, T? T? C. TO H. L. PRESTON
DRIVER, ALDONA TO ROBT. T. MURPHY
DUBIRTH, NANCY TO ROBERT GOLAHAN

DUBOIS, MARTHA TO JAMES HELTON
DUBOISE, JAMES P. TO MISS JULIAN TENPENNY 7-25-1867
DUBOISE, JOHN IRVIN TO MISS SUSAN JANE HOLLIS 3-8-1844 (3-14-1844)
DUBOISE, MARY A. TO CHARLES ELKINS
DUBOYS, JAMES M. TO MISS NANCY HAYS 1-1-1857 (1-15-1857)
DUGGAM, PRESTLEY TO MISS MARY HANCOCK 6-18-1844 (6-18-1844)
DUGGAN, AARON TO NARCISS BROWN 4-2-1840
DUGGAN, HENRY S. TO MISS SARAH E. MCKNIGHT 12-20-1847 (12-21-1847)
DUGGAN, SUSAN TO JAMES HIGGINS
DUGGIN, JULIANN TO DAVID SAULS
DUGGIN, THOS. TO EUNICE JONES 11-26-1873 (11-27-1873)
DUGGIN, W. P. TO MARY J. MCKNIGHT 7-31-1873
DUGGON, HENRY S. TO SELINA TITTLE 6-6-1839
DUKE, ALEXANDER TO MISS ANN ALMON 3-17-1869 (3-18-1869)
DUKE, B. HARRY TO MISS MELINDA EDWARDS 12-23-1847
DUKE, ELIZABETH TO ISAAC BROOKS
DUKE, GIDEON TO BETSY KING 2-12-1840 (2-13-1840)
DUKE, I. J. TO MISS MARRY EDWARDS 8-29-1853 (8-30-1853)
DUKE, J. M. TO RACHAL C. LYNN 12-6-1865 (12-7-1865)
DUKE, JOHN A. TO VICY C. HALY 10-15-1852 (10-16-1852)
DUKE, JOHN TO MISS NANCY PARKER 4-17-1867 (4-18-1867)
DUKE, MONROE TO MISS SARAH LYNN 8-31-1867 (9-1-1867)
DUKE, MORDECAI M. TO MISS ELEANOR RHEA 3-17:1847
DUKE, N. R. J. TO VENTURIAN HALEY
DUKE, S. H. TO J. H. BEASON
DUKE, SARAH ANN TO DAVID HALEY
DUKE, SARAH P. TO JESSE G. LEWIS
DUKE, WILLIAM TO CYNTHIA MORGAN 3-19-1838 (3-22-1838)
DUKIN, J. F. TO MISS M. J. PRATOR 10-27-1858 (10-28-1858)
DUNCAN, CLARISSA TO JOHN R. ASHLEY
DUNCAN, ELIZA A. TO JESE SIMMONS
DUNCAN, ELIZABETH TO JOSHUA DAVIS
DUNCAN, J. D. TO REBECCA A. ENSEY 9-10-1872
DUNCAN, JAMES TO ISSABELLA B. BOTKINS 3-16-1843
DUNCAN, JANE TO EDMUND MCFERRIN
DUNCAN, L. G. TO W. G. PENDLETON
DUNCAN, L. L. TO HENRY N. FINLEY
DUNCAN, L. T. TO MISS MARY E. SCOTT 4-9-1867 (NO RETURN)
DUNCAN, MANERVA TO ISAAC LEMONS
DUNCAN, MARTHA A. TO J. B. DAVENPORT
DUNCAN, MARY ANN TO WILLIAM WHITAMORE
DUNCAN, MATISA TO RANSON TODD
DUNCAN, PETER B. TO LISA A. SISSAM 3-3-1856 (3-4-1856)
DUNCAN, POLLY TO JESSE WILLIAMS
DUNCAN, REBECCA A. TO T. R. WRIGHT
DUNCAN, SARAH ANN TO WM. C. ALFORD
DUNCAN, W. B. D. TO MISS R. D. RAINS 3-18-1854 (1-17-1854) (SIC)
DUNKIN, OWEN TO MISS NANCY S. WYLY 3-9-1853 (3-10-1853)
DUNN, WM. J? TO MISS NANCY C. KNOX 2-14-1848 (2-17-1848)
DURRETT, RHAMY TO MARCUS PRATOR
DUSTON, J. E. TO AMANDY REED 7-30-1872 (8-1-1872)
EADES, SALLY TO JAMES BURKES
EADS, MATHEW W. TO MISS VINA A. ESPEY 6-18-1856 (6-19-1856)
EADS, SAMUEL TO MISS PERMELA MOORE 3-2-1852 (NO RETURN)
EAKES, GEORGE TO REBECCA EKINS 7-2-1858 (7-14-1858)
EARLS, NATHAN TO MISS ELISABETH AUSTON 4-9-1857 (4-10-1857)
EARP, G. W. TO M. L. BYNUM 3-6-1872 (3-7-1872)
EARVIN, JOHN W. TO MISS MARY COLEMAN 2-19-1867
EASON, EMILY TO ALFRED MCFERRIN
EASON, HARRIET TO WILLIAM J. GIVENS

EASON, JANE TO B. J. BETHEL
EASON, R. F. TO MISS NANNIE? A. ATCHLEY 7-30-1868
EDDING, PLESANT TO NANCY MERRITT 9-25-1852 (NO RETURN)
EDDINGS, WM. R. TO ELIZABETH MUNCY 12-8-1852
EDDINGTON, HUGH TO MARTHA J. OSMENT 10-21-1862 (10-22-1862)
EDGE, ELISHA TO HARIETT DENBY 1-30-1839 (2-1-1839)
EDWARD, J. W. TO MISS LUIZA F. CARTER 6-6-1859 (NO RETURN)
EDWARD, NANCY TO WM. C. PHILIPS
EDWARDS, ALFORD TO MISS JANE LEWIN 12-19-1857 (NO RETURN)
EDWARDS, CHARITY TO JOHN MOON
EDWARDS, ELIZABETH TO GEORGE W. HOLLIS
EDWARDS, M. L. TO MISS M. J. BLANCET 11-5-1856 (NO RETURN)
EDWARDS, MARRY TO I. J. DUKE
EDWARDS, MARTHA E. TO JOHN MOON
EDWARDS, MARY E. TO G. T. TURNER
EDWARDS, MARY TO JOSEPH W. HOPKINS
EDWARDS, MELINDA TO B. HARRY DUKE
EDWARDS, NANCY A. TO JOHN H. REED
EDWARDS, NANCY TO JAMES H. LANIER
EDWARDS, SUSANNAH TO LEWIS J. HOLLIS
EDWARDS, UPHEY TO JOHN ST. JOHN
EDWARDS, WILLIAM TO ELIZA PAYNE 9-27-1842
EDWARDS, WM. H. TO SARAH E. STACY 5-3-1864 (NO RETURN)
EKENS, LIZA JANE TO M. M. PRATER
EKINS, REBECCA TO GEORGE EAKES
ELAM, FLORA TO NELSON HOKES
ELAM, FRANCES C. TO JOHN WILERFORD
ELAM, HENRY TO ELIZABETH PENDLETON 10-22-1840 (10-24-1840)
ELAM, MARY ANN TO JOHN WILSON
ELAM, REUBEN TO MISS POLLY LANCE 12-24-1843 (12-27-1843)
ELANDER, SARAH TO W. C. DONNELL
ELDER, EDWARD TO MISS ELIZABETH ORAND 1-9-1855
ELEDGE, MARTHA TO SAMUEL GILLEY
ELGIN, MARY A. TO S. J. DILLON
ELKIN, ROBT. L. TO ELIZA T. FOSTER 8-10-1872
ELKINS, ARTA M. TO GORDON MORGAN
ELKINS, C. TO WILLIAM THOMAS
ELKINS, CALIDONIA TO ISAAC SMITH
ELKINS, CHARLES TO MISS MARY A. DUBOISE 4-29-1848 (4-30-1848)
ELKINS, D. L. TO ELIZABETH T. ELKINS 10-6-1862 (10-7-1862)
ELKINS, D. L. TO EMILY E. WALKUP 11-29-1850 (12-1-1850)
ELKINS, DILLARD S. TO MISS MARY E. CUMMINGS 10-2-1844
ELKINS, DOSIA E. TO WILLIAM F. SOWELL
ELKINS, ELIZABETH T. TO D. L. ELKINS
ELKINS, H. R. TO ELIZA ANN HIGGINS 2-4-1868
ELKINS, H. R. TO MISS R. E. NEELY 7-9-1859 (7-10-1859)
ELKINS, HAMPTON TO MISS MARY GOODING 3-2-1854 (NO RETURN)
ELKINS, HARIETT D. TO N. L. NEELY
ELKINS, J. P. TO MISS HARRIET J. PARRIS 1-6-1869 (NO RETURN)
ELKINS, J. P. TO MISS HARRIETT J. PARRIS 1-6-1859
ELKINS, JAMES TO MISS JANE LEWIS 7-4-1859 (NO RETURN)
ELKINS, JOHN D. TO JULIA ANN TITTLE 9-4-1839 (9-5-1839)
ELKINS, JOHN TO MANDY LOWRANCE 2-27-1873 (2-30-1873) (SIC)
ELKINS, JOHN W. TO LUCINDA ESQUE 6-29-1850 (6-30-1850)
ELKINS, LEROY LAFAYETTE TO MISS MARY CAROLINE YOUNG 4-5-1856 (4-6-1856)
ELKINS, LUCINDA TO C. L. PRATER
ELKINS, LUCY ANN TO STANFORD PITMAN
ELKINS, M. G. TO MISS MARY JANE VANDAGRIFF 12-7-1854
ELKINS, M. J. TO J. B. PARRIS
ELKINS, MALISSA CAROLINE TO BENJAMIN MELTON

ELKINS, MARGARET TO WALTER L. TODD
ELKINS, MARGARETT E. TO JAMES PRATER
ELKINS, MARTHA E. TO ABRAHAM BARETT
ELKINS, MARTHA VIRGINIA TO JACOB B. FOWLER
ELKINS, MARY C. TO HOUSTON MCCABE
ELKINS, MARY C. TO THOMAS MERRITT
ELKINS, MARY J. TO JOHN R. FOSTER
ELKINS, N. A. TO WM. MARKUM
ELKINS, NANCY TO JAMES MEARS
ELKINS, POLLY TO PETER DOZIER
ELKINS, RACHELL J. TO ANDREW YOUNGBLOOD
ELKINS, SANDY J. TO MALISSA ELLEDGE 1-23-1865 (1-24-1865)
ELKINS, SARAH ANN TO JOHN TITTLE
ELKINS, SHADERICK W. TO MISS LOUSANNA DELOACH 8-19-1848 (NO RETURN)
ELKINS, SILAS TO MISS SARAH F. THOMAS 3-4-1871 (NO RETURN)
ELKINS, STACY C. TO JOHN A. YOUNG
ELKINS, SUSANNAH TO DANIEL MANUS
ELKINS, T. D. TO MISS MARY ANN FOSTER 8-6-1866 (8-7-1866)
ELLADGE, WM. C. TO MARY MCCLAIN 12-23-1846 (12-24-1846)
ELLEDGE, CHARLES TO CALLIE READY 12-28-1870 (12-29-1870)
ELLEDGE, JAMES B. TO EDNY S. MAYFIELD 9-20-1873 (9-21-1873)
ELLEDGE, MALISSA TO SANDY J. ELKINS
ELLEDGE, SARAH ANN TO SAMUEL VANCE
ELLEDGE, SARAH E. TO JNO. E. TURNER
ELLEDGE, SUSAN TO J. E. TURNER
ELLEDGE, T. B. TO J. P. CUMMINS
ELLEDGE, WILLIAM F. TO NANCY ANN WOOD 10-3-1839 (10-4-1839)
ELLIDGE, PAOMPEY? TO MARY JONES 2-29-1872
ELLIOTT, A. C. TO MISS MARY A. MCCULLOUGH 8-29-1871 (8-30-1871)
ELLIS, MARY ANN TO ASA ANDERSON
ELLISON, JOSEPH M. TO MOLLIE MITCHELL 12-24-1868 (12-25-1868)
ELLISON, MARTHA TO LAFAYETT JONES
ELROD, A. T. TO MISS SUSAN JUSTIC 12-12-1871
ELROD, ADAM TO JANE LOWING 8-2-1838
ELROD, B. F. TO MISS ANNIE MILLIKIN 9-6-1871
ELROD, ELIZA B. TO WM. B. FERREL
ELROD, ELIZABETH TO JAMES H. MITCHELL
ELROD, I. J. TO W. E. JUSTICE
ELROD, J. M. TO MISS M. M. COUCH 10-30-1869 (10-31-1869)
ELROD, MARGARET TO JOHN FERREL
ELROD, MARTHA T. TO JOSEPH HANES
ELROD, NANNIE A. TO F. J. LORANCE
ELROD, S. H. TO MARY JONES 10-24-1860 (NO RETURN)
EMERY, ELIZABETH S. TO JEREMIAH ROMINE
ENGLISH, ANDREW TO MISS ROXIE TEAGUE 4-20-1866 (4-22-1866)
ENGLISH, JOHN D. TO MARY J. MARTIN 1-10-1852 (1-12-1852)
ENGLISH, NANCY TO JOHN ESQUE
ENGLISH, SARAH TO W. A. MARTIN
ENNIS, ISSABELLA TO HARMAN H. HOPKINS
ENOS, HENRY TO ELIZA PARTIN 1-1-1841 (1-7-1841)
ENOS, HENRY TO MISS NELLY KINNAMON 10-12-1848
ENSEY, ELIGIA A. TO MISS HONEY COOPER 2-7-1853 (2-10?-1853)
ENSEY, JAMES A. H. TO MISS MARGARETT ANN FERRELL 3-9-1868 (3-12-1868)
ENSEY, REBECCA A. TO J. D. DUNCAN
ENSEY, W. S. TO LUCINDA ANDERSON 7-14-1873
EPSEY, JAMES R. TO MARRY L. LEIGH 7-27-1854 (7-29-1854)
ERSRY, WM. L. TO MARY J. PARKER 11-19-1852 (11-22-1852)
ERVIN, NANCY E. TO G. W. D. PALLETT
ESCUE, CHARLES TO MISS MALISSA GILLIAM 8-30-1866 (8-28?-1866)
ESCUE, NANCY TO WILLIAM GOODING

ESCUE, PERLINA TO J. W. BARRATT
ESKHUE, G. G. TO NANCY R. GOOD 7-24-1857 (7-26-1857)
ESPEY, CHARLES TO MISS KATHERINE FINLY 6-11-1856
ESPEY, ELIZABETH TO JOHN FINLEY
ESPEY, HENRIETTA TO HYRAM TODD
ESPEY, JEMIMA TO HOLLIS COOPER
ESPEY, MARGARETT J. TO JAMES JAMISON
ESPEY, SARAH L. TO CLENDENEN PAUL
ESPEY, VINA A. TO MATHE W. EADS
ESPY, CHARLES TO SUSAN A. HERALD 7-11-1872 (7-12-1872)
ESPY, M. J. TO J. W. ST. JOHN
ESPY, NANCY TO WILLIAM RING
ESPY, NARCISSA TO ROBERT JAMISON
ESPY, ROBERT TO ELIZABETH DEAUBOISE 3-23-1838 (3-27-1838)
ESQUE, CHARLES TO MISS MARY GANNON 10-30-1847 (10-31-1847)
ESQUE, ELIZA TO JOHN DENNIS
ESQUE, JOHN TO NANCY ENGLISH 2-3-1842
ESQUE, LUCINDA TO JOHN W. ELKINS
ESQUE, MARY R. TO JAMES M. TUCKER
ESSARY, MARTHA F. TO PETER PRICE
ESSARY, REBECCA E. TO JAMES L. CRAFT
ESTES, EDWARD TO MISS MARY ANN PARKER 12-8-1847
ESTES, MARGARETT ANN TO GIDEON THOMPSON
ESTES, RACHEL TO PETER ADAMS
EVANS, C. C. TO MARY STOR 9-28-1872 (9-29-1872)
EVANS, C. E. TO THOMAS J. WOODS
EVANS, CHARLES E. TO MISS SARAH CHUMLY 1-4-1855
EVANS, DAVID TO MISS ELIZA MELTON 4-20-1848 (NO RETURN)
EVANS, E. A. TO D. B. WORLEY
EVANS, JAMES M. TO ELIZABETH STONE 12-22-1842 (12-23-1842)
EVANS, JAMES M. TO MISS JULIA MULLINS 11-9-1865
EVANS, JULIA ANN TO CHARLES A. COX
EVANS, LEMUEL D. TO MISS ETHALINDA KIRSEY 8-27-1850
EVANS, NANCY A. TO STEPHEN A. ANDERSON 8-13-1863 (NO RETURN)
EVANS, NANCY C. TO JESSE BARRATT
EVANS, POLLY E. TO E. G. FERRELL
EVANS, SALLIE L. TO JOSEPH A. BAILEY
EVANS, SARRAH TO CAMPBELL GUNTER
EVON, ELIZABETH TO ISAAH NEELY
EWEL, LATEN TO MILLY WILLIAMS 2-22-1864 (NO RETURN)
EWELL, JOHN TO MISS ELIZABETH BUSH 1-7-1847
EWELL, SARAH TO WM. TODD
EWING, JOHN L. TO MARY JANE MCADOO 12-9-1839 (12-19-1839)
EWING, NANCY M. TO JOHN B. THOMPSON
EWING, TENNIE TO SAMUEL ROBERSON
FAGAN, ALBERT T. TO ISSABELLA ELIZABETH ANN KATES 3-19-1842
FAGAN, ELIZA TO WILLIAM MCGILL
FAGAN, ELIZABETH A. TO J. C. SMITH
FAGAN, GRANVILLE TO MISS ANN M. MCFADDAN 9-18-1854
FAGAN, I. N. TO J. W. MCBROOM
FAGAN, JAMES H. TO CAROLINE COX 8-11-1849 (8-12-1849)
FAGAN, M. J. TO T. A. GAITHER
FAGAN, MOLLIE E. TO HARTWELL HOUSE
FAGAN, ROBERT L. TO MISS CYNTHIA GAITHER 2-16-1846
FAIESTAR, N. H. TO A. G. CAMPBELL
FALKENBERY, ISABELLA TO R. F. SULLIVAN
FAN, ALEXANDER TO MARTHA A. HARRIS 4-21-1864
FANEN, REBECCA TO JOHN POWEL
FANN, ALFORD TO MISS M. S.? HIBDON 2-28-1852
FANN, CAROLINE TO BRICE M. RICHARDSON

FANN, FRANCIS TO MISS SARAH BARRATT 12-17-1845
FANN, G. TO MISS T. H. SNEED 9-26-1857
FANN, GRUNDY TO M. B. HARRIS 7-12-1860 (NO RETURN)
FANN, GRUNDY TO MISS CAROLINE SAULS 3-5-1844 (3-10-1844)
FANN, J. Q. TO MISS ELIZABETH GAITHER 2-23-1871 (2-27-1871)
FANN, JAMES TO MISS SARAH J. HARRIS 9-1-1869 (9-2-1869)
FANN, JEMIMA TO WILLIAM REED
FANN, JNO. A. TO MARY C. GANN 10-28-1873 (10-29-1873)
FANN, JULIE Q. TO SAMUEL TUCKER
FANN, MARY J. TO T. J. BUSEY
FANN, MELISSA TO D. B. REED
FANN, MELISSA TO JESSE SMITH
FANN, PELINA TO NATHANIEL GANN ?
FANN, SARAH A. TO D. H. TEDDER
FANN, WM. TO MARTHA WILSON 6-25-1864
FARE, D. L. TO A. G. MCKNIGHT
FARE, MARY A. TO MOSES W. MCKNIGHT
FARLER, HENRY TO LUCINDA HART 2-12-1841 (2-14-1841)
FARLER, MAHALA TO THOMAS MERRIMAN
FARLER, MARY TO DANIEL THOMAS
FARLER, PATTON TO MISS HANEY PHILIPS 1-30-1844 (2-2-1844)
FARLER, TABITHA TO EDWARD WATERS
FARLEY, JOHN JEFFERSON TO MISS SARAH THOMAS 3-6-1847 (3-7-1847)
FARLEY, LETTY TO THOMAS M. PRATER
FARLEY, NANCY J. TO CRAVIN WATERS
FARLEY, PATTON TO DOVEY WALLS 1-1-1872
FARLEY, TEBIPHA TO W. R. J. PRATOR
FARLY, CHARLES TO MISS MARTHA C.PRATER 1-4-1855 (1-5-1855)
FARR, BETTIE K. TO JAMES S. BARTON
FARRELL, HARRISON W. TO MISS SARAH JANE FERRELL 3-17-1868
FARRELL, SARAH JANE TO ROBERT S. MURFREY
FAULKAM, JAMES TO PARTHANA MILLIKIN 2-7-1858
FAULKENBERG, BENJAMIN TO MISS DELITHA WATERS 1-24-1850 (NO RETURN)
FAULKENBERG, JAMES TO MARGARET BRAGG 5-5-1840
FAULKENBERG, JOHN TO JANE RUTHERFORD CATHEY 10-23-1839 (10-24-1839)
FERGASON, F. M. TO MISS CHARITY BULLARD 10-31-1870 (11-3-1870)
FERREL, ELIZABETH J. TO THOMAS WHORTON
FERREL, JAMES TO MARTHER ST. JOHN 9-16-1865
FERREL, JOHN TO MISS MARGARET A. ELROD 8-24-1844 (8-25-1844)
FERREL, JORDON TO JULIA TAYLOR 8-22-1865 (8-28-1865)
FERREL, MARGARET TO JOHN MCBROOM
FERREL, WM. B. TO ELIZA B. ELROD 8-29-1839
FERRELL, C. TO MISS M. SULLENS 7-16-1859 (NO RETURN)
FERRELL, CENNINE TO JAMES BALEY
FERRELL, E. G. TO MISS MARY E. PATTRICK 9-23-1869
FERRELL, E. G. TO MISS POLLY E. EVANS 1-14-1867 (1-16-1867)
FERRELL, ELIZA ANN TO JOHN F. WEEDON
FERRELL, ELIZA P. TO EM HART
FERRELL, ELIZABETH TO C. H. GASAWAY
FERRELL, ENOCH TO MISS SUSANAH SULLINS 12-20-1859 (NO RETURN)
FERRELL, FANNIE TO DAVID BURKETT
FERRELL, J. B. TO FRANCES A. RIGSBY 8-31-1872 (9-1-1872)
FERRELL, JAMES W. TO MISS DELILA MOORE 5-13-1870 (5-15-1870)
FERRELL, JOHN TO SARAH SPURLOCK 2-15-1844
FERRELL, LAURA TO EZEKIEL BARTON
FERRELL, M. L. TO W. H. SULLIVAN
FERRELL, MALISA A. TO JOHN A. TATE
FERRELL, MARGARETT ANN TO JAMES A. H. ENSEY
FERRELL, MARINDA TO WILLIAM SPURLOCK
FERRELL, MARTHA TO JAMES D. TAYLOR

FERRELL, MARY ELIZABETH TO WILLIAM T. PENDLETON
FERRELL, MARY JANE TO JOHN F. WEEDON
FERRELL, MARY TO ANDY MITCHELL
FERRELL, MARY TO JOHN A. SPURLOCK
FERRELL, ROXANAH TO PEYTON B. CURLEE
FERRELL, RUTH TO SAMUEL SULLINS
FERRELL, SARAH JANE TO HARRISON W. FARRELL
FERRELL, SUSAN J. TO MICHAEL BOGLE
FERRELL, W. G. TOMARY SULLIVAN 3-27-1864
FERRELL, WILLIAM TO MANCA RIDEOUT 10-3-1873 (10-4-1873)
FERRELL, WILLIAM TO MISS SARAH YOUNG 8-1-1843
FERRELL, WM. TO CLAY J. BOLEY 12-31-1873 (1-1-1874)
FERRELL, YOUNG TO MISS ADALINE CUMMINS 12-19-1866 (12-20-1866)
FERRILL, E. W. TOMISS J. W. HARE 2-10-1858
FERRILL, M. R. TO TH. BREWER
FIELDS, MARTIN TO MISS SCYNTHA GOINS 3-28-1867
FIGHT, OBEDIAH TO MISS SARAH A. MCCULLOUGH 2-9-1870 (2-16-1870)
FINCH, KATHARINE E. TO JOSEPH DAVIS?
FINLEY, ALEATHY TO JEREMIAH J. OWEN
FINLEY, ALEXANDER TO MISS MANERVA J. LEIGH 3-7-1850
FINLEY, ANALIZA TO G. W. THURSTON
FINLEY, CHRISTENEY C. TO LEGRAND HERRALL
FINLEY, E. TO K. C. SULLIVAN
FINLEY, EFFA TO JOHN A. WEBBER
FINLEY, FRANCES TO W. J. SMITH
FINLEY, GEO. TO MISS MARENER GAITHER 3-14-1871
FINLEY, GEO. W. TO MARTHA J. LYNN 8-4-1873 (8-7-1873)
FINLEY, HENRY TO L. L. DUNCAN 9-27-1865
FINLEY, J. C. TO MISS E. GAITHER 11-7-1870 (11-8-1870)
FINLEY, JAMES TO MISS JEMIMA MALISSA COOPER 1-30-1851 (NO RETURN)
FINLEY, JANE P. TO J. G. TAYLOR
FINLEY, JOHN TO ELIZABETH ESPEY 2-8-1843 (2-9-1843)
FINLEY, MANERVA J. TO PETER J. LEWIS
FINLEY, MARGARET P. TO ZACHARIAH CONLEY
FINLEY, MARY A. TO GEORGE PARKER
FINLEY, NANCY TO WILLIAM B. WHITTEMORE
FINLEY, NANCY TO WILLIAM C. CATHY
FINLEY, SARAH JANE TO BRADLEY HAM
FINLEY, THOMAS TO MISS LUCY CATHEY 4-10-1847
FINLY, ALEX TO MALINDA WEST 7-21-1873 (NO RETURN)
FINLY, CATHARIN JANE TO JOHN A. PARKER
FINLY, ELENOR TO ANDREW S. SIMPSON
FINLY, ELIZABETH TO JAMES H. HAITHCOCK
FINLY, KATHARINE TO CHARLES ESPEY
FINLY, REBECA TO DAVID WILLIAM
FISHER, A. N. TO MISS TENNESSEE E. WEEDAN 1-22-1856
FISHER, JOHN TO MISS MARIAH E. PORTERFIELD 11-20-1844 (11-21-1844)
FISHER, MARIAN E. TO WM. MCFERIN
FISHER, MARIAN TO OSIN ALEXANDER
FISHER, SARAH E. TO JAMES H. BELL
FITCH, PARLIE TO WILLIAM BARRETT
FITE, DANIEL TO MISS MARGARETT JANE SUTTON 12-23-1850 (12-25-1850)
FITE, J. C. TO MISS SARAH L. ODOM 8-28-1871 (9-3-1871)
FITE, JOHN A. TO MISS H. A. PATY 2-7-1871 (2-9-1871)
FITSPATRICK, SUSAN TO WM. L. PRESTON
FLEMMING, ALBERT M. TO MISS MATILDA BURNETT 7-24-1841 (7-25-1841)
FLETCHER, HARIETT TO THOMAS MEDLOCK
FLETCHER, LOUISA TO H. L. W. CAPSHAW
FLETCHER, MAY TO B. H. AKEN
FLOYD, S. E. TO M. M. ODOM

FORCANA, KATHERIN TO WILLIAM COOPER
FORD, AMANDA T. TO GEORGE W. UNDERHILL
FORD, D. S. TO MARY E. RIGSBY 12-16-1871 (12-17-1871)
FORD, D. S. TO MISS P. D. MAKUM 10-31-1859 (11-9-1859)
FORD, DANIEL TO PAMELIA A. SPURLOCK 2-22-1839 (NO RETURN)
FORD, EASTER L. TO WILLIAM PITMAN
FORD, GORLEY? T. S. TO MISS ISABELLA MANKIN 9-13-1859 (NO RETURN)
FORD, HARIETT TO G. W. COOPER
FORD, HARRY E. TO MISS SARAH GUNTHE 7-27-1854
FORD, J. P. TO ANNA COOPER 1-12-1865 (1-27-1865)
FORD, JAMES W. TO JEMIMA M. TODD 10-30-1865 (11-1-1865)
FORD, LARKIN TO MISS R. C. JIMMERSON 11-24-1870
FORD, LAVISA H. TO LEMUEL D. BURKE
FORD, LUANNA J. TO JOSEPH H. SISSOM
FORD, MARTHA C. TO W. B. BLAIRE
FORD, MARY TO THOMAS OLIVAR
FORD, MARY TO WM. SMITH
FORD, NANCY E. TO JOHN A. JAMESON
FORD, NANCY TO WILLIAM MCNICKLE
FORD, ORVELL H. TO MISS P. KNOX 9-14-1865 (9-21-1865)
FORD, S. J. TO M. C. BURKETT
FORD, THOMAS TO MISS ----- HANCOCK 12-23-1850 (NO RETURN)
FORD, THOMAS TO MISS ELIZA J. RANEY 12-21-1854
FORD, W. J. TO MISS D. J. DAVIS 12-28-1870 (12-29-1870)
FOSTER, ANN TO JAMES CUMMINS
FOSTER, BETTIE P. TO T. B. CURLEE
FOSTER, ELIZA T. TO ROBT. L. ELKIN
FOSTER, HANAH TO WM. N. FOSTER
FOSTER, ISAAC TO MISS SYRILDA YORK 6-9-1868 (6-14-1868)
FOSTER, J. D. TO MISS M. A. MARKUM 8-27-1859 (NO RETURN)
FOSTER, JOHN R. TO MISS MARY J. ELKINS 9-6-1870 (9-27-1870)
FOSTER, KATHARINE TO JOHN O. TACKETT
FOSTER, LUCINDA TO J. B. CROUCH
FOSTER, MARY ANN TO T. D. ELKINS
FOSTER, POLLY ANN TO WILLIAM J. STONE
FOSTER, PORTER, TO MISS MARGARETT A. STONE 9-4-1841
FOSTER, ROBERT M. TO MISS ZENOBIA F. SOAPE 12-5-1850
FOSTER, SARAH JANE TO SAMUEL PRESTON
FOSTER, W. L. TO EMILY H. PATERSON 7-24-1865 (7-26-1865)
FOSTER, WM. N. TO MISS HANAH FOSTER 11-22-1856 (NO RETURN)
FOUSTEN, ANN TO JOHN KEATON
FOWLER, BURRELL TO MISS MARTHA CONTY 11-15-1854
FOWLER, JACOB B. TO MISS MARTHA VIRGINIA ELKINS 5-21-1846
FOWLER, JAMES M. TO FRANCES E. LANCE 12-7-1868
FOWLER, JESSEE TO MISS CHARLOTTE WINNETT 2-20-1866 (2-21-1866)
FOWLER, JOHN TO M. F. YOUNGBLOOD 10-16-1873
FOWLER, JOSEPHINE TO JAMES SMITH
FOWLER, LAURA A. TO WILLIAM HART
FOWLER, NANCY TO JACOB KUYKENDALL
FOWLER, PATTON TO MISS NANCY E. PRATOR 6-13-1855
FOX, JAMES M. TO MISS MARTHA P. KNOX 1-19-1866 (1-23-1866)
FRANCIS, A. A. TO MISS M. E. COOPER 12-15-1870
FRANCIS, A. F. TO V. P. MCADOO 12-3-1873 (12-4-1873)
FRANCIS, ARMSTED TO ELIZABETH SUMMAR 10-14-1840 (NO RETURN)
FRANCIS, C. C. TO MISS LAVISA SUMMAR 3-9-1868
FRANCIS, C. J. TO J. N. MCADOE
FRANCIS, E. P. TO R. T. HANCOCK
FRANCIS, J. D. TO MISS P. E. SUMMER 1-30-1856 (1-31-1856)
FRANCIS, LUCINDA TO P. P. JOHNSON
FRANCIS, M. C. TO MISS L. J. SUMNAR 2-26-1858 (2-28-1858)

FRANCIS, M. H. TO MISS MARY M. BRYSON 10-21-1867
FRANCIS, MALINDA TO RICHARD L. VANDAGRIFF
FRANCIS, MALISSA TO D. B. WILLARD
FRANCIS, MARTHA TO JAMES W. WILSON
FRANCIS, MARY ANN TO JOS. D. OWEN
FRANKLIN, PETER F. TO MISS ELIZABETH WADE 10-11-1849 (10-31-1845?)
FRANKS, L. B. TO MISS FANNY NEW 6-18-1866 (6-21-1866)
FRASURE, ROBERT TO MALINDA BUSH (LICENSE DATE OMITTED) (9-14-1851(
FREEMAN, AVANDER TO ALMARINDA TODD 6-6-1856 (6-15-1856)
FREEMAN, ELIZABETH TO ROBERT J. JAMES
FREEMAN, J. H. TO MISS MATTIE J. WOOD 9-21-1858 (NO RETURN)
FREEMAN, JAKE TO HANNAH J. JONES 9-16-1873 (9-22-1873)
FREEMAN, NANCY A. E. TO W. J. VASSER
FREEZE, EMALINE TO ABRAHAM GRAY
FREEZE, HIRAM TO SARAH JONES 12-26-1844
FREEZE, JOHN TO MISS MATTIE A. HOGWOOD 10-19-1867 (10-20-1867)
FRENCH, JOHN M. TO MISS MARY E. GREEN 1-7-1868 (1-8-1868)
FRY, ELIZABETH TO JAMES M. WHEELING
FRY, NANCY TO JOHN BOLIN
FUGETT, FRANCES TO HENRY CLAY
FUGETT, SUSAN TO WASHINGTON HARE
FUGETT, WASHINGTON TO ELVIRA TAYLOR 12-8-1865
FUGITT, EMILY TO MARTIN FUGITT
FUGITT, JANE W. TO THOMAS B. BREVARD
FUGITT, MARTIN TO EMILY FUGITT 8-24-1865
FUGITT, SALLIE TO E. T. DILLON
FUGITT, SAML. (COL) TO JOSEPHINE WOOD 2-22-1873
FUGITT, TOWNSEND TO MISS ANN BROWN 9-19-1853
FUGITT, WM. TO LUCINDA GLASPER 12-11-1873
FULLER, JAMES TO MISS ELIZABETH C. GIVENS 7-11-1867
FULLER, SUSAN TO ABNER MCKNIGHT
FURMAN, ANN E. TO PLEASANT T. HENDERSON
FUSTON, ELIZABETH TO WILLIAM KEETAN
FUSTON, JOSIAH TO ELIZABETH KEETON 5-19-1856
FUSTON, JOSIAH TO SALLY RIGSBY 12-23-1865
FUSTON, LEROY TO MISS MALISSA HOLLANDSWORTH 2-13-1869 (2-14-1869)
FUSTON, LUCINDA TO ALFORD OWEN
FUSTON, MARGARETT TO C. H. GASAWAY
FUSTON, MELVINA TO WILLIAM HIGGANS
FUSTON, SARAH TO HENRY BARRUTT
FUSTON, SARAH TO J. M. HERNDON
GAINS, J. B. TO EMELINE COOPER 2-1-1860 (NO RETURN)
GAITHEN, BASWELL TO ISABELLA BURK 2-1-1865
GAITHER, ANGELINE TO ELIJAH S. KNOX
GAITHER, ANN TO THOMAS CAMBELL
GAITHER, BAZEL TO MISS MARY A. COX 2-14-1849
GAITHER, CYNTHIA TO ROBERT L. FAGAN
GAITHER, E. TO J. C. FINLEY
GAITHER, ELIZA JANE TO JOHN H. SAULS
GAITHER, ELIZABETH F. TO P. B. CURLEE
GAITHER, ELIZABETH TO J. Q. FANN
GAITHER, ELIZABETH TO THOMAS E. JONES
GAITHER, ISAAC TO MISS S. E. BRAGG 4-3-1871 (4-?-1871)
GAITHER, JACKSON TO JOANNA R. GANNON 11-8-1873 (11-9-1873)
GAITHER, JOHN W. TO AMANDA R. CURLEE 8-27-1866 (8-28-1866)
GAITHER, M. E. TO T. G. BASSHAM
GAITHER, M. L. C. TO W. A. SAFFLE
GAITHER, MAHALA TO N. O. PERRY
GAITHER, MARENER TO GEO. FINLEY
GAITHER, MARTHA TO ABNER B. BOWEN

GAITHER, MARY E. TO HUBBARD MORGAN
GAITHER, MARY H. TO P. B. CURLEE
GAITHER, MARY JANE TO DANIEL TENPENNY
GAITHER, MERAN L. TO WM. H. YONG
GAITHER, PLEASANT TO MISS ELVIRA SULLIVAN 11-8-1866
GAITHER, R. L. TO MISS MARGARET E. BRANDON 1-30-1866 (2-1-1866)
GAITHER, SARAH TO ALBERT G. MILLIKIAN
GAITHER, SILAS TO REBECCA J. BRAGG 11-2-1865
GAITHER, T. A. TO MISS M. J. FAGAN 3-31-1866 (4-1-1866)
GAITHER, THOMAS F. TO MISS MARY ELIZABETH HORN 1-24-1848 (1-27-1848)
GAITHER, W. P. TO MISS S. A. E. CARUTHERS 3-3-1856 (3-4-1856)
GAITHER, WILSON TO MISS KATHARINE TUCKER 4-8-1843 (4-9-1843)
GAITHER, ZELPHA TO FRANKLIN READY
GALAHARE, JULY TO JAMES W. TARLTON
GAM, JOHN H? TO MISS ELIZABETH M. BENNETT 9-18-1855
GAM, MARRY? J. TO WM. H. GAN
GAMON, DILLARD L. TO MISS ELIZABETH SMITH 11-5-1850 (NO RETURN)
GAN, ALLAMINTA TO JOSHUA BUTCHER
GAN, CALIDONIA TO JOHN F. DAVENPORT
GAN, DANIEL TO MISS MARTHA GAN 6-13-1854
GAN, MARTHA TO DANIEL GAN
GAN, SARAH TO JOSEPH DEVANPORT
GAN, WM. H. TO MARRY? J. GAM 1-4-1853 (1-5-1853)
GANDY, E. A. TO JOHN E. MITCHELL
GANN, BRITTON TO MISS ANN MANUS 6-10-1868
GANN, CYNTHIA TO ADAM TITTLE
GANN, ELIZA TO ROBERT BOGLE
GANN, JAMES TO MISS ELIZABETH BASHAM 3-4-1856
GANN, JOHN H. TO MISS SUSAN C. STANLEY 3-23-1867 (3-24-1867)
GANN, JOHN TO MISS CRIDA BRANDON 1-6-1869
GANN, JOHN TO MISS LUCINDA BRANDON 1-9-1868 (2-8-1868)
GANN, M. C. TO MISS LAVINA COLLINS 11-17-1866 (11-18-1866)
GANN, MARGARET A. TO BENJAMIN L. GILLUM
GANN, MARY C. TO JNO. A. FANN
GANN, MARY J. TO WM. H. GANN
GANN, NATHAN TO MISS JEMIMA WILSON 3-2-1868 (3-4-1868)
GANN, NATHANIEL TO MISS P. J. HARRIS 2-28-1856
GANN, ROBERT TO MISS MARTH STANLY 8-20-1844 (8-21-1844)
GANN, ROBERT TO SALLIE LAFEVERS 2-21-1873
GANN, ROBT. TO SARAH AMUS 9-19-1872 (NO RETURN)
GANN, RUSSEL TO MISS ELIZABETH ASHFORD 7-29-1857
GANN, TENNESSEE TO LAFAYETT BETHELL
GANN, WM. H. TO MISS MARY J. GANN 1-4-1853 (1-5-1853)
GANN?, NATHANIEL TO PELINA FANN 12-21-1865 (12-28-1865)
GANNN, SAMUEL M. TO MISS LOCKEY J. HERRYMAN 7-22-1868 (7-23-1868)
GANNON, GEORGE TO REBECCA PACE 9-3-1842 (9-6-1842)
GANNON, HARVY A. TO LIDEY SIMPSON 8-30-1863
GANNON, JAMES P. TO TENNIE W. BROOKS 10-11-1873 (10-12-1873)
GANNON, JOANNA R. TO JACKSON GAITHER
GANNON, JOANNA TO WILLIAM A. SULLIVAN
GANNON, JOHN P. TO RIDY E. TRAVIS 2-23-1860
GANNON, JOHN TO MISS MANERVA HAYS 12-18-1849 (NO RETURN)
GANNON, MARTHA ANN TO NATHAN MCBROOM
GANNON, MARTHA TO DAVID HAYS
GANNON, MARY ANN TO ELI B. BARRETT
GANNON, MARY TO CHARLES ESQUE
GANNON, NITHA A. TO PETER SIMPSON
GANNON, ROXANNA TO JOHN BRANDON
GANNON, SAML. TO SUSANNAH STACY 12-12-1839 (12-13-1839)
GANNON, SAMUEL TO MISS MARTHA E. SAPP 3-7-1846 (3-8-1846)

GANNON, SARAH C. TO JAMES M. READY
GANNON, SARAH TO DILLARD TODD
GANNON, WM. E. TO REBECCA HAYS 3-24-1864
GARAWAY, JAMES R. TO MISS CAROLINE MORRIS 3-16-1858 (3-17-1858)
GARDNER, MARTHA A. TO D. W. MITCHELL
GARIS, W. G. D. TO MISS S. F. BABBITT 9-27-1858
GARIS, W. G. O. TO S. F. BABBETT 2-18-1859
GARITY, PATTRICK TO MISS SARAH M. HALE 7-15-1867 (7-20-1867)
GARMAN, G. W. TO MISS E. R. VANCE 10-1-1857
GARMENT, T. M. TO MISS ELIZABETH MILIGAN 6-15-1854
GARMON, THOMAS TO MISS MARTHA GILLEY 12-28-1857
GARNER, MATILDA J. TO JAMES A. BOND
GARNER, WM. H. TO MISS HARRIETT KEELY 11-5-1859 (11-8-1859)
GARRIS, WILLIAM G. D. TO MISS S. F. BABET 2-18-1859
GARRISON, C. B. TO MISS M. A. KENNEDY 11-23-1867 (11-25-1867)
GASAWAY, C. H. TO MISS ELIZABETH FERRELL 12-3-1853 (NO RETURN)
GASAWAY, C. H. TO MISS MARGARET FUSTON 4-1-1856 (NO RETURN)
GASAWAY, M. L. TO G. W. GRIZZLE
GASAWAY, RUFUS TO ELIZABETH MARTIN 3-14-1873 (3-16-1873)
GASSOWAY, GEORGIANA TO JOB MARCUN
GATES, G. W. TO OLLEY BLAIRE 10-9-1865 (10-14-1865)
GATHER, SARAH L. TO JOHN H. JONES
GAY, WM. TO SARAH R. BREWER? 12-7-1852 (12-8-1852)
GEONS, BLUFORD H. TO MISS SINTHY J. DOOD 2-2-1859 (NO RETURN)
GEORG, AMANDA J. TO JAMES A. HAILEY
GEORGE, JAMES O. TO MARTHAANN TROTT 8-21-1838
GEORGE, JOHN A. TO NANCY ALEXANDER 1-20-1842
GEORGE, MARIAH TO WILLIAM L. COVINGTON
GEORGE, MARRY J. TO R. K. STEPHEN
GEORGE, MARY S. TO JAMES A. MITCHELL
GEORGE, MILES B. TO FRANCES TENPENNY 8-23-1865 (9-2-1865)
GEORGE, PLEASANT TO VINA HARDIN 8-13-1869 (8-14-1869)
GEORGE, RACHEL TO THOMAS POWELL
GIBSON, ELIZABETH TO WILLIAM H. BUSEY
GIBSON, JAMES TO MISS ESTHER REED 12-15-1849
GIBSON, MARY E. TO STEVEN HERRIMAN
GIBSON, RICHARD D. TO MISS JEMIMA SOUTHERN 4-13-1843 (4-17-1843)
GILLAM, J. M. TO MISS NANCY BRYSON 7-2-1860 (NO RETURN)
GILLEY, A. S. TO MISS SARAH C. HOLLANDSWORTH 2-28-1867 (2-29-1867)
GILLEY, CHARLES TO JANE ANN BELL 4-1-1842 (5-15-1842)
GILLEY, EMALINE TO WILLIAM WILSHER
GILLEY, EZZY TO ELISHA MELTON
GILLEY, HARRIET C. TO GEORGE RITCHEY
GILLEY, ISAAC G. TO S. C. BOGLE 8-20-1870 (NO RETURN)
GILLEY, IZZA TO ELIGAH CRABTREE
GILLEY, J. R. Y. TO SARAH BUSH 2-8-1860 (NO RETURN)
GILLEY, JANE TO JOHN PRESTON
GILLEY, JESSE N. TO MISS LUCINDA BYNUM 10-5-1869 (NO RETURN)
GILLEY, JOHN TO MISS ELIZABETH ANN RIGBY 1-2-1854 (1-5-1854)
GILLEY, JUDAH F. TO JEREMIAH C. WALKER
GILLEY, M. B. TO MISS MARY E. MURFREE 8-23-1869
GILLEY, M. J. TO W. J. VANHOOZER
GILLEY, MALINDA TO J. H. MCCRARY
GILLEY, MARTHA TO THOMAS GARMON
GILLEY, MARY E. TO W. H. MERRITT
GILLEY, MARY M. TO JOHN HAWKINS
GILLEY, SAMUEL TO MISS MARTHA ELEDGE 10-15-1870 (10-16-1870)
GILLEY, SARAH E. TO JAMES CAMPBELL
GILLEY, T. F. TO MISS L. J. JONES 12-8-1868 (12-10-1868)
GILLEY, TERISIAN TO WM. CAMPBELL

GILLIAM, MALISSA TO CHARLES ESCUE
GILLUM, BENGAMIN TO MISS LUCINDA HELTON 12-3-1869
GILLUM, BENJAMIN L. TO MISS MARGARET A. GANN 2-13-1866 (2-14-1866)
GILLUM, HENRY TO MELVINA HARRIS 8-27-1865
GILLUM, S. E. TO P. A. HIBDON
GILLY, AMOS TO MISS ELIZABETH TITTLE 2-12-1854 (2-15-1854)
GILLY, DORCUS TO WM. A. JERNIGAN
GILLY, ISZA TO ELIGAH CRABTREE
GILLY, MARY A. TO JAMES BURKET
GILLY, N. I. TO H. A. LEWIS
GILLY, WILLIAM TO HANNAH BLANTON 4-14-1838 (4-20-1838)
GILSON, ROBERT TO MISS POLLY SOUTHERLAND 3-25-1846 (3-26-1846)
GINOE?, W. Z. TO NANCY A. JAMISON 12-20-1859 (NO RETURN)
GIVAN, BLUFORD H. TO MISS SMITHY J. DODD 2-2-1859 (NO RETURN)
GIVENS, ELIZABETH C. TO JAMES FULLER
GIVENS, FORDY TO GEORGE DEVENPORT
GIVENS, MARY F. TO JESSE L. TODD
GIVENS, MARY TO C. D. MELTON
GIVENS, S. J. TO MISS S. J. MELTON 12-22-1866 (12-23-1866)
GIVENS, SALLIE TO BAILAM RIGSBY
GIVENS, WILLIAM A. TO MISS ELIZA A. NICHOLS 3-3-1845 (NO RETURN)
GIVENS, WILLIAM C. TO NANCY BRALLEY 12-24-1842
GIVENS, WILLIAM J. TO MISS HARRIET EASON 1-20-1851 (1-21-1851)
GIVINS, AMERICA TO I. N. B. MURFREE
GIVINS, M. TO L. L. LEWIS
GLASPER, LUCINDA TO WM. FUGITT
GLAZEBROOKS, JAMES TO MISS NANCY A. PHILIPS 7-17-1845
GOAD, G. B. TO MISS MARGRET TODD 5-6-1854 (3-5-1855)
GOAD, LOUISA TO R. W. PATTERSON
GOAD, WILLIAM TO MRS. MALINDA BUNCH 3-31-1869
GODWIN, BENJAMIN A. TO MISS REBECCA BRANDON 5-4-1843
GOEN, LABORN TO ORTIME CLARK 7-18-1855 (RETURNS MISSING)
GOFF, L. P. TO MISS ANN C. MELTON 3-29-1870 (3-30-1870)
GOFF, L. P. TO SARAH BRIM 11-21-1873
GOFF, MARTHA ANN TO J. E. WIMBERLY
GOINGS, RODA TO JOHN CRAWFORD
GOINS, CARTER TO CATHARINE SCOTT 5-23-1868 (5-28-1868)
GOINS, EDMOND TO MISS ZADE A. HOLLANDWORTH 4-19-1856 (4-20-1856)
GOINS, JOHN B. TO CHATATA CRAFT 12-28-1855
GOINS, SCYNTHA TO MARTIN FIELDS
GOLAHAN, ROBERT TO NANCY DUBIRTH 8-23-1839
GOOD, HARRIET C. TO W. D. T. THOMPSON
GOOD, M. P. TO J. C. PHILLIPS
GOOD, MARY A. TO HENRY N. THOMAS
GOOD, MARY ANN TO DANIEL M. POLOCK
GOOD, N. C. TO J. M. ANDERSON
GOOD, NANCY R. TO G. G. ESKHUE
GOOD, NANCY TO WILLIAM HALEY
GOOD, R. C. TO ANN HELTON 2-13-1872
GOOD, WM. TO ANGELINE LASETER 11-11?-1851 (11-21-1851)
GOODIN, SUSANAH TO THOMAS K. BEATY
GOODIN, WILLIAM TO SABELLA BRANDON 11-21-1838 (NO RETURN)
GOODING, ABRAHAM TO MISS OLIVE SIMPSON 9-19-1857 (9-20-1857)
GOODING, EMELINE TO J. W. COOK
GOODING, JAMES TO ISABELLA TODD 10-17-1872
GOODING, LUCINDA TO JOHN W. STACY
GOODING, MARTHA TO CHARLES POFF
GOODING, MARTHA TO JAMES MCCLAIN
GOODING, MARY TO HAMPTON ELKINS
GOODING, RADID? TO A. J. BEATY

GOODING, RICHARD TO MISS ESTHER C. CARRICK 12-22-1866 (12-27-1866)
GOODING, ROBERT TO CAROLINE WIMBY 7-21-1860 (7-26-1860)
GOODING, SARAH TO ARTHUR N. SMOOT
GOODING, SARAH TO W. T. LEMMONS
GOODING, WILLIAM TO MISS FANNY HOLT 8-4-1841 (8-6-1841)
GOODING, WILLIAM TO MISS NANCY ESCUE 3-28-1854 (3-30-1854)
GOODING, WILLIAM TO MISS PARLEE STANFIELD 11-5-1869 (11-17-1869)
GOODLOE, A. M. TO MISS M. E. SMITH 6-17-1856
GOODLOE, ALLEMIRA M. TO BRYANT HAN
GOODLOE, B. R. TO MISS EUGENIA CROCKER 4-9-1867
GOODLOE, E. A. TO A. E. MCKNIGHT
GOODWIN, R. D. TO JANE SIMMONS 3-10-1865
GORDEN, GEORGE H. TO MISS LAVISA BRANDON 10-6-1841 (NO RETURN)
GORDON, AMANDA TO THOMAS BEARGIN
GORDON, J. H. TO MISS ANN E. MITCHELL 12-24-1870 (12-25-1870)
GORDON, JOHN TO MISS HARRIETT PATTON 10-28-1847
GORDON, JULIAN TO RICHARD MARTIN
GORDON, LEWIS TO LUCINDA MARTIN 6-22-1867 (6-21?-1867)
GORDON, MOLLIE TO GEO. MITCHELL
GORDON, ROBERT TO MISS SARAH HAYS 1-20-1848
GORDON, ROBERT TO MISS VINA A. ROBINSON 7-9-1845
GORDON, W. M. TO MISS MARY A. HOOKER 12-7-1870 (12-23-1870)
GOTCHER, W. M. TO MISS FANNY DICKENS 11-2-1847 (11-3-1847)
GOWEN, CHARITY TO NATHAN GOWIN
GOWEN, H. N. TO M. A. E. BROWN 1-7-1873
GOWEN, JAMES J. TO MISS MARTHA E. MOORE 2-17-1853 (7-20-1853)
GOWEN, JULIA Y. TO NICHOLAS C. TILFORD
GOWENS, SARAH TO RICHARD BOWLIN
GOWER, BETTIE TO W. M. BREWER
GOWIN, JOHN TO MISS RHODA GOWIN 3-29-1855 (RETURNS MISSING)
GOWIN, NATHAN TO MISS CHARITY GOWEN 3-29-1855 (SOLEMNIZED, NO DATE)
GOWIN, RHODA TO JOHN GOWIN
GRAHAM, --- M. TO MISS S. E. JUSTICE 2-14-1856
GRAHAM, J. M. TO LUTHUR S. RAMSEY
GRAHAM, MATTIE D. TO E. P. CHAPMAN
GRAHAM, SALLIE TO E. J. LORANCE
GRAHAM, T. N. TO MISS EDNEY WHEELER 3-2-1871
GRAHAM, W. J. TO MISS M. E. JUSTICE 8-19-1858 (NO RETURN)
GRAHAM, W. J. TO MISS M. J. JUSTICE 8-3-1870 (8-7-1870)
GRAY, ABRAHAM TO EMALINE FREEZE 1-1-1866 (1-4-1866)
GRAY, JEMIMA E. TO W. J. WILLIAMS
GRAY, N. E. TO R. T. MCKNABB
GRAY, NANCY E. TO THOMAS H. WILLIAMS
GRAY, RACHEL CAROLINE TO THOMAS MCCOLLOUGH
GRAY, SAMUEL W. TO NANCY ELEANOR SAGELY 2-18-1843 (2-19-1843)
GRAY, SILAS M. TO MISS MARTHA E. HOLLIS 8-15-1854 (8-17-1854)
GRAY, W. W. TO MATTIE A. PRATER 9-27-1873 (9-28-1873)
GRAY, WILLIAM TO ELIZABETH WEBBER 8-4-1842 (8-5-1842)
GRAY, WM. TO TEMPA CAROLINE BROWN 12-27-1853
GREAR, ELIZABETH TO MOSES PERRY
GREEAR, DAVID TO MISS EDITH JONES 5-1-1843 (5-2-1843)
GREEAR, DAVID TO SALLY HARRIS 9-7-1839 (9-11-1839)
GREEAR, POLLY ANN TO PHILIP D. BEATY
GREEAR, THOMAS L. TO RACHAEL SOUTHERLAND 6-4-1842 (6-5-1842)
GREEN, JOHN C. TO MISS JANE E. BURK 1-7-1852 (1-11-1852)
GREEN, MARY E. TO JOHN M. FRENCH
GREER, JAMES C. TO OLIVE LANE 3-8-1838 (3-9-1838)
GRIFFIN, CAROLINE E. TO WM. MARTIN
GRIGGS, MICHAEL TO MISS LUCINDA PITTS 7-7-1859 (7-27-1859)
GRIMES, BRITTON TO MISS ELIZABETH HAYS 8-10-1843

GRIMES, G. G. C. TO MISS SARRAH J. SMITH 1-13-1853
GRIMES, GENINNIA TO ANDREW RAWLINGS
GRIMETT, PATSEY TO MOSE SNEED
GRINDSTAFF, JAMES TO ELIZABETH RITCH 5-26-1870
GRIZLE, WILLIAM TO POLLY MELTON 8-15-1840 (8-16-1840)
GRIZZEL, JOHN TO ELIZABETH HAMMONS 8-16-1872 (8-18-1872)
GRIZZEL, MARTHA N. TO JOHN N. DENNIS
GRIZZEL, SARAH E. TO E. W. TASSIE
GRIZZEL, SUSAN TO ROBERT MOLLEY
GRIZZEL, WILLIAM TO MRS. DOVEY CAMPBELL 8-15-1870 (8-17-1870)
GRIZZELL, IZZAN TO JAS. ARNETT
GRIZZELL, SARAH A. TO JAMES HAILEY
GRIZZLE, DANIEL TO MISS MARGARETT WOOD 9-26-1849 (9-27-1849)
GRIZZLE, G. W. TO MISS M. L. GASAWAY 3-7-1856 (3-10-1856)
GRIZZLE, ISAAC TO MISS ELIZABETH JONES 10-14-1847 (10-20-1847)
GRIZZLE, JAMES TO MISS MARTHA MELTON 9-14-1850 (9-16-1850)
GRIZZLE, PAUMP? TO RODY MARTIN9-27-1871
GRIZZLE, POLK TO MISS PARLEE MATHIS 8-7-1866 (8-9-1866)
GRIZZLE, RICHARD TO MISS PELINA J. BURGER 2-27-1867 (2-29-1867)
GROOM, A. E. TO A. G. OWENS
GROOM, FRANCES TO H. E. MCADOO
GROSS, HARRISON TO MARY BROWN 6-2-1866 (6-3-1866)
GULLETT, SAMUEL TO MISS MARTHA JANE CLEMENTS 7-25-1843
GUNTER, A. J. TO JOHN C. PRIME
GUNTER, A. TO ZEB BOWREN
GUNTER, ADALINE TO ISAAC BURGER
GUNTER, C. C. TO MISS C. NANCY MOORE 4-19-1853 (NO RETURN)
GUNTER, C. D. TO MARY INGLIS 11-29-1873 (11-27?-1873)
GUNTER, C. Y. TO MARY COOK 6-28-1873 (6-29-1873)
GUNTER, CAMPBELL TO MISS SARRAH EVANS 3-7-1855 (3-9-1855)
GUNTER, CLAIBORNE Y. TO MISS VIRGINIA KERSEY 9-27-1846 (9-28-1846)
GUNTER, ISAAC TO MISS MARY LAWRENCE 11-8-1853
GUNTER, JAMES M. TO MISS DISA PITMAN 2-8-1846
GUNTER, JOHN L. TO MISS TISBY A. BARRETT 1-23-1868
GUNTER, JOSEPHINE TO FRANCIS MELTON
GUNTER, MARGARETT TO J. B. LASETER
GUNTER, MARTHA TO MICAJAH MARCUM
GUNTER, MARY TO JAMES P. K. LANCE
GUNTER, SARAH TO JOHN D. MCDOUGALD
GUNTER, W. J. TO MISS REBECCA J. HIPP 12-24-1870 (12-25-1870)
GUNTER, WILLIAM TO SARRYAN? KERSEY 12-10-1853 (NO RETURN)
GUNTER, WILLIAM W. TO MISS ELIZABETH RAMSEY 7-12-1845 (7-13-1845)
GUNTHE, SARAH TO HARRY E. FORD
GURTY, MARY E. TO A. J. MCCABE
GUY, A. J. TO SARAH A. KERBY 12-27-1872 (NO RETURN)
GUY, JAMES TO NARCISSA PUCKET 6-1-1865

HADLEY, MELISSA TO MARK A. POPE
HADLEY, NANCY TO WESTLEY HERIMAN
HAGWOOD, H. B. TO SARAH E. CARTER 12-24-1873 (12-25-1873)
HAILEY, CAPHUS C. TO MISS SARA BURK 1-5-1856
HAILEY, CLEMENTINE TO HENRY WATERS
HAILEY, ELIZABETH TO MARK MEARS
HAILEY, J. A. TO MISS L. A. LYNN 8-30-1871 (8-31-1871)
HAILEY, JAMES A. TO MISS AMANDA J. GEORG 9-1-1858 (NO RETURN)
HAILEY, JAMES TO MISS SARAH A. GRIZZELL 8-23-1870 (8-28-1870)
HAILEY, TILDEY TO MCCASLIN MUNCEY
HAILEY, W. B. TO MISS M. E. RING 11-24-1869 (11-25-1869)
HAILY, ANN E. TO J. D. CAMPBELL
HAINEY, JOHN TO MARIAH MARCHBANKS 2-26-1840 (2-25-1840)(SIC)
HAITHCOCK, JAMES H. TO ELIZABETH FINLY 2-23-1844 (2-25-1844)
HAITHCOCK, POLLY TO SAMUEL H. STACY
HALE, CREED W. TO MISS NANCY JANE ASHFORD 5-8-1849
HALE, ELVIRA F. TO JAMES O. RITCH
HALE, L. TO J. W. WARREN
HALE, MARY O. TO GEORGE J. BOTTEN
HALE, MARY TO DAVID PATTON
HALE, NANCY C. TO PRESLEY A. ADAMSON
HALE, SARAH M. TO PATTRICK GARITY
HALE, THOMAS TO MARY MALISSA KEETON 1-19-1864 (1-21-1864)
HALE, THOMAS TO MISS MARY E. DODD 11-22-1869 (11-23-1869)
HALEY, ALLEN TO MISS MARTHA YOUNG 4-10-1847
HALEY, B. TO J. H. JANSON
HALEY, DAVID TO MISS SARAH ANN DUKE 1-11-1848
HALEY, GEORGE TO MISS ABAGAIL RHEA 9-23-1848 (9-28-1848)
HALEY, GEORGE TO MISS MARY BOWEN 2-20-1857 (NO RETURN)
HALEY, JAMES TO ELISABETH DICKENS 9-19-1840 (9-20-1840)
HALEY, JOHN W. TO JERUSHA WILLIAMS 6-12-1840 (6-14-1840)
HALEY, JOSHUA TO MISS ELEANOR HAYNES 1-3-1846 (2-26-1846)
HALEY, MARY A. TO H. PENDLETON
HALEY, NANCY E. TO A. L. HANCOCK
HALEY, S. A. TO N. J. BURK
HALEY, VENTURIAN TO N. R. J. DUKE 10-24-1860 (NO RETURN)
HALEY, WILLIAM TO NANCY GOOD 12-13-1855 (NO RETURN)
HALL, ALBERT E. TO MISS NANCY C. SPRY 3-3-1868
HALL, C. H. TO MISS SARAH MORRIS 2-1-1869
HALL, FLEMING W. TO MISS ELIZA A. PETTY 5-15-1844 (5-16-1844)
HALL, JAMES TO MISS MARY BURKET 8-1-1857 (8-3-1857)
HALL, JOHN W. TO MISS MARY ANN LAWING 8-31-1850 (9-1-1850)
HALL, JONATHAN TO MISS LOUISA LAMIRA WHARREY 12-9-1841
HALL, M. A. TO BENJAMIN ST CLAIR
HALL, MARGARETT TO ROBERT S. MILES
HALL, MARY E. TO W. M. BROWN
HALL, MARY TO THOMAS J. BREWER
HALL, PRESTON TO MISS MARGARETT WHERRY 9-25-1849 (NO PROPERTY FOUND)
HALL, R. TO MISS ELIZABETH WILLSON 12-2-1853 (12-4-1853)
HALL, WILLIAM J. TO MATILDA TROLLINGER 2-5-1844 (NO RETURN)
HALL, WILLIAM J. TO MISS ELIZABETH YOUNG 8-19-1846 (8-20-1846)
HALL,H. B. TO MISS CELISA JANE WALE 2-28-1848 (2-29-1848)
HALLEYBURTON, O. G. TO BITTIE MCFERREN 9-26-1872
HALPAYNE, MARTHA B. TO JAMES ROUGHTON
HALY, ELIZABETH TO DAVID REED
HALY, VICY C. TO JOHN A. DUKE
HAM, BRADLEY TO MISS SARAH JANE FINLEY 12-24-1866 (12-25-1866)
HAMILTON, HARVEY TO PENEY REED 1-8-1864 (NO RETURN)
HAMILTON, MARY TO RICHARD J. HOLSTON

HAMLET, NANCY TO ISAAC WILLIAMS
HAMMEN, MALINDA TO WESLEY A. MORGAN
HAMMON, JOHN TO MISS JANE YOUNG 11-1-1841 (NO RETURN)
HAMMON, LARKIN TO MISS POLLY SAPP 10-30-1841 (10-31-1841)
HAMMOND, MARY TO WM. HENDRICKSON
HAMMONDS, JOICE V. TO WARD BARRETT
HAMMONS, ELIZBETH TO JOHN GRIZZEL
HAMMONS, I. I. TO MARGARET N. ODOM 4-1-1865 (1-2?-1865)
HAMMONS, JASPER TO ELIZABETH KEATON 3-17-1864 (3-18-1864)
HAMMONS, JOHN J. TO NANCY T. YOUNG 7-29-1865 (7-30-1865)
HAMMONS, REESE TO MISS RUTHY STARR 12-4-1866 (12-5-1866)
HAMMONS, SALLY TO JOHN MOODY
HAMMONS, SARAH P. TO GEORGE ASHFORD
HAN, BRYANT TO ALLEMIRA M. GOODLOE 10-4-1854 (10-5-1854)
HANCOCK, A. L. TO M. J. VANDERGRIFF 4-1-1872
HANCOCK, A. L. TO MISS NANCY E. HALEY 3-1-1859 (NO RETURN)
HANCOCK, A. T. TO JOHN M. ALLEN
HANCOCK, ALAMINTA TO N. T. JEWEL
HANCOCK, CAROLINE TO J. A. KING
HANCOCK, CHARLES TO MISS NANCY HUBBARD 11-9-1867 (11-10-1867)
HANCOCK, CINDA TO JOHN ODOM (COL)
HANCOCK, E. C. TO R. M. RAMSEY
HANCOCK, ELIZA A. TO PETER S. TURNEY
HANCOCK, ELIZABETH TO SAM CHAMBERS
HANCOCK, FRANCES TO LEWIS HANCOCK
HANCOCK, JAMES TO TEMPY ADAMS 9-30-1865
HANCOCK, JERRY TO ELIZA MCKNIGHT 3-?-1873 (4-3-1873)
HANCOCK, JOHN TO MALISSA SELLARS 9-15-1865 (9-16-1865)
HANCOCK, JOSEPH TO MARY ADAMS 10-6-1866 (10-7-1866)
HANCOCK, LEWIS TO FRANCES HANCOCK 12-2-1852 (NO RETURN)
HANCOCK, LUCETTA TO JOS. O. HOLLINGSWORTH
HANCOCK, M. P. TO J. R. TURNER
HANCOCK, MARY TO PRESTLEY DUGGAM
HANCOCK, MISS ----- TO THOMAS FORD
HANCOCK, R. M. TO MISS S. E. HANCOCK 2-3-1857
HANCOCK, R. T. TO MISS E. P. FRANCIS 9-9-1869
HANCOCK, REBECCA F. TO DAVIES CHAMBLY
HANCOCK, RICHARD TO MISS MARTHA WARREN 8-5-1854 (8-6-1854)
HANCOCK, S. E. TO R. M. HANCOCK
HANCOCK, SALLIE TO JACK MARTIN
HANEE?, SALLY ANN TO HENRY R. PERRY
HANES?, JOSEPH TO MARTHA T. ELROD 12-20-1851 (12-23-1851)
HANEY, MARY ANN TO BENGAMIN E. MANOUS
HANEY, POLLY TO JOHN RING
HANEY, SARAH TO CLARK D. WORLEY
HANKINS, ROBERT TO SARAH POWEL 7-21-1863 (NO RETURN)
HANONS, ELIZABETH TO JAMES CANTRELL
HARDIN, VINA TO PLEASANT GEORGE
HARE, J. W. TO E. W. FERRILL
HARE, JOHN P. TO MISS MATTIE Z. THOMPSON 12-25-1867
HARE, LUCINDA D. TO SAMUEL P. MCKNIGHT
HARE, M. L. TO A. D. MCKNIGHT
HARE, MATTIE P. TO JOHN B. HOLMES
HARE, NANNIE TO G. H. JONES
HARE, WASHINGTON TO SUSAN FUGETT 1-31-1867
HARGES, LIDIA TO VOLENTINE COBERT
HARGUS, JERUSHA TO JOHN ANDERSON
HARMON, M. C. TO WM. R. MARTIN
HARP, RACHAEL TO EMANUEL WATKINS
HARP, THORNTON TO MARY MALINDA MOODY 2-16-1843 (2-16-1843)

HARPER, HUNTER TO ELLA RIDEOUT 12-10-1873
HARPER, JOSEPH P. TO NANCY TODD 4-18-1839 (NO RETURN)
HARRELL, H. L. TO MISS REBECCA ANN MCMAHAN 1-13-1868 (1-16-1868)
HARRIS, AMANDA TO HIRAM BRANDON
HARRIS, AMBROSE TO EVALINE RIDEOUT 11-25-1867 (11-28-1867)
HARRIS, D. P. TO MISS REBECCA L. PRESTON 1-16-1866
HARRIS, DORCAS TO WESTLEY BOXLEY
HARRIS, EMILY TO A. W. WEST
HARRIS, FRANCES TO JAMES A. PETTY
HARRIS, G. W. TO MISS RUTH SAULS 9-14-1850 (NO RETURN)
HARRIS, J. J. TO MISS E. A. PEDON 7-29-1871 (7-30-1871)
HARRIS, JAMES N. L. TO MISS JANE C. MOORE 1-9-1856
HARRIS, JOHN L. TO MISS SARAH BRYSON 8-5-1845
HARRIS, M. B. TO GRUNDY FANN
HARRIS, MARTHA A. TO ALEXANDER FAN
HARRIS, MARTHA J. TO RUFUS D. PEAY
HARRIS, MARY ANN TO JOHN HOLLIS
HARRIS, MARY J. TO T. D. SUMMAR
HARRIS, MARY TO HENRY MEDFORD
HARRIS, MARY TO W. C. WILLIAMS
HARRIS, MELVINA TO HENRY GILLUM
HARRIS, P. J. TO NATHANIEL GANN
HARRIS, PHILIP TO MISS CAROLINE PETTY 4-17-1845
HARRIS, RANSOM P. TO SARAH TUCKER 3-23-1843
HARRIS, S. H. TO MISS M. J. MORGAN 7-29-1871 (NO RETURN)
HARRIS, SALLY TO DAVID GREEAR
HARRIS, SARAH E. TO LOUIS F. W. WITHERSPOON
HARRIS, SARAH J. TO JAMES FANN
HARRIS, WILLIAM J. TO MISS EMILY M. RICHARDSON 2-21-1849
HARRIS, ZEPHANIAH TO ELIZABETH BRANDON 10-27-1840 (NO RETURN)
HARRISON, WILLIAM H. TO MISS MARTHA JANE LAWRENCE 7-25-1867
HARROD, JOHN A. TO MISS FANNIE B. MARTIN 1-30-1871 (2-2-1871)
HART, DAVID MASSAN TO MISS LOCKEY JANE LANCE 1-15-1856 (1-17-1856)
HART, EM TO ELIZA P. FERRELL 12-10-1873 (12-11-1873)
HART, JAMES M. TO NANCY S. LANER 12-12-1855 (12-13-1855)
HART, L. N. TO JOHN PARTON
HART, LUCINDA TO HENRY FARLER
HART, WILLIAM T. TO MISS MARTHA J. WOODS 6-9-1870
HART, WILLIAM TO LAURA A. FOWLER 11-5-1864 (11-8-1864)
HARVEY, FRANCIS M. TO BARBARY COLEMAN 11-27-1865 (11-29-1865)
HAS, MANERVA TO JOHN GANNON
HATCHINS, JOSEPHINE TO GEORGE W. MOORE
HATFIELD, DELITHA TO SOLOMON SPICER
HATFIELD, J. W. TO MISS MARY J. BYFORD 10-14-1847 (NO RETURN)
HATFIELD, MARY TO PEYTON L. COOPER
HATFIELD, ROBERT TO MISS SARAH JANE MONGOMERY 2-2-1848 (2-7-1848)
HATFIELD, WILLIAM C. TO MISS ELMIRA C. SPRADLIN 1-3-1846 (1-4-1846)
HATTSON, MARY TO JOHN T. DABBES
HAWKINS, H. P. TO R. F. LONG .
HAWKINS, JACOB B. TO MISS SUSAN MARTIN 9-6-1849
HAWKINS, JO B. TO MARY E. MELTON 9-20-1873 (9-21-1873)
HAWKINS, JOHN TO MARY MELTON 12-28-1872 (1-5-1873)
HAWKINS, JOHN TO MISS M. E. JONES 7-19-1853 (7-21-1853)
HAWKINS, JOHN TO MISS MARY M. GILLEY 5-8-1841 (5-9-1841)
HAWKINS, MARTHA P. TO W. B. LOWRY
HAWKINS, MARY TO JOSEPH L. OSMENT
HAWKINS, PARELEE TO S. E. JONES
HAWKINS, WM. B. TO MISS P. A. WIMBERLY 8-18-1858
HAY, ANLIZA TO JAMES A. ALEXANDER
HAYES, ALEXANDER TO MISS IBIA HELTON 1-10-1867

HAYES, ELIAS TO MISS MARTHA HIPP 12-28-1868 (12-29-1868)
HAYES, LOUISA F. TO SIMEON WHITTEMORE
HAYES, MARY M. TO JOHN H. CLIFFORD
HAYES, PEYTON H. TO MISS ADALINE OGLESBY 12-21-1868 (12-22-1868)
HAYES, T. E. TO M. E. TATUM 12-10-1873
HAYES, W. M. TO MISS L. S. CLIFFORD 6-5-1867 (6-6-1867)
HAYNES, ELEANOR TO JOSHUA HALEY
HAYS, B. TO MISS NANCY ANN BURK 12-21-1853 (12-22-1853)
HAYS, BENJAMIN J. TO MARY SMITH 3-7-1843
HAYS, DAVID TO MARTHA GANNON 6-19-1844 (6-20-1844)
HAYS, ELIZABETH TO BRITTON GRIMES
HAYS, FANNY TO ABEL MCBROOM
HAYS, FRANCES TO ALFRED TENPENNY
HAYS, J. C. TO MISS MARY J. TRAVIS 2-25-1857 (NO RETURN)
HAYS, JOHN TO ELIZABETH PITARD 5-19-1856 (5-25?-1856)
HAYS, JOHN TO ROWANN PITARD 12-23-1841
HAYS, JULIE A. TO S. D. MULLINS
HAYS, MARANDA M. TO DENNIS BANK
HAYS, MARY TO ROBERT C. MCBROOM
HAYS, NANCY TO JAMES M. DUBOYS
HAYS, RACHAEL TO JAMES MCBROOM
HAYS, REBECCA TO WM. E. GANNON
HAYS, S. F. TO MISS N. ARMSTRONG 12-24-1857
HAYS, SARAH ANN TO WILLIAM MULLINS
HAYS, SARAH TO ROBERT GORDON
HAYS, WILLIAM B. TO MISS REBECCA KETHCART 8-9-1847
HAYS, WM. B. TO MARGART BRAGG 11-15-1852 (11-16-1852)
HAZLEWOOD, CYRENE C. TO HENRY V. STATOM
HEARNDON, M. J. TO NELSON RIGSBY
HEATHCOCK, ANNA TO ISAH SISSOM
HEATHCOCK, JOHN TO MISS MARTHA HOLLIS 10-25-1848 (10-26-1848)
HEATHERLY, GEO. TO CYNTHIA A. BEVINS 2-1-1873 (2-4-1873)
HEELTON, CALVIN TO MISS ETTER KEATH 2-13-1871
HELLENSULAR, ELIZABETH TO A. MARKUM
HELMS, CREED TO ELIZABETH A. PACE 4-7-1840
HELTON, ANN TO R. C. GOOD
HELTON, IBIA TO ALEXANDER HAYES
HELTON, JAMES TO MISS MARTHA DUBOIS 7-19-1849
HELTON, LUCINDA TO BENGAMIN GILLUM
HELTON, NANCY F. TO ABRAHAM BRANDON
HEMMAN, MARGARET TO AARON READY
HENDERSON, J. T. TO MISS FRANCES COVINGTON 4-9-1865
HENDERSON, JAMES T. TO MISS SUSAN C. SEAWELL 5-20-1845
HENDERSON, JULIA ANN TO ADAM TITTLE
HENDERSON, M. G. TO MISS S. A. BARRETT 9-24-1867 (NO RETURN)
HENDERSON, MARGARETT TO THOMAS N. PRIM
HENDERSON, MARY TO NATHANIEL M. TAYLOR
HENDERSON, PLEASANT T. TO MISS ANN E. FURMAN 5-26-1845 (5-28-1845)
HENDIX, WILLIAM M. TO MARY E. CRANE 3-15-1849
HENDRICKS, N. M. TO MISS SARAH JOHNSON 7-12-1854 (NO RETURN)
HENDRICKSON, ELIZABETH TO JAMES M. COMER
HENDRICKSON, J. R. TO MISS MERRY ANN MERRITT 4-17-1852 (4-18-1852)
HENDRICKSON, JOHN TO ELIZABETH BULLARD 4-27-1860
HENDRICKSON, JOHN TO MINTEE HUTCHINS 10-13-1862 (NO RETURN)
HENDRICKSON, MARY TO WILLIAM J. MELTON
HENDRICKSON, NATHAN TO MISS SARAH JOHNSON 7-12-1854 (7-13-1854)
HENDRICKSON, WM. TO MISS MARY HAMMOND 10-18-1849
HENDRIX, SARAH TO JAMES ARNET
HENDRIXSON, JOHN TO ELIZABETH MCDOUGAL 7-25-1863 (11-26-1865)
HENEBREW, JOHN R. TO MISS ELIZABETH WOODS? 6-14-1858 (6-?-1858)

HERALD, JENETTA TO HOWEY ARNOLD
HERALD, SUSAN A. TO CHARLES ESPY
HERIMAN, JOHN TO SUSAN WILLIAMS 7-1839 (10-21-1840)
HERIMAN, JOSIAH TO FREELY CAPSHAW 4-12-1838
HERIMAN, NANCY TO JACKSON MORGAN
HERIMAN, WESTLEY TO NANCY HADLEY 1-23-1839
HERMMON, WESLEY O MISS MARY JONES 7-20-1871 (7-21-1871)
HERNDEN, M. F. TO MISS ELIZA E. BOGLE 10-23-1858 (10-24-1858)
HERNDON, J. M. TO MISS SARAH A. TITTLE 2-14-1857 (2-15-1857)
HERNDON, J. M. TO SARAH FUSTON 5-30-1872 (5-31-1872)
HERNDON, JAMES M. TO MISS SARAH T. WOODALL 1-8-1847
HERNDON, M. M. TO J. G. LAHEW
HERNDON, W. J. TO MISS MARGARET J. MCADOW 1-12-1867 (1-20-1867)
HEROD, D. T. TO MISS SOPHIA E. MARTIN 6-30-1860 (7-4-1860)
HEROLD, ISSABELLA TO AMERICA ARNOLD
HERRAL, MARY TO THOMAS UNDERWOOD
HERRALD, SARRAH J. TO W. H. WARREN
HERRALL, LEGRAND TO MISS CHRISTENEY C. FINLEY 1-22-1866 (1-25-1866)
HERRELL, ANN E. TO HUGH L. THOMPSON
HERRELL, E. P. TO MARTHA HOLLIS 2-7-1865
HERREMAN, NANCY TO H. C. SPURLOCK
HERRIMAN, AMANDA TO ANTHONY ORRAND
HERRIMAN, JOHN TO MARY ANN REEVES 1-2-1843
HERRIMAN, JOHN TO MISS REBECCA JOHNSON 3-6-1869
HERRIMAN, MARY TO PINKNEY TUCKER
HERRIMAN, STERLING B. TO MISS ELIZABETH SPURLOCK 4-27-1850 (4-28-1850)
HERRIMAN, STEVEN TO MARY E. GIBSON 5-8-1865
HERRIMON, JOHN TO SHOPHIA READY 3-22-1864 (3-24-1864)
HERRIN, SALLY TO WILLIAM BRASHEARS
HERRYMAN, JOHN S. TO MISS EMALINE J. ST. JOHN 5-4-1869 (5-5-1869)
HERRYMAN, LOCKEY J. TO SAMUEL M. GANNON
HERRYMAN, MARY E. TO ZACHARIAH SULLIVAN
HERTER?, A. TO MISS M. E. MCKNIGHT 2-13-1861 (NO RETURN)
HIBDON, C. C. TO JOEL THOMAS
HIBDON, JOHN TO MISS TILDY SULLIVAN 12-21-1857
HIBDON, M. S. TO ALFORD FANN
HIBDON, P. A. TO MISS S. E. GILLUM 10-12-1870
HIBDON, SUSAN TO WM. A. DAVENPORT
HIBDON, WILLIAM C. TO CHARITY M. BARRETT 9-19-1856
HICKEMBOTTOM, ELIZABETH TO ALEXANDER SULLENS
HICKENBOTTAM, ELIZABETH TO ALEXANDER SULLENS
HICKS, ELIZABETH TO JESSEMIN KNIGHT
HICKS, ELIZABETH TO ROBERT M. JONES
HICKS, G. D. TO JANE SHERLEY 11-22-1865
HICKS, RUTH TO WILLIAM J. RAGLAND
HIET, MARY TO JOHN BARHAM
HIGDON, SALATHA J. TO S. W. ROBERTSON
HIGDON, SARAH E. TO ELIGAH NEELEY
HIGGANS, JOHN TO MISS LOCKY J. PATRICK 9-21-1850 (9-22-1850)
HIGGANS, JULY ANN TO DAVID HUTCHINS
HIGGANS, MARY TO JEREMIAH OCONNER
HIGGANS, NANCY TO ISAAC MARCUM
HIGGANS, ROBERT W. TO MISS SUSAN SULLENS 8-9-1849
HIGGANS, WILLIAM TO MELVINA FUSTON 1-17-1864 (1-18-1864)
HIGGENBOTTOM, JAMES TO MARINDA A. COUSLEY 1-21-1858 (1-25-1858)
HIGGENS, SABRINA TO JOSIAH HOLLINSWORTH
HIGGINS, AMANDA S. TO J. W. STEPHENS
HIGGINS, ELIGAH TO MISS SARY ANN KELLY 5-28-1853
HIGGINS, ELIJAH C. TO MISS AMANDA J. WAMACK 8-15-1870 (8-18-1870)
HIGGINS, ELIZA ANN TO H. R. ELKINS

HIGGINS, ELIZA TO JAMES P. PENY
HIGGINS, ISAAC TO MISS BARBARY ANN TITTLE 1-17-1867
HIGGINS, JAMES TO ELIZABETH YORK 1-9-1870
HIGGINS, JAMES TO EMALINE MELTON 1-28-1841
HIGGINS, JAMES TO SUSAN DUGGAN 1-22-1839 (1-24-1839)
HIGGINS, JANE TO JOSEPH F. MASON
HIGGINS, JULIAN TO ROBERT DAVIS
HIGGINS, LOCKY JANE TO SAMUEL TITTLE
HIGGINS, LUCY TO CALVIN BROWN
HIGGINS, LUCY TO GEORGE W. MILLIGAN
HIGGINS, MARGARET TO JOHN NOKES
HIGGINS, MARGARETT TO E. N. WALKUP
HIGGINS, MARY E. TO ALSA WEBB
HIGGINS, MARY TO BENJAMIN PENDLETON
HIGGINS, MISS POLLY TO JOHN HUTCHINS
HIGGINS, PEGGY TO WILLIAM DENNES
HIGGINS, PRESLEY TO MARY MULLENAX 1-18-1865 (NO RETURN)
HIGGINS, R. L. TO MISS MARY E. RIGSBY 12-20-1869 (12-22-1869)
HIGGINS, RANCE TO MISS PARALEE MARTIN 4-14-1871
HILL, DABNY TO MISS ELIZABETH LASWELL 10-17-1853 (10-18-1853)
HILL, ELI TO LUCY RICHARDSON 12-6-1869
HILL, ELIZA TO THOMAS CARRICK
HILL, ELIZABETH TO NATHAN S. JOHNSON
HILL, GILBERT TO MANERVA CHAMBERS 7-11-1870
HILL, JAMES TO MISS MARY PETTY 9-20-1848 (9-21-1848)
HILL, JOHN N. TO MISS AMANDA J. SUMMERS 11-19-1867 (11-20-1867)
HILL, LUCINDA TO JOSEPH SMITH
HILL, WILLIAM R. TO MISS NANCY ELEANOR MOORE 3-6-1848 (3-7-1848)
HILL, WM. T. TO REBECCA E. WATTS 5-11-1872
HILL, WM. TO C. I. SESSIN 1-6-1855 (NO RETURN)
HILLIS, ELIZABETH JANE TO RAYFORD CANNON
HIPP, A. R. TO MISS L. A. BAILEY 12-26-1866
HIPP, EMELINE TO JOHN H. LYNN
HIPP, MARTHA TO ELIAS HAYES
HIPP, N. J. TO J. T. MCMAHAN
HIPP, REBECCA J. TO W. J. GUNTER
HIPP, SALLIE B. TO A. B. BARRETT
HODGE, JAMES L. TO MISS JOSEPHINE BURGER 9-12-1867
HODGES, SARAH E. TO M. S. WARD
HOGWOOD, JAMES R. TO MISS AMANDA J. CARTER 9-23-1868 (9-24-1868)
HOGWOOD, MATTIE A. TO JOHN FREEZE
HOLDER, B. H. TO MISS MARY WARREN 4-15-1867
HOLEMANE, L. TO MISS J. C. TRAVIS 12-11-1855 (NO RETURN)
HOLLAND, AMANDY A. TO J. M. BURCH
HOLLAND, ELIZABETH TO JOSEPH A. SPICER
HOLLAND, JOHN TO MISS SARAH B. KIRK 1-3-1866 (1-18-1866)
HOLLAND, MARY K. TO WM. MARES
HOLLAND, SARAH S. TO WM. C. PHILIPS
HOLLAND, SPEAKER TO MISS ELIZABETH STEWART 3-23-1871
HOLLANDSWORTH, CAHAL TO C. MORRIS 10-9-1865 (10-10-1865)
HOLLANDSWORTH, FRANCIS TO MISS NANCY J. MELTON 12-25-1869 (12-27-1869)
HOLLANDSWORTH, H. TO NANCY E. NEELEY 9-3-1872
HOLLANDSWORTH, IRA TO MISS SARAH WOOD 7-26-1870
HOLLANDSWORTH, JAMES F. TO MISS RUTHY BUTCHER 3-13-1866 (3-15-1866)
HOLLANDSWORTH, JOHN TO MISS BETTIE VINSON 8-3-1870
HOLLANDSWORTH, JOHN TO MISS ELIZA J. CRABTREE 7-23-1868
HOLLANDSWORTH, LIZZIE TO D. B. VINSON
HOLLANDSWORTH, MALISSA TO LEROY FUSTON
HOLLANDSWORTH, MARY TO THOS. BARRETT
HOLLANDSWORTH, N. T. TO JAMES F. YOUNGBLOOD

HOLLANDSWORTH, N. TO MARY BARRETT 4-22-1873 (4-23-1873)
HOLLANDSWORTH, SARAH C. TO A. S. GILLEY
HOLLANDSWORTH, SUSAN TO WM. BARRETT
HOLLANDWORTH, GAILEN TO M. J. HUTCHINS 10-3-1871
HOLLANDWORTH, WM. TO NANCEY JETTON 9-18-1871 (9-20-1871)
HOLLANDWORTH, ZADE A. TO EDMOND L. GOINS
HOLLINGSWORTH, IRA TO SARAH A. NEELY 1-4-1865 (1-5-1865)
HOLLINGSWORTH, JOS. O. TO LUCETTA HANCOCK 3-24-1864
HOLLINGSWORTH, NANCY A. TO J. D. MURPHY
HOLLINSWORTH, ADEN TO MISS LUCRETIA MURFREY 5-8-1845
HOLLINSWORTH, CHARLES W. TO MISS MARY VANDAGRIFFE 8-17-1849 (8-19-1849)
HOLLINSWORTH, IRA TO ELIZABETH MILLIGAN 6-4-1840
HOLLINSWORTH, JOHN TO CHARLOTTE DENNIS 7-10-1840
HOLLINSWORTH, JOSIAH TO SABRINA HIGGENS 11-23-1842 (11-25-1842)
HOLLIS, A. E. TO THOS. E. JAMES
HOLLIS, D. C. TO J. Y. NICHOL
HOLLIS, E. MATILDA TO JOSEPH H. NEELY
HOLLIS, ELIZABETH TO LEWIS W. BOND
HOLLIS, GEORGE W. TO ELIZABETH EDWARDS 8-1-1839 (NO RETURN)
HOLLIS, HARRIET TO JAMES DAVIS
HOLLIS, J. B. TO MISS MARY CRESON 2-17-1866 (2-18-1866)
HOLLIS, J. E. TO CAROLINE CATES 11-14-1864
HOLLIS, J. H. TO JANE TENPENNY 8-14-1860 (NO RETURN)
HOLLIS, J. L. TO MISS ALICE E. TODD 2-28-1866 (3-1-1866)
HOLLIS, J. W. D. TO MISS E. M. ORAND 11-26-1856 (NO RETURN)
HOLLIS, JOHN H. TO MISS JOANAH F. SIMPSON 9-9-1869
HOLLIS, JOHN TO ELIZABETH TODD 11-19-1849 (NO RETURN)
HOLLIS, JOHN TO MARY ANN HARRIS 1-13-1841
HOLLIS, LAMIRA L. TO LUKE LASATER
HOLLIS, LEWIS J. TO SUSANNAH EDWARDS 7-9-1839 (7-11-1839)
HOLLIS, LOUISA CAROLINE TO JONATHAN DOZIER
HOLLIS, LUCY M. TO WILLIAM D. STACY
HOLLIS, M. L. TO W. H. YOUREE
HOLLIS, MANDY TO MORGE MCKNIGHT
HOLLIS, MARGARETT A. TO JOHN S. NUGAN
HOLLIS, MARTHA E. TO SILAS M. GRAY
HOLLIS, MARTHA TO E. P. HERRELL
HOLLIS, MARTHA TO JOHN HEATHCOCK
HOLLIS, MARY E. TO HARVEY T. WILLIAMS
HOLLIS, MARYANN TO WILLIAM J. WALKUP
HOLLIS, MAYN TO C. W. SNIPES
HOLLIS, PAULINA TO WILLIAM THOMPSON
HOLLIS, R. M. TO W. MCREAD
HOLLIS, SUSAN JANE TO JOHN IRVIN DUBOISE
HOLLIS, WILLIAM C. TO MISS MARTHA DELOACH 6-28-1841
HOLLOWMAN, OLLEY TO FRANKLIN NEELEY
HOLMES, JOHN B. TO MISS MATTIE P. HARE 1-2-1867 (1-3-1867)
HOLMS, MARY R. TO J. W. NICHOL
HOLSTON, RICHARD J. TO MISS MARY HAMILTON 9-20-1849
HOLT, BLACKBURN TO MISS EMALINE STACY 12-9-1868 (12-13-1868)
HOLT, FANNY TO WILLIAM GOODING
HOLT, H. N. TO MISS MARTHA C. WILLIAMS 2-9-1869 (2-28-1869)
HOLT, ISABELLA A. TO ABRAM H. STACY
HOLT, MARGARET TO MATTHEW T. PUMPHREY
HOLT, MILLY TO MARTIN S. HOOVER
HOLT, MINERVA TO SOLOMON TRAVIS
HOLT, NANCY TO IRA I. BRYANT
HOLT, THOMAS TO ELIZABETH RING 10-6-1842
HOLT, WILLIAM TO MISS ELIZABETH BRYANT 8-17-1867
HOLTERMAND, JOHN TO RHODY MELTON 2-7-1863 (2-8-1863)

HOLY, TILDY TO MCCASLEN MUNY
HOLYFIELD, SALLY TO HENRY SPICER
HOOKER, ELIZABETH F. TO H. L. BUSH
HOOKER, MARY A. TO W. M. GORDON
HOOPER, JAMES TO MISS POLLY YOUNGBLOOD 7-25-1846 (7-26-1846)
HOOPER, MARTHA TO F. G. THOMPSON (SEE COOPER, MARTHA J.--COULD BE READ EITHER WAY)
HOOPER, NANCY E. TO ARCHELAUS YOUNGBLOOD
HOOSER, G. W. TO SARAH D. MITCHELL 12-9-1859 (NO RETURN)
HOOVER, BENGAMIN TO MISS MARY J. TODD 9-23-1869
HOOVER, ELIZABETH TO JOHN BYNUM
HOOVER, HENRY W. TO MISS MARY JANE E. KNOX 1-3-1848 (1-6-1848)
HOOVER, ISAAC TO MISS JANE TODD 2-6-1867 (2-7-1867)
HOOVER, J. M. TO BARCELONA STROUD 3-28-1872
HOOVER, MARTIN S. TO MILLY HOLT 6-20-1839 (NO RETURN)
HOOVER, MARTIN S. TO SUFFRONA ROBINSON 6-14-1838
HOOVER, MARY TO ALEXANDER MCBROOM
HOOVER, MARY TO WILLIAM MCKEE
HOOVER, MILLIA TO THOMAS J. HOOVER
HOOVER, NEWTON TO MISS MARY MASON 8-9-1871 (8-10-1871)
HOOVER, THOMAS J. TO MILLIA HOOVER 12-11-1865 (12-12-1865)
HOOVER, THOS. J. TO MISS SUSAN MITCHEL 12-9-1858
HOOVER, WM. TO JANE R. CARNAHAN 7-22-1872
HOPE, F. M. TO N. E. RAINS 11-7-1865
HOPKINS, ELIJAH TO MISS NANCY PRICE 8-21-1844 (8-23-1844)
HOPKINS, HARMAN H. TO ISSABELLA ENNIS 2-19-1842 (2-20-1842)
HOPKINS, JOEL TO MISS EASTHER PETTY 5-13-1843 (NO RETURN)
HOPKINS, JOSEPH W. TO MISS MARY EDWARDS 11-25-1848 (11-21?-1848)
HOPKINS, LUCY ANN TO L. L. C. CUMMINS
HOPKINS, SAMUEL A. TO MISS MARTHA E. SEALES 12-16-1856 (NO RETURN)
HORN, JOHN TO MISS ELIZABETH USSELTON 2-26-1866 (NO RETURN)
HORN, MARY ELIZABETH TO THOMAS F. GAITHER
HORN, THOMAS W. TO MISS NANCY ELEANOR PATTON 12-20-1848 (NO RETURN)
HORRAL, SARAH M. TO JOHN NIGHT
HOUGHS, L. TO MARY CARRELL 11-4-1852
HOUSE, E. J. TO W. S. MELTON
HOUSE, ELIZABETH TO CASWELL SULLIVAN
HOUSE, HARTWELL TO MISS MOLLIE E. FAGAN 7-23-1867 (7-25-1867)
HOUSE, W. D. TO MISS JANIE PHILLIPPS 12-22-1870
HOUSE, WILLIAM TO JANE SULLIVAN 1-13-1852
HOWARD, ELMIRA TO JOSIAH SPURLOCK
HOWETH, JAMES A. TO MISS NANCY J. MINGLE 9-13-1847 (9-14-1847)
HOWETH, NANCY J. TO ISAAC MCBROOM
HUBBARD, M. A. F. TO W. H. MATHEWS
HUBBARD, NANCY TO CHARLES HANCOCK
HUBBARD, NANCY TO DANIEL BRYSON
HUGHS, ADALINE TO WM. MCCARLIN
HULEHENS, WILLIAM TO JANE STARR 12-28-1854
HUNT, T. J. TO M. A. MILLSTED 12-28-1872 (12-29-1872)
HUNT, T. J. TO MISS M. A. LORANCE 3-31-1859
HUNTER, MARY A. TO JOHN BLUE
HUTCHEANS, DAVID TO MISS EMERLINE DENIS 4-13-1859 (5-2-1859)
HUTCHENS, FRANCES L. TO JESSEE MOORE
HUTCHENS, M. J. TO GAILEN HOLLANDWORTH
HUTCHENS, VINA C. TO ALEXR. BRASHEARS
HUTCHENSON, M. H. TO ISUL LONG
HUTCHERSON, NANCY TO A. E. UNDERHILL
HUTCHINS, AARON TO MISS SARAH STAR 5-15-1841 (NO RETURN)
HUTCHINS, DAVID TO MISS JULY ANN HIGGANS 5-11-1848
HUTCHINS, JOHN TO MISS POLLY HIGGINS 8-28-1840 (8-30-1840)
HUTCHINS, LAVINA C. TO ZACHARIAH T. MOORE

HUTCHINS, MINTEE TO JOHN HENDRICKSON
HUTCHINS, PATSY TO JAMES SMITHSON
HUTCHINS, SARAH ANN TO JOSEPH LANCE
INGLIS, DIANITIA TO FRANKLIN PARKER
INGLIS, EVAN A. TO MISS ELIZABETH BYFORD 9-14-1844 (9-17-1844)
INGLIS, M. E. TO T. E. PRATOR
INGLIS, MARY TO C. D. GUNTER
INGLIS, URIAH F. TO MISS SARAH MARBERRY 11-19-1846
IRVIN, H. A. TO MISS M. J. BRANDON 2-10-1868 (2-18-1868)
ISAM, R. C. TO JOSEPH UNDERWOOD
IVEY, PHILIP TO DELEY A. DICKENS 9-1-1865 (NO RETURN)
JACO, E. J. TO NANCY P. PERCELL 11-27-1871 (12-9-1871)
JACO, MARY C. TO LEVI BARRETT
JACOBS, ARMINDA TO THOS. PEMELTON
JACOBS, ELIZABETH TO CALVIN LOW
JACOBS, MALVINA TO D. F. PARKER
JAMES, A. F. TO MISS MANDY ODAM 1-11-1859
JAMES, A. F. TO MISS MANDY ODOM 1-11-1859 (NO RETURN)
JAMES, A. F. TO MISS NANCY ADAMS 2-13-1852 (2-4?-1852)
JAMES, DANIEL TO MISS NANCY MANERVA MEACE 4-1-1841
JAMES, F. M. TO MISS ELIZA DEVENPORT 1-5-1859 (NO RETURN)
JAMES, ROBERT J. TO ELIZABETH FREEMAN 1-30-1840
JAMES, SAMUEL R. TO MRS. LUCY BATES 8-10-1850 (8-11-1850)
JAMES, THOS. E. TO A. E. HOLLIS 1-5-1857 (1-7-1857)
JAMESON, JOHN A. TO MISS NANCY E. FORD 9-23-1867 (10-3-1867)
JAMISON, JAMES TO MARGARETT J. ESPEY 2-6-1856 (2-7-1856)
JAMISON, NANCY A. TO W. Z. GINOE?
JAMISON, ROBERT TO NARCISSA ESPY 7-12-1855
JAMISON, T. G. TO S. J. SMITH 11-16-1857 (11-19-1857)
JAMISON, WILLIAM A. TO MISS JANE ADALINE WEBBER 8-12-1867 (8-18-1867)
JAMISON, WILLIAM TO EMALINE BELL 6-18-1840 (NO RETURN)
JANSON, J. H. TO B. HALEY 7-12-1860
JARNAGIN, CARY TO HALY WHITFIELD 11-29-1838 (NO RETURN)
JARNAGIN, NEEDHAM TO SARAH NIVENS 11-9-1842
JARNEGIN, WM. A. TO MISS MARTHA J. COUTHEN 5-5-1858 (NO RETURN)
JARRATT, MARY C. TO J. T. MITCHELL
JARRETT, ISAAC TO MAY E. CARUTHERS 6-21-1854 (6-22-1854)
JENNINGS, LEANDER TO AMERICA C. OVERALL 12-12-1867
JERNIGAN, ANDREW J. TO MISS REBECCA JANE TODD 4-2-1859 (3?-6-1859)
JERNIGAN, J. C. TO MRS. REBECCA SISSOM 12-24-1868
JERNIGAN, L. W. TO MARY J. WHITFIELD 12-27-1865
JERNIGAN, RICHARD TO SARAH SISSOM 4-25-1873 (4-27-1873)
JERNIGAN, WM. A. TO MISS DORCUS GILLY 10-11-1855 (10-16-1855)
JETTON, ALEXANDER TO MISS ELIZABETH MILLIGAN 10-20-1857
JETTON, DANIEL TO MISS SARAH A. MELTON 11-1-1859 (NO RETURN)
JETTON, ELLER TO JOHNSON RIDEOUT
JETTON, GRANVILLE TO MISS T. A. CHAPELL 12-30-1854 (1-4-1855)
JETTON, GRANVILLE TO MRS. SARAH E. CORN 1-29-1852
JETTON, JAMES TO SOPHY PETTY 12-7-1871
JETTON, JOHN B. TO ISABELA JANE STEWART 4-2-1840 (NO RETURN)
JETTON, JULIA TO JOHN WEEDON
JETTON, MARTHA TO THOMAS LEDBETTER
JETTON, MARY E. TO JAMES T. E. MCKNIGHT
JETTON, MARY TO DILLARD MELTON
JETTON, NANCY TO WM. HOLLANDWORTH
JETTON, SARAH E. TO JOHN W. STONE
JETTON, SARAH R. TO AMZI B. MCKNIGHT
JETTON, SARAH TO SAMUEL YOUNG
JETTON, T. J. TO MISS S. P. BURGER 7-31-1854
JETTON, WILLIAM TO MISS MARY MARKUM 5-28-1869

JETTON, WM. TO L. R. MCGEE 11-20-1873
JEWEL, N. T. TO MISS ALAMINTA HANCOCK 9-23-1869 (9-25-1869)
JEWELL, JACOB W. TO MARGRET W. SHELTON 2-1-1840 (2-2-1840)
JIMERSON, E. TO T. J. CARIC
JIMERSON, NARCISSA TO ROBERT S. RICKETS
JIMMERSON, R. C. TO LARKIN FORD
JOHNSON, CHARLES TO MISS SARAH JANE JOHNSON 6-19-1867 (NO RETURN)
JOHNSON, ELIZABETH M. TO WILLIAM A. COLVERT
JOHNSON, ISAAC N. TO SARAH ANN MARSHALL 3-13-1848 (3-14-1848)
JOHNSON, ISAAC N. TO SARAH M. THOMAS 7-26-1850 (7-30-1850)
JOHNSON, JAMES N. TO MISS MARY E. REED 5-23-1868 (5-22?-1868)
JOHNSON, JOHN B. TO EMA M. THOMAS 1-26-1856
JOHNSON, JOHN T. TO MISS ELIZABETH PHILLIPS 12-24-1869 (12-25-1869)
JOHNSON, LIBE TO ELIZABETH TEEPLES 10-8-1863 (NO RETURN)
JOHNSON, MIARIAH TO URIAH BUSH
JOHNSON, NATHAN S. TO MISS REBECCA ELIZABETH HILL 12-?-1848 (12-16-1848)
JOHNSON, NELSON TO MISS MARY A. PATRICK 3-23-1851
JOHNSON, P. P. TO MISS LUCINDA FRANCIS 10-1-1844 (10-2-1844)
JOHNSON, REBECCA TO JOHN HERRIMAN
JOHNSON, RICHARD P. TO ELIZABETH E. WEBBER 4-14-1838 (4-20-1838)
JOHNSON, SARAH JANE TO CHARLES JOHNSON
JOHNSON, SARAH TO N. M. HENDRICKS
JOHNSON, SARAH TO NATHAN HENDRICKSON
JONES, A. V. TO MARY MCCABE 10-16-1873 (10-19-1873)
JONES, AARON F. TO MAHALY CARTER 8-5-1852
JONES, ALABAMA TO JOHN E. JONES
JONES, ANNE F. TO JOSEPH F. SMITH
JONES, B. F. TO MARY M. COX 7-25-1864 (8-4-1864)
JONES, B. M. TO MISS ELIZA DEVENPORT 1-5-1859 (1-6-1859)
JONES, BA--- TO ROBERT RIGSBY
JONES, CELIA TO MARION JONES
JONES, CHRISTENEY TO S. S. BRANDON
JONES, D. A. TO MISS LUCINDA KIRK 4-8-1869 (4-9-1869)
JONES, E. J. TO J. J. JONES
JONES, EDITH TO DAVID GREEAR
JONES, ELIZABETH C. TO JAMES H. YOUNGBLOOD
JONES, ELIZABETH TO ISAAC GRIZZLE
JONES, ENOCH TO MARY BURGER 2-8-1854
JONES, EUNICE TO THOS. DUGGIN
JONES, G. H. TO MISS NANNIE HARE 12-11-1869 (12-15-1869)
JONES, H. J. TO W. O. BURGER
JONES, HANNAH J. TO JAKE FREEMAN
JONES, HARRIETT C. TO WM. STATTS
JONES, HENRY TO ROXANAH RICHARDSON 9-29-1866 (9-30-1866)
JONES, J. J. TO MISS E. J. JONES 1-30-1869 (1-31-1869)
JONES, JAMES A. TO MISS CELIA COX 1-13-1866
JONES, JAMES TO MISS HARRIETT MAZY 8-31-1854 (9-7-1854)
JONES, JOHN E. TO MISS ALABAMA JONES 2-19-1850 (NO RETURN)
JONES, JOHN H. TO SARAH L. GATHER 4-3-1838
JONES, JOHN M. TO MISS MARTH MCDOW 11-9-1849 (NO RETURN)
JONES, JOHN TO ELIZABETH MARTIN 1-10-1844 (1-12-1844)
JONES, JOHN TO MISS MANERVA COOK 1-19-1850
JONES, JOSPHENE? TO RICHARD LASETER
JONES, JULY A. TO LAYFAYETTE BOGLE
JONES, KATHARINE TO JAMES CARTER ·
JONES, L. J. TO T. F. GILLEY
JONES, LAFAYETT TO MISS MARTHA ELLISON 6-24-1870 (6-26-1870)
JONES, M. E. TO J. H. LASTER
JONES, M. E. TO JOHN HAWKINS
JONES, M. T. TO L. F. BOGLE

JONES, MALINDA TO JAMES PEERCE
JONES, MARGRET TO W. T. MARTIN
JONES, MARION TO MRS. CELIA JONES 9-27-1869
JONES, MARTHA ANN TO WM. WOOD
JONES, MARY E. TO THOMAS W. DAVENPORT
JONES, MARY TO ISAAC THEIRS
JONES, MARY TO PAOMPEY? ELLEDGE
JONES, MARY TO RICHARD B. MARTIN
JONES, MARY TO S. H. ELROD
JONES, MARY TO WESLEY HERMMAN
JONES, MATTIE L. TO J. D? BENNETT
JONES, NANCY C. TO R. A. KING
JONES, NANCY P. TO JAMES P. BARRETT
JONES, PINKNEY TO LUCINDA VANDAGRIPH 1-7-1840 (NO RETURN)
JONES, ROBERT M. TO ELIZABETH HICKS 8-25-1842 (NO RETURN)
JONES, ROXANAH TO ISAAC C. WORLEY
JONES, S. E. TO PARELEE HAWKINS 2-8-1872 (NO RETURN)
JONES, SAMUEL TO MISS MARGRETT M? ORAND 5-13-1856 (HANDED IN WITHOUT RETURN)
JONES, SARAH TO HIRAM FREEZE
JONES, SARRAH M. TO JAMES H. BRYSON
JONES, SUSAN L. TO JOHN C. DAVENPORT
JONES, T. B. TO MARTHA C. TODD 7-7-1873 (NO RETURN)
JONES, THOMAS E. TO MISS ELIZABETH GAITHER 10-26-1843
JONES, W. C. TO MISS CHRISTENY MINGLE 8-4-1858
JONRAN, LUCINDA TO WM. VOSSER
JONSEN, MARGARETT TO HAMES BARRETT
JOURDAN, JOHN TO MISS FANNY THROWER 7-25-1843 (NO RETURN)
JOYS, MARTHA JANE TO REDMON BYNUM
JURNIGAN, EDMUND TO MARGARET MANOUS 11-11-1865 (11-12-1865)
JUSTIC, SUSAN TO A. T. ELROD
JUSTICE, ALICE TO F. E. WATSON
JUSTICE, H. A. TO MISS E. A. DANIEL 11-4-1858
JUSTICE, JOHN B. TO MISS MARGARETTE ANN WARREN 8-26-1848 (9-5-1848)
JUSTICE, M. E. TO W. J. GRAHAM
JUSTICE, M. J. TO W. J. GRAHAM
JUSTICE, ROBERT N. TO MISS ELIZABETH C. RUCKER 1-16-1866
JUSTICE, S. E. TO --- M. GRAHAM
JUSTICE, W. E. TO MISS I. J. ELROD 12-23-1857 (NO RETURN)
KATES, ISSABELLA ELIZABETH ANN TO ALBERT T. FAGAN
KEATH, ETTER TO CALVIN HEELTON
KEATH, L. TO Z. BOWLIN
KEATH, SARAH E. TO ELIJAH BESHERS
KEATON, CHARLOTTE TO JOHN BOGLE
KEATON, ELIZABETH TO JASPER HAMMONS
KEATON, F. B. TO JACOB K. KING
KEATON, GABRIEL TO MARY A. KING 2-7-1865
KEATON, H. L. TO MISS ANNIE T. DAVIS 1-2?-1871 (1-29-1871)
KEATON, HENRY TO MISS CLARISSA DISTING 9-17-1846 (9-20-1846)
KEATON, JOHN TO ANN FOUSTEN 7-12-1842 (7-14-1842)
KEATON, JOHN TO NANCY E. TURNEY 3-19-1873 (3-20-1873)
KEATON, MARY P. TO JEREMIAH COLLINS
KEATON, PETER N. J. TO MISS NANCY T. A. MCGEE 10-4-1869 (10-10-1869)
KEATON, W. T. TO M. E. READY 1-1-1872 (1-4-1872)
KEEL, LOUISA TO LUKE SHERLEY
KEEL, T. M. TO MISS E. ALEXANDER 12-4-1856 (NO RETURN)
KEELE, ANDERSON TO MARIAH MITCHELL 1-4-1866? (1-4-1867)
KEELE, MARGARET J. TO JOHN H. MULLIN
KEELE, SARAH TO JOSEPH NICHOL
KEELE, THOMAS TO NANCY KUYKENDALL 11-14-1865 (11-16-1865)
KEELE?, JAMES A. TO MISS SARAH M. TRAVIS 9-16-1858

KEELY, HARRIETT TO WM. H. GARNER
KEENY, JAMES TO MISS CYRENA CUMMINGS 7-18-1843 (7-20-1843)
KEENY?, R. A. TO MISS SARAH A. BOGLE 11-4-1857
KEES, ERASMUS S. TO MISS ELIZABETH MAXEY 12-13-1843 (NOT EXECUTED)
KEETAN, WILLIAM TO MISS ELIZABETH FUSTON 3-17-1855 (3-20-1855)
KEETON, ELIZABETH TO JOSIAH FUSTON
KEETON, MARY MALISSA TO THOMAS HALE
KEETON, ROBIN TO MISS LUIZA KEY 8-30-1852
KEETON, SARAH J. TO A. KING
KEITH, NANCY TO NATHAN MATHEWS
KELL, LOUISA TO LUK SHIRLEY
KELL, REBECA C. TO W. W. BELL
KELLY, JACOB A. TO LAURA ANN PATRICK 9-20-1842 (9-26-1842)
KELLY, REEPES? P. TO MISS N. M. ODOM 12-23-1850 (NO RETURN)
KELLY, SARY ANN TO ELIGAH HIGGINS
KELLY, WILLIAM B. TO MISS LUCINDA KING 1-13-1847 (1-14-1847)
KELTON, SARAH M. E. TO MICHAEL LORANCE
KENNADY, B. L. TO W. T. H. WHORTON
KENNADY, FRANCES M. TO R. S. SPIELLE
KENNEDY, J. W. TO MISS LYDIA H. BETHELL 1-12-1869 (1-14-1869)
KENNEDY, JOSIE TO RUFUS RITCH
KENNEDY, M. A. TO C. B. GARRISON
KENNEDY, M. A. TO MISS ELIZABETH B. TOLBERT 9-7-1849 (NO RETURN)
KENSAR, REBECCA ANN TO JAMES P. BARRET
KERBY, ELIZABETH TO JACK TUCKER
KERBY, MILITA TO JOHN MEANIS
KERBY, SARAH A. TO A. J. GUY
KERKLIN, E. J. TO JOHN B. WILLIAMS
KERSE, LUAN TO WILLIAM C. SMITHSON
KERSEY, ELIZABETH TO JACOB B. TATE
KERSEY, MARY J. TO JOHN CONLEY
KERSEY, SARRYAN? TO WILLIAM GUNTER
KERSEY, THANEY TO ENOCH PATTERSON
KERSEY, VIRGINIA TO CLAIBORNE Y. GUNTER
KERSY, EATHCINDY TO JOHN MASON
KERTZ, KATHARIN TO J. C. PRATOR
KETHCART, REBECCA TO WILLIAM B. HAYS
KEY, LUIZA TO ROBIN KEETON
KEYTON, GEORGE? H. TO REBECA E. LANIER? 10-8-1851 (10-9-1851)
KINCAID, NANCY TO CULLEN BRADBURY
KINCAID, THOMAS TO MISS ELIZABETH CUMMINS 9-5-1850 (9-6-1850)
KING, A. TO MISS SARAH J. KEETON 2-3-1852 (2-6-1852)
KING, ALAMENTA TO ALEXANDER VANDERGRIFF
KING, B. A. TO MATTIE J. PATTON 7-14-1873 (7-16-1873)
KING, BETSY TO GIDEON DUKE
KING, GEORGE TO MISS KATHARINE A. PEALER 8-21-1847 (8-24-1847)
KING, J. A. TO CAROLINE HANCOCK 2-20-1860 (NO RETURN)
KING, J. J. TO MISS M. A. KING 2-19-1867 (2-21-1867)
KING, JACOB A. TO MISS LURANEY WILLIAMS 10-21-1846
KING, JACOB K. TO MISS T. B. KEATON 1-12-1867 (1-13-1867)
KING, JAMES H. H. TO IBBY ELIZABETH MATHIS 9-12-1860 (NO RETURN)
KING, JNO. E. TO MIRIAH STRAND 8-2-1873 (8-3-1873)
KING, LIDY P. TO JOEL A. KNIGHT
KING, LUCINDA TO WILLIAM B. KELLY
KING, LYDA TO W. J. KNIGHT
KING, M. A. TO J. J. KING
KING, M. E. TO N. S. BOGLE
KING, MARGARET E. TO J. A. COOPER
KING, MARTIN TO MISS SARAH WILLIAMS 2-25-1848
KING, MARY A. TO GABRIEL C. KEATON

KING, NANCY E. TO JAME H. DODD
KING, NANCY E. TO JESSE MCGEE
KING, R. A. TO MISS NANCY C. JONES 6-26-1867
KING, SAMPSON J. TO NANCY A. PARTON 7-21-1865
KING, WILLIAM J. TO MISS MARTHA E. BOGLE 11-1-1866
KING, WILLIAM TO MISS SALLY PEALER 12-12-1849
KING, WM. M. TO NANCY L. MARKUM 12-13-1873 (12-14-1873)
KING, WM. TO MISS NANCY MOON 12-17-1855
KINNAMON, NELLY TO HENRY ENOS
KIPP, G. B. TO MISS NANCY M. A. DICKENS 1-5-1848 (NO RETURN)
KIRBY, JULENA TO LAVENDER SUTTEN
KIRBY, R. TO GEORGE ST. JOHN
KIRBY, ROBT. S. TO SARAH J. SMITHSON 10-4-1871 ((NO RETURN)
KIRBY, THOS. TO NANCY POWELL 10-12-1864
KIRK, E. TO JOHN ST. JOHN
KIRK, LUCINDA TO D. A. JONES
KIRK, SARAH B. TO JOHN HOLLAND
KIRKLIN, ISAAC TO MISS CINDY R. DARABERRY 11-27-1852
KIRLOCK, AMENA C. TO J. L. BRASHERS
KIRSEY, ETHALINDA TO LEMUEL D. EVANS
KIRSEY, FRANCES TO WM. BRATON
KITTRELL, GEORGE TO MISS CAROLINE STEWART 12-4-1867 (12-5-1867)
KITTRELL, PRUDIE TO H. B. RUSHING
KNIGHT, JAMES M. TO MISS SARAH THOMAS 1-22-1849 (NO RETURN)
KNIGHT, JAMES TO MISS SARAH ANN ASE 3-4-1858
KNIGHT, JESSEMIN TO ELIZABETH M. HICKS 10-28-1855 (10-20?-1855)
KNIGHT, JOEL A. TO LIDY P. KING 12-28-1871
KNIGHT, W. J. TO MISS LYDA KING 7-7-1856 (7-10-1856)
KNOTT, R. F. TO MISS FANNIE MCBROOM 6-3-1871 (6-4-1871)
KNOX, ELIJAH S. TO MISS ANGELINE GAITHER 8-2-1849
KNOX, ISSABELLA ANN R. TO NATHAN J. LYON
KNOX, J. R. TO MISS R. A. PEAY 1-14-1866 (1-15-1866)
KNOX, JAMES B. TO MISS SALINA JANE COX 1-5-1850 (1-7-1850)
KNOX, JOE A. TO ELIZABETH MORGAN 4-22-1864 (4-24-1864)
KNOX, JOHN G. TO MISS ELIZABETH SMITH 3-19-1868 (3-22-1868)
KNOX, MARINDA M. M. TO LUKE LASETER
KNOX, MARTHA P. TO JAMES M. FOX
KNOX, MARY JANE TO HENRY W. HOOVER
KNOX, MARY TO ROBERT CRAMNER
KNOX, NANCY C. TO WM. J? DUNN
KNOX, NANCY P. TO ORVELL H. FORD
KNOX, S. J. TO G. T. MOON
KNOX, S. W. TO MISS NANCY E. MEDOW 5-15-1856 (NO RETURN)
KNOX, SOPHIA E. TO ARTUA MCCRARY
KNOX, SYNTHA E. TO E. D. OWNBY
KNOX, THOMAS TO DISEY LUSTER 6-21-1867
KNOX, WILLIAM A. TO MISS NANCY J. TODD 9-15-1849 (9-?-1849)
KNOX, WILLIAM TO MISS MARY C. COOPER 8-30-1856 (NO RETURN)
KURKENDALL, CYNTHA TO SIMON KURKENDALL
KURKENDALL, SIMON TO MISS CYNTHA L. KURKENDALL 10-18-1855 (10-19-1855)
KUYKENDALL, EASTER J. TO SILAS R. CURTIS
KUYKENDALL, JACOB TO MISS NANCY FOWLER 6-6-1854 (NO RETURN)
KUYKENDALL, NANCY TO THOMAS KEELE
KUYKENDALL, NORRIS TO MARY BEATY 12-3-1844
KUYKENDALL, TELITHA F. TO JOHN WILLIAMS
LACKEY, SARAH TO JOSEPH MOORE
LACKEY, WILLIAM K. TO NANCEY M. MCKNIGHT 10-19-1839 (10-27-1839)
LAFEVERS, R. S. TO MARTHY A. SULLIVAN 5-28-1857
LAFEVERS, SALLIE TO ROBERT GANN
LAFEVERS, SARY TO FRANCIS BOWERS

LAFEVERS, WM. J. TO MISS MARRY J. MCCABE 4-12-1853 (NO RETURN)
LAMBERT, DAVID TO MARY UNDERWOOD 7-18-1863 (NO RETURN)
LAMBERT, DAVID TO PURITY LASETER 9-4-1839
LAMBERT, ELIZABETH TO JOHN REED
LAMBERT, J. E. TO MISS MARTHA A. BURGETT 3-?-1856 (3-2-1856)
LAMBERTH, ANDERSON TO REBECCA ANNE BUSH 8-26-1840 (8-27-1840)
LAMBERTH, DAVID TO ELIZABETH WRON 6-17-1840 (6-18-1840)
LAMBERTH, HARRISON H. TO MISS NEY LAMBERTH 2-17-1847 (2-18-1847)
LAMBERTH, JAMES TO MARGARET F. PATTON 7-31-1838
LAMBERTH, JANEY TO HARRISON H. LAMBERTH
LAMBIRTH, MARYANN TO URIAH BUSH
LAMBUTH, MARY ANN TO HUGH REED
LANCE, CATHARINE TO JOHN MILLIGAN
LANCE, FRANCES E. TO JAMES M. FOWLER
LANCE, J. L. TO MISS M. J. THOMPSON 11-10-1858 (11-11-1858)
LANCE, JAMES P. K. TO MISS MARY GUNTER 10-5-1867 (10-6-1867)
LANCE, JAS. R. TO MARTHA M. MELTON 9-1-1873 (9-2-1873)
LANCE, JOHN TO MISS SARAH LITRELL 10-13-1841
LANCE, JOSEPH TO MISS SARAH ANN HUTCHINS 5-3-1847
LANCE, LOCKEY JANE TO DAVID MASSAN HART
LANCE, MANERVA TO JOHN W. BARRETT
LANCE, POLLY TO REUBEN ELAM
LANCE, WM. H. TO MISS SARRAH M. MILLAR 10-3-1857 (10-7-1857)
LANDSDEN, JOHN TO MARY MICKEY 9-13-1867 (9-14-1867)
LANE, OLIVE TO JAMES C. GREER
LANER, NANCY S. TO JAMES M. HART
LANG, MARGARETT TO JAMES H. BARRETT
LANIER, CHARLES B. TO MISS ELIZA MELTON 9-20?-1854 (9-21-1854)
LANIER, JAMES H. TO MISS NANCY EDWARDS 10-21-1858
LANIER, REBECA E. TO GEORGE H. KEYTON
LANIER, WM. J. TO MISS RUTHA COOPER 10-14-1858 (NO RETURN)
LANSDEN, SARAH P. TO WILLIAM C. DONNELLE
LANSDEN, SUSAN C. TO ZACHARIAH SMITH
LANSLEY, ISSABELLA TO NILE A. MITCHEL
LARANCE, SARAH J. TO S. D. TRAVIS
LASATER, CINDERELLA TO JACOB DERRYBERRY
LASATER, LUKE TO MISS LAMIRA L. HOLLIS 11-7-1848
LASATER, MARY ELIZABETH TO JAMES F. STACY
LASATER, NANCY ANN TO NATHAN C. TABOUR
LASATER, PURITY TO WILLIAM SIMMONS
LASETER, ANGELINE TO WM. GOOD
LASETER, HARDY TO SARAH CLEMMENTS 10-3-1838
LASETER, J. H. TO MISS M. A. SAFFLE 3-10-1869 (3-11-1869)
LASETER, LUKE TO MARINDA M. M. KNOX 12-19-1838
LASETER, MARIAH TO JONATHAN YORK
LASETER, MARY TO ALFORD BIVENS
LASETER, MARY TO JAMES REED
LASETER, NANCY E. TO G. C. YOUREE
LASETER, PEYTON TO MISS MARY FRANCES BOWEN 8-16-1866 (8-17-1866)
LASETER, PURIETY TO DAVID LAM BERT
LASETER, RICHARD TO MISS JOSPHENE? JONES 8-3-1871
LASITER, J. B. TO MISS MARGARETT GUNTER 7-25-1868 (7-29-1868)
LASITER, J. B. TO MISS SARAH MERRITT 3-18-1870 (NO RETURN)
LASITER, SINIA E. TO NATHAN SPATTON
LASTER, J. H. TO MISS M. E. JONES 3-6-1871 (NO RETURN)
LASWELL, ELIZABETH TO DABNY HILL
LAW, CHARLY TO SARAH MOON 7-12-1856
LAW, JANE TO S. W. BYNUM
LAWING, MARY ANN TO JOHN W. HALL
LAWRANCE, M. W. TO S. E. TODD 9-19-1860 (NO RETURN)

LAWRENCE, JAMES T. TO MISS LUCY E. CUMMINS 10-6-1869 (10-7-1869)
LAWRENCE, MARTHA JANE TO WILLIAM H. HARRISON
LAWRENCE, MARY TO ISAAC GUNTER
LAWSON, MARY TO ARCHIBALD SOUTHERLAND
LAYMAN, NANCY TO H. J. COOPER
LEA, MAT TO JOHN W. COOK
LEACH, NANCY TO WM. L. MEADOR
LEAL, L. A. TO K. M. MASON
LEDBETTER, ALFORD TO ZANIE A. POWELL 5-10-1873
LEDBETTER, ELI TO POLLY ASHFORD 4-25-1838 (NO RETURN)
LEDBETTER, JAMES TO MISS SALINA REEVES 5-?-1849 (5-11-1849)
LEDBETTER, NANCY TO ALEXANDER MCDOUGALD
LEDBETTER, THOMAS TO MISS MARTHA JETTON 8-3-1868 (8-?-1868)
LEDBETTER, WILLIAM TO SUSAN SULLENS 4-16-1842 (4-17-1842)
LEE, CHARLES TO MARTHA J. WOMBERLY 11-16-1865 (NO RETURN)
LEE, OZBURN TO MARY STACY 3-2-1839 (NO RETURN)
LEECH, JOHN C. TO MISS JULIA ANN BLANKS 12-29-1845 (1-12-1846)
LEECH, M. J. TO ROBERT DAVENPORT
LEECH, WILLIAM C. TO MISS AMANDA E. THOMAS 9-12-1847
LEFEVER, MARTHA TO THOS. M. PITMAN
LEFEVERS, SARY TO FRANCIS BOWERS
LEIGH, ELIZABETH W. TO JOSHUA CRESON
LEIGH, JOHN TO JANE SHORES 12-21-1856 (1-1-857)
LEIGH, MANERVA J. TO ALEXANDER FINLEY
LEIGH, MARRY L. TO JAMES R. ESPEY
LEIGH, MARY TO JOHN WILSON
LEIGH, NANCY C. TO THOMAS J. ROBERTS
LEIGH, WARE TO MISS SARAH CRESON 10-22-1846
LEIGH, WILLIAM J. TO MISS REBECCA J. CUMMINGS 12-25-1868 (1-7-1869)
LEMAY, S. E. TO S. MANESS
LEMAY, T. P. TO MISS M. BARRETT 7-9-1853 (NO RETURN)
LEMMONS, ISAAC N. TO MARTHA J. TODD 8-14-1872 (8-15-1872)
LEMMONS, SARAH E. TO SAMUEL A. TENPENNY
LEMMONS, W. T. TO MISS SARAH GOODING 2-3-1869 (2-11-1869)
LEMONS, ISAAC TO MISS MANERVA DUNCAN 10-25-1845 (EXECUTED--NO DATE)
LEMONS, JACOB M. TO MISS ELIZABETH C. PELHAM 12-19-1867
LENING, N. J. TO MISS S. F. BALEY 12-28-1870
LENOX, NANCY K. TO THOMAS BYFORD
LEONARD, CYRENA A. TO BERRY WILLIAMS
LESTER, KATHARINE TO WM. H. COUCH
LETT, JEMIMA ANN TO SHEROD MAYS
LEWELLEN, ELLEN TO COPEN SMITH
LEWIN, JANE TO ALFORD EDWARDS
LEWIS, H. A. TO MISS N. I. GILLY 9-21-1870 (9-22-1870)
LEWIS, J. W. TO MISS NANCY E. WEST 11-29-1859 (NO RETURN)
LEWIS, JANE TO JAMES ELKINS
LEWIS, JESSE G. TO MISS SARAH P. DUKE 10-5-1869 (10-10-1869)
LEWIS, L. L. TO MISS M. GIVINS 2-22-1859 (NO RETURN)
LEWIS, LUCINDA TO J. SIMMONS
LEWIS, MARGARET A. TO JAMES W. BROWN
LEWIS, MARTHA E. TO JAMES SUMMERS
LEWIS, PETER J. TO MANERVA J. FINLEY 12-12-1868
LEWIS, S. H. TO S. L. COOPER
LEWIS, S. T. TO MALISA P. MATHIS 12-27-1871 (12-28-1871)
LEWIS, WILLIAM C. TO MISS PELINA A. DERABERRY 4-2-1870
LILLARD, BRIST TO MARY WOODS 11-25-1873
LINCH, L. B. TO J. F. BROILES
LITLE, W. M. TO MISS JULIANN QUALLS 8-4-1858 (8-?-1858)
LITRELL, JANE TO WILLIAM YOUNG
LITRELL, SARAH TO JOHN LANCE

LITRELL, WILFORD TO MISS POLLY MELTON 11-23-1841 (11-27-1841)
LITTERAL, SAUNDERS TO ELIZABETH BOYD 9-14-1838
LITTLE, CAMELEE TO J. P. MILLIGAN
LITTLE, SARAH TO J. A. RIGSBY
LOGAN, BETTIE TO J. R. PARRIS
LOGAN, M. TO J. M. WOOTON
LOGUE, ANDREW TO MISS MAY MOFFITT 4-12-1847
LOLLIN, MARGARETT TO PHILLIP COOPER   ·
LONG, HANAH P. TO JOSEPH M. CLARK
LONG, ISUL TO M. H. HUTCHENSON 12-13-1873 (12-14-1873)
LONG, R. F. TO MISS H. P. HAWKINS 1-9-1858 (1-11-1858)
LORANCE, E. J. TO MISS SALLIE GRAHAM 1-1-1867
LORANCE, F. J. TO NANNIE A. ELROD 2-8-1865
LORANCE, G. R. TO MISS JULIAN WIMBERLY 9-28-1869
LORANCE, J. M. TO M. T. TODD 2-22-1872 (NO RETURN)
LORANCE, M. A. TO T. J. HUNT
LORANCE, M. W. TO MARY E. COSBEY 8-23-1873 (8-24-1873)
LORANCE, MANERVA TO HENRY D. STONE
LORANCE, MICHAEL TO MISS SARAH M. E. KELTON 12-20-1869 (12-21-1869)
LORANCE, R. C. TO MISS T. P. AKERS 2-23-1870 (2-24-1870)
LORANCE, WM. W. TO MISS R. J. WINNETT 12-31-1868
LORD, MITCHEL TO MISS PERMELIA ANN CLEMENTS 10-15-1840
LOW, CALVIN TO ELIZABETH JACOBS 9-14-1863 (NO RETURN)
LOW, THOS. N. TO SARAH E. SUMMER 8-9-1864
LOWE, C. T. TO R. J. MOORE 5-1-1873 (5-14-1873)
LOWE, ELIZABETH TO ELIHU J. MILLER
LOWE, FRANCES E. TO J. B. SMITH
LOWE, FRANCES M. TO ROBERT H. PATTON
LOWE, HARRIET TO JONATHAN J. BRANDON
LOWING, JANE TO ADAM ELROD
LOWIS, WM. C. TO MISS E. RETTON 10-5-1858
LOWRANCE, M. H. TO G. R. ALLEN
LOWRANCE, MANDY TO JOHN ELKINS
LOWRY, W. B. TO MARTHA P. HAWKINS 9-18-1871 (9-19-1871)
LUNDSDON, MARY TO HARRY ODOM
LUSTER, DISEY TO THOMAS KNOX
LUSTER, LETTICIA TO NATHANIEL PERRY
LUSTER, SALLY TO JOSEPH PRESTON
LVANER?, SARAH TO ANUL MELTON
LYNN, JOHN H. TO EMELINE HIPP 7-22-1872 (8-1-1872)
LYNN, L. A. TO J. A. HAILEY
LYNN, LAVISA J. TO J. W. WARRICK
LYNN, MARTHA J. TO GEO. W. FINLEY
LYNN, MARY E. TO JOHN L. PENDLETON
LYNN, RACHAL C. TO J. M. DUKE
LYNN, SARAH TO MONROE DUKE
LYON, GEORGE W. TO MISS MARY A. MCKNIGHT 12-23-1850 (12-24-1850)
LYON, N. J. S. TO MISS EMALINE SISSOM 11-17-1866 (11-18-1866)
LYON, NATHAN J. TO ISSABELLA ANN R. KNOX 12-7-1842 (12-8-1842)
LYONS, CATHERINE TO AL? RUSHING
LYONS, ED TO MISS LANY MILLER 1-12-1871
LYONS, FRANK TO MOLLIE TODD 9-8-1872
MABRY, ABE TO ABIGALE MCKNIGHT 12-3-1867 (12-5-1867)
MACLAN, HARRIET TO J. F. THOMAS
MACLIN, HARRIET TO S. F. THOMAS
MAGLOCKLIN, SARAH JANE TO JAMES VASSER
MAGON?, JACKSON TO NANCY MOORE 11-1-1851 (11-2-1851)
MAIES, WILLIAM TO ANN CURTIS 4-11-1842
MAINES, ARRMANDA TO JOHN MOONYHAM
MAJORS, HANNAH A. TO HENRY TROTT

MAKUM, P. D. TO D. S. FORD
MALONE, ERSKINE TO MISS ELIZA MCEWIN 9-1-1846
MALONE, JOHN J. TO REBECCA BRASHEARS 7-13-1842 (NO RETURN)
MANES, D. E. TO MISS A. BARRETT 12-17-1858
MANESS, GEORGE W. TO RUTHY CAPPS 2-8-1852
MANESS, I. TO MISS S. E. LEMAY 7-9-1853
MANEY, H. J. TO MISS MARTHA A. DOUGHERTY 3-15-1869 (3-16-1869)
MANEY, PRISCILLA TO JAMES R. BRIGHT
MANEY, VIRGINIA TO EDWARD DONOHO
MANFRES, GEORGE TO MARIAH MILLIGAN 6-21-1869 (6-22-1869)
MANIS, E. D. TO MALVIRA TEPLES 3-27-1864
MANIUS, M. A. TO ROBERT MOONAHAM
MANKIN, ISABELLA TO GORLEY? T. S. FORD
MANOUS, BENGAMIN E. TO MISS MARY ANN HANEY 8-21-1867 (8-22-1867)
MANOUS, MARGARET TO EDMUND JURNIGAN
MANUS, ANN TO BRITTON GANN
MANUS, DANIEL TO SUSANNAH ELKINS 6-11-1840
MANUS, ELIJAH TO MARY ANN PATRICK 2-14-1845 (2-13?-1845)
MANUS, M. H. TO EMLEY MUNCY 11-20-1873
MANUS, MALISSA TO J. R. TAYLOR
MANUS, MARIAN TO WILLIAM MANUS
MANUS, N. TO V. E. MANUS 8-3-1860 (NO RETURN)
MANUS, NATHAN TO MISS NANCY A. STEEPLES 11-11-1853 (NO RETURN)
MANUS, THOMAS TO MISS JANE THOMAS 9-25-1847 (NO RETURN)
MANUS, V. E. TO N. MANUS
MANUS, WILLIAM TO MISS MARIAN MANUS 2-26-1841 (2-27-1841)
MARBERRY, SARAH TO URIAH F. INGLIS
MARCHBANKS, JAMES TO ELIZABETH H. BROWN 11-1-1839 (11-2-1839)
MARCHBANKS, MARIAH TO JOHN HAINEY
MARCUIS, JACOB TO MISS MARGARETT THOMAS 6-10-1852
MARCUM, CHARLES TO MISS SARAH C. BLAIR 5-15-1856 (NO RETURN)
MARCUM, CHARLES TO MISS SARAH C. BLUE 5-15-1856
MARCUM, ELIZA TO GREEN W. BETHEL
MARCUM, ISAAC TO MISS NANCY HIGGANS 2-11-1851 (2-14-1851)
MARCUM, JOHN TO MISS NANCY OWEN 9-9-1853 (9-12-1853)
MARCUM, MELVINA J. TO JOHN S. BALY
MARCUM, MICAJAH TO MISS MARTHA GUNTER 1-30-1850
MARCUM, PAULINA TO JOHN BURKETT
MARCUN, JOB TO MISS GEORGIANA GASSOWAY 3-3-1849 (NO RETURN)
MARE, M. N. TO MRS. M. E. WILLIAMS 7-19-1860 (NO RETURN)
MARES, ELIZABETH TO JACKSON MORGAN
MARES, WM. TO MARY K. HOLLAND 11-23-1862
MARKER, H. B. TO MARTHA A. SEALS 12-2-1863 (12-3-1863)
MARKUM, A. TO ELIZABETH HELLENSULAR 7-6-1860 (7-15-1860)
MARKUM, ALFRED TO MISS MARY DENNIS 11-11-1869 (11-14-1869)
MARKUM, ANTHON A. TO ROBT. MCGEE
MARKUM, ARCH TO A. H. OWEN 5-4-1864 (5-8-1864)
MARKUM, BERRY TO MISS MATILDA BURKETT 8-26-1843
MARKUM, CALAFORNIA TO JACOB BAILEY
MARKUM, FRANCES TO JAMES VINSON
MARKUM, M. A. TO J. D. FOSTER
MARKUM, MARTHA A. TO J. N. YORK
MARKUM, MARY TO WILLIAM JETTON
MARKUM, NANCY L. TO WM. M. KING
MARKUM, WM. TO N. A. ELKINS 1-24-1872 (1-25-1872)
MARLIN, MERRY JANE TO WM. WOODROFF
MARSHALL, ELIZA JANE TO THOMAS COX
MARSHALL, MARTHA C. TO WILLIAM J. SMITH
MARSHALL, SARAH ANN TO ISAAC N. JOHNSON
MARTIN, AMZI W. TO MISS ISABELLA E. MCKNIGHT 3-12-1841 (3-25-1841)

MARTIN, ANTHONY TO JOSE MOORE 7-12-1873
MARTIN, CHARLES TO MISS HATTIE COVINGTON 12-28-1868 (12-30-1868)
MARTIN, ELIZABETH TO JOHN JONES
MARTIN, ELIZABETH TO RUFUS GASAWAY
MARTIN, FANNIE B. TO JOHN A. HARROD
MARTIN, JACK TO MISS SALLIE HANCOCK 9-24-1870 (9-27-1870)
MARTIN, JACKSON TO JOSEPHINE MOORE 2-25-1869
MARTIN, LEWIS G. TO ALLEY CONN 3-4-1839
MARTIN, LUCINDA TO LEWIS GORDON
MARTIN, MALISA TO JIM THOMPSON
MARTIN, MARTHA TO JAMES OFFICER
MARTIN, MARY J. TO JOHN D. ENGLISH
MARTIN, PARALEE TO JOHN DICKEY
MARTIN, PARALEE TO RANCE HIGGINS
MARTIN, RICHARD B. TO MISS MARY JONES 9-9-1850 (NO RETURN)
MARTIN, RICHARD TO JULIAN GORDON 1-27-1869
MARTIN, RODY TO PAUMP? GRIZZLE
MARTIN, ROSLIN L. TO JAMES I. DOUGLASS
MARTIN, SELINA TO GEO. MCBROOM
MARTIN, SOPHIA E. TO D. T. HEROD
MARTIN, SUSAN J. TO WILLIAM B. WRIGHT
MARTIN, SUSAN TO JACOB B. HAWKINS
MARTIN, THOMAS S. TO MISS EMALIZA BOWEN 10-24-1844
MARTIN, W. A. TO SARAH ENGLISH 8-19-1872 (8-21-1872)
MARTIN, W. T. TO MISS MARGRET JONES 11-21-1870 (11-23-1870)
MARTIN, WM. R. TO MRS. M. C. HARMON 7-28-1870 (NO RETURN)
MARTIN, WM. TO CAROLINE E. GRIFFIN 12-17-1855 (12-20-1855)
MARTIN, WM. TO MISS SARAH ANN BULLEN 4-1-1871
MARTIN, ZENAS A. TO ELIZA E. MCKNIGHT 5-18-1840 (5-20-1840)
MASON, ALICE TO HENRY MCKNIGHT
MASON, J. T. TO MISS ELIZA J. VANCE 11-27-1867 (11-28-1867)
MASON, JAMES TO CASSINDA SMITH 11-15-1838 (11-18-1838)
MASON, JOHN TO EATHCINDY KERSY 10-22-1860 (NO RETURN)
MASON, JOSEPH F. TO MISS JANE HIGGINS 11-20-1868 (11-27-1868)
MASON, K. M. TO MISS L. A. LEAL 12-29-1869 (12-30-1869)
MASON, MARY TO NEWTON HOOVER
MASON, N. F. TO S. J. BELL 7-18-1860 (7-19-1860)
MASON, REGNEER H. TO FLORA M. STONE 12-4-1849 (12-8-1849)
MASON, SARAH E. TO T. M. NEEL?
MASON, WILLIAM C. TO MISS S. A. SPURLOCK 9-1-1869 (9-2-1869)
MASSEY, MARTHA TO SAMUEL NELSON
MASSIE, W. M. TO MISS ELIZA DILLON 12-14-1869
MATHEWS, CHARLOTTE TO WILLIAM DODD
MATHEWS, J. W. TO MISS ANNIE WILLIAMS 12-?-1870 (12-7-1870)
MATHEWS, JOHANNA E. TO JAMES L. COLVERT
MATHEWS, JOHN W. TO MARY DODD 1-19-1842 (1-20-1842)
MATHEWS, JOHN W. TO MISS MARY E. DAVIS 5-3-1856 (5-26-1856)
MATHEWS, MARY E. TO A. B. MCKNIGHT
MATHEWS, NANCY TO JOHN M. ORR
MATHEWS, NATHAN TO NANCY KEITH 3-26-1840 (3-31-1840)
MATHEWS, PAULINA J. P. TO A. M. WEEDON
MATHEWS, SAMUEL TO MISS MILLEY SUMMAR 7-22-1847
MATHEWS, SARAH C. TO R. T. BOND
MATHEWS, SARAH TO REUBEN DAVENPORT
MATHEWS, W. H. TO MISS M. A. F. HUBBARD 11-30-1869 (12-2-1869)
MATHEWS, WALTER TO ANTALIZA ASHFORD 7-21-1842 (NO RETURN)
MATHIS, CLARINDA TO R. H. WILLIAMS
MATHIS, IBBY ELIZABETH TO JAMES H. H. KING
MATHIS, MALISA P. TO S. T. LEWIS
MATHIS, NANCY F. TO LEVI MORRIS

MATHIS, PARLEE TO POLK GRIZZLE
MAXERY, RICHARD TO ELIZABETH M. BATSON 10-26-1839 (10-29-1839)
MAXEY, DANIEL TO ANNA C. MCDOUGAL 12-28-1864 (NO RETURN)
MAXEY, ELIZABETH TO ERASMUS S. KEES
MAXEY, LEWIS TO MISS SARAH PHILIPS 10-21-1868 (10-22-1868)
MAXEY, NANCY TO DAVID M. PRATER
MAXEY, P. P. TO MARTHA H. BALY 1-6-1864 (1-7-1864)
MAXEY, PEGGY JANE TO BENJAMIN L. STACY
MAXEY, POLLY TO SAMUEL? WHITTER
MAYES?, SUSAN A. TO JAMES MEANTS
MAYFIELD, EDNY S. TO JAMES B. ELLEDGE
MAYO, BENGAMIN F. TO MISS STACY MELTON 7-21-1870 (NO RETURN)
MAYS, SHEROD TO JEMIMA ANN LETT 4-7-1842
MAZEY, W. W. TO MISS MARGARETT J. YOUNG 12-26-1866 (1-3-1867)
MAZY, HARRIETT TO JAMES JONES
MAZY, LOUISA A. TO E. J. YOUNG
MCADAM, A. TO ABNER MOORE
MCADOE, J. N. TO MISS C. J. FRANCIS 12-24-1866 (12-25-1866)
MCADOO, H. E. TO MISS FRANCES GROOM 12-21-1870 (12-22-1870)
MCADOO, J. C. TO MISS C. R. SUMMAR 10-12-189 (10-14-1869)
MCADOO, MARY JANE TO JOHN L. EWING
MCADOO, N. C. TO GEO. ALEXANDER
MCADOO, V. P. TO A. F. FRACIS
MCADOW, AELISA TO BENJAMIN PENDLETON
MCADOW, AZALINE TO JOHN D. COOPER
MCADOW, ELIZA TO A. C. TATUM
MCADOW, HANAH TO ABRAHAM ODOM
MCADOW, L. F. TO D. WITHERSPOON
MCADOW, MARGARET J. TO M. T. SIMMS
MCADOW, MARGARET J. TO W. J. HERNDON
MCADOW, P. A. TO WM. A. T. MOORE
MCALEXANDER, J. TO MAHAMA SULLIVAN 11-18-1872 (11-21-1872)
MCALEXANDER, REBECCA TO JAMES N. WATSON
MCBORREN, ISAAC TO MARYANN TENPENNY 2-17-1852
MCBRIDE, POLLY TO JACOB UNDERWOOD
MCBROOM, ALEXANDER D. TO MISS CHARLENY TENPENNY 8-12-1856 (NO RETURN)
MCBROOM, ALEXANDER TO MARY HOOVER 12-21-1871
MCBROOM, B. T. TO MISS KISSIA J. MCBROOM 9-23-1869
MCBROOM, BETTIE TO JAMES R. CARTER
MCBROOM, BETTIE TO S. O. MCKNIGHT
MCBROOM, E. J. TO W. T. MINGLE
MCBROOM, ELIZABETH A. TO S. E. BRAGG
MCBROOM, FANNIE TO R. F. KNOTT
MCBROOM, FLORA TO SAMPSON MCBROOM
MCBROOM, GEO. TO SELINA MARTIN 6-6-1872
MCBROOM, ISAAC TO MRS. NANCY J. HOWETH 8-19-1869
MCBROOM, J. W. TO MISS I. N. FAGAN 4-4-1871 (4-5-1871)
MCBROOM, JAMES TO MISS RACHEL HAYS 1-3-1850
MCBROOM, JESSEE TO FRANCES E. MULLINS 11-4-1873
MCBROOM, JOHN TO MARGARET FERREL 10-5-1863
MCBROOM, JOHN TO MISS ROXANNA ALEXANDER 11-15-1848 (11-16-1848)
MCBROOM, KISSIA J. TO B. T. MCBROOM
MCBROOM, MANERVA ANN TO JOHN M. TAYLOR
MCBROOM, NANCY E. TO JAMES T. SULLIVAN
MCBROOM, NANCY TO JOHN STEPHEN
MCBROOM, NATHAN TO MISS MARTHA ANN GANNON 12-11-1856
MCBROOM, RACHEL TO DANIEL BARTON
MCBROOM, ROBERT C. TO MISS MARY HAYS 1-8-1846 (NO RETURN)
MCBROOM, SAMPSON TO FLORA MCBROOM 11-17-1865 (11-19-1865)
MCBROOM, SARAH J. TO WILLIAM BARTON JR.

MCBROOM, W. H. TO MISS E. A. MCGILL 9-15-1870
MCBROOM?, ABEL TO MISS FANNY HYS 4-3-1841 (NO RETURN)
MCCABE, A. J. TO MISS MARY E. GURTY 5-20-1853 (NO RETURN)
MCCABE, CORNELIA A. TO JAMES H. TODD
MCCABE, HOUSTON TO MARY C. ELKINS 1-23-1860 (NO RETURN)
MCCABE, JAMES A. TO SARAH TODD 7-12-1872 (7-14-1872)
MCCABE, MARRY J. TO WM. J. LAFEVARS
MCCABE, MARY C. TO WILLIAM THOMAS
MCCABE, MARY J. TO W. L. TODD
MCCABE, MARY TO A. V. JONES
MCCABE, WM. B. TO MISS AMERICA ANN ADCOCK 6-7-1853 (6-9-1853)
MCCABE?, JOHN C. TO MISS ELIZABETH MERIT 6-18-1845
MCCAFFREY, MALISSA TO JOHN NEVAL
MCCARLIN, WM. TO MISS ADALINE HUGHS 12-15-1859 (NO RETURN)
MCCASLIN, C. E. TO LUCINDA BYNUM 7-30-1873 (7-31-1873)
MCCASLIN, EMALINE TO JAMES P. MCGILL
MCCASLIN, LOGAN TO BETTY COOPER 9-12-1860 (9-?-1860)
MCCASLIN, MARGARETT E. TO WILLIAM C. SOAPE
MCCGREGGER, WM. B. TO MISS S. J. MCGREGGER 11-15-1856 (NO RETURN)
MCCLAIN, JAMES P. TO MISS MARTHA PETTY 11-12-1865
MCCLAIN, JAMES TO MISS MARTHA GOODING 8-20-1847 (NO RETURN)
MCCLAIN, JANE TO JOHN RODGERS
MCCLAIN, M. J. TO J. I. REED
MCCLAIN, MARY TO WM. C. ELLADGE
MCCOLLOUGH, THOMAS TO RACHEL CAROLINE GRAY 9-18-1838 (9-19-1838)
MCCRARY, ABRAM TO MARY SMITH 12-16-1869
MCCRARY, ARTHUR TO MISS SOPHIA E. KNOX 8-16-1844 (8-19-1844)
MCCRARY, J. H. TO MISS MALINDA GILLEY 5-16-1866 (5-17-1866)
MCCRAY, NANCY TO JOHN E. BRANDON
MCCULLAR, SAMUEL TO MISS MARY CAWTHON 10-7-1870 (10-18-1870)
MCCULLER, R. S. TO P. J. BALTIMORE
MCCULLOCH, MARTIN TO MISS MELBERRY ROBERTS 2-13-1866 (2-18-1866)
MCCULLOUGH, ALEXANDER J. TO MISS REBECCA STACY 10-14-1841 (10-21-1841)
MCCULLOUGH, JOHN A. TO ELVIRA MCDANIEL 3-14-1843 (3-15-1843)
MCCULLOUGH, MARY A. TO A. C. ELLIOTT
MCCULLOUGH, R. J. TO J. L. TAYLOR
MCCULLOUGH, RODA S. TO BENJAMIN WILLIAMS
MCCULLOUGH, SARAH A. TO OBEDIAH FIGHT
MCCULLOUGH, WILLIAM W. TO MALVINA ANN WHARRY 1-11-1843 (1-12-1843)
MCDANEL, RODA A. TO A. W. CRANE
MCDANIEL, DAVID TO ADALINE D. REYNOLDS 7-16-1842 (7-18-1842)
MCDANIEL, ELVIRA TO JOHN A. MCCULLOUGH
MCDANIEL, JAMES TO NANCY REYNOLDS 12-10-1839
MCDOUGAL, ANNA C. TO DANIEL MAXEY
MCDOUGAL, ELIZABETH TO JOHN HENDRIXSON
MCDOUGAL, JOHN W. TO MISS ELIZA J. TODD 4-7-1870
MCDOUGAL, JOHN W. TO MISS MARGARET J. ST. JOHN 9-3-1866 (EXECUTED--NO DATE)
MCDOUGALD, ALEXANDER TO NANCY LEDBETTER 1-11-1847 (1-18-1847)
MCDOUGALD, JOHN D. TO SARAH GUNTER 1-2-1843 (1-5-1843)
MCDOUGLE, ELIZA TO WM. SPICER
MCDOUGLE, GUNTER TO MISS MALISA ST. JOHN 1-20-1871 (NO RETURN)
MCDOUGLE, JOHN TO SUTTY ST. JOHN 10-2-1860 (NO RETURN)
MCDOW, MARTH TO JOHN M. JONES
MCELROY, JAMES TO MARGARET PATTON 9-4-1865 (12-5-1865)
MCELROY, JOHN JAMES TO MISS MARY ANN PATTON 2-25-1846 (3-2-1846)
MCELROY, S. N. TO M. M. PORTERFIELD 11-16-1871
MCEWEN, JOHN DIXSON TO MISS HANNAH EMALINE TATE 5-25-1848
MCEWIN, ELIZA TO ERSKINE MALONE
MCEWIN, JOSEPH TO EMALIZA THOMAS 4-6-1839 (4-7-1839)
MCEWIN, SARAH TO ELIAS ALEXANDER READY

MCFADDAN, ANN M. TO GRANVILLE FAGAN
MCFARLAND, BENJAMIN P. TO MISS ERVINA? C. MCKNIGHT 8-9-1847 (8-12-1847)
MCFERIN, L. B. TO MARY E. WEBB 2-7-1865
MCFERIN, MARY J. TO R. A. REAGAN
MCFERIN, WM. TO MARIAN E. FISHER 8-17-1863 (NO RETURN)
MCFERREN, BITTIE TO O. G. HALLEYBURTON
MCFERREN, FANNIE F. TO JOHN W. PAGE
MCFERRIN, ALFORD TO REBECCA A. CUMMINS 11-16-1872 (11-17-1872)
MCFERRIN, ALFRED TO EMILY EASON 8-23-1865 (8-25-1865)
MCFERRIN, BURTON L. TO MISS MARTHA YOUNG 6-1-1843
MCFERRIN, E. C. TO J. R. OLIVER
MCFERRIN, EDMUND TO JANE DUNCAN 8-24-1865 (NO RETURN)
MCFERRIN, J. A. TO MISS TENNIE WOOD 1-1-1871
MCFERRIN, LOUISA TO JOSEPH WRIGHT
MCFERRIN, MARY E. TO JOHN H. OLIVER
MCFERRIN, WILLIAM H. TO MISS SARAH J. MITCHELL 11-8-1866
MCFERRIN, ZEKE TO LUTISIA BARNES 9-20-1873 (9-22-1873)
MCGEE, JANE TO JOHN VANDAGRIFF
MCGEE, JESSE TO MISS NANCY E. KING 10-19-1848
MCGEE, L. R. TO WM. JETTON
MCGEE, NANCY T. A. TO PETER N. J. KEATON
MCGEE, ROBT. TO ANTHON A. MARKUM 9-12-1872
MCGEE, WILLIAM TO MISS LAVINA ANN SOPHIA COX 7-28-1841 (7-29-1841)
MCGILL, E. A. TO W. H. MCBROOM
MCGILL, JAMES P. TO EMALINE MCCASLIN 9-8-1842 (9-13-1842)
MCGILL, JANE TO DAVID M. PATTON
MCGILL, M. A. TO J. C. CARNAHAN
MCGILL, MARTHA TO J. G. ANDERSON
MCGILL, P. T. TO E. H. ALLMON
MCGILL, SARAH E. TO J. A. SUMMERS
MCGILL, WILLIAM TO MISS ELIZA FAGAN 8-15-1845 (8-?-1845)
MCGLOCKLIN, ELEANOR TO DANIEL W. MITCHEL
MCGLOTHLIN, W. C. TO MISS MATILDA J. YONG 12-21-1858 (12-22-1858)
MCGREGGER, S. J. TO WM. B. MCGREGGER
MCGUIRE, THOS. G. TO MISS MARTHA J. SIMPSON 9-8-1849 (9-9-1849)
MCKEE, WILLIAM TO MARY HOOVER 12-11-1865 (12-12-1865)
MCKNAB, R. T. TO N. E. GRAY 10-17-1865 (10-19-1865)
MCKNABB, J. F. TO MISS L. J. TODD 1-20-1866 (1-31-1866)
MCKNIGHT, A. B. TO MISS MARY E. MATHEWS 10-22-1851 (NO RETURN)
MCKNIGHT, A. D. TO MISS M. L. HARE 2-1-1853 (2-3-1853)
MCKNIGHT, A. E. TO E. A. GOODLOE 7-7-1859 (NO RETURN)
MCKNIGHT, A. G. TO MISS D. L. FARE 11-3-1857
MCKNIGHT, ABIGALE TO ABE MABRY
MCKNIGHT, ABNER TO SUSAN FULLER 12-28-1867
MCKNIGHT, AMZI B. TO MISS SARAH R. JETTON 11-3-1868
MCKNIGHT, CHARLES TO HARRIET MCKNIGHT 8-21-1865 (8-26-1865)
MCKNIGHT, EASTER S. TO RAMZEL H. RODGERS
MCKNIGHT, ED TO BABE BARRETT 12-14-1872 (12-15-1872)
MCKNIGHT, ELIM TO M. M. COLLINS 5-18-1854
MCKNIGHT, ELIZA E. TO ZENAS A. MARTIN
MCKNIGHT, ELIZA TO JERRY HANCOCK
MCKNIGHT, ELIZABETH TO ALBERT SMITH
MCKNIGHT, ERVINA C. TO BENJAMIN F. MCFARLAND
MCKNIGHT, G. D. A. TO MISS ELEANOR F. ANDREWS 9-5-1849 (NO RETURN)
MCKNIGHT, HARRIET TO CHARLES MCKNIGHT
MCKNIGHT, HENRY TO ALICE MASON3-9-1873 (3-20-1873)
MCKNIGHT, ISABELLA E. TO AMZI W. MARTIN
MCKNIGHT, ISSABELLA A. TO DAVID N. RALSTON
MCKNIGHT, JAMES L. TO MISS MARGARETT JANE MCKNIGHT 11-5-1845 (11-6-1845)
MCKNIGHT, JAMES T. TO MISS MARY E. JETTON 11-25-1846 (SOLEMNIZED 1846)

MCKNIGHT, JOHN N. TO MISS CHARLOTA MOON 9-1-1859 (NO RETURN)
MCKNIGHT, JOSEPH D. TO MISS ARTALIA P. STEPHENS 3-20-1868 (3-22-1868)
MCKNIGHT, M. E. TO A. HERTER?
MCKNIGHT, MARGARETT E. TO WILLIAM H. SMITH
MCKNIGHT, MARGARETT JANE TO JAMES L. MCKNIGHT
MCKNIGHT, MARY A. TO GEORGE W. LYON
MCKNIGHT, MARY ANN TO AARON TRIMBLE
MCKNIGHT, MARY F. TO W. P. CARTER
MCKNIGHT, MARY J. TO W. P. DUGGIN
MCKNIGHT, MORGE TO MISS MANDY HOLLIS 8-5-1871 (8-6-1871)
MCKNIGHT, MOSES W. TO MARY A. FARE 9-24-1855 (RETURNS MISSING)
MCKNIGHT, NANCEY M. TO WILLIAM K. LACKEY
MCKNIGHT, NANCY TO JESSE WEATHERLY
MCKNIGHT, NANNIE A. TO D. R. CARTER
MCKNIGHT, RUBEN TO MISS L. RUCKER 10-14-1870 (NO RETURN)
MCKNIGHT, S. H. A. TO MISS MARY F. ANDREW 11-9-1847 (11-11-1847)
MCKNIGHT, S. O. TO BETTIE MCBROOM 12-18-1873 (NO RETURN)
MCKNIGHT, SAMUEL P. TO MISS LUCINDA D. HARE 2-12-1849 (NO RETURN)
MCKNIGHT, SARAH E. TO HENRY S. DUGGAN
MCKNIGHT, SARAH E. TO JAMES H. BYRNE
MCKNIGHT, SARAH J. TO J. M. ANDREWS
MCKNIGHT, SARAH M. TO SAMUEL H. BRYSON
MCKNIGHT, SHANNON TO THURZA EMALINE WITHERSPOON 9-28-1846 (NO RETURN)
MCKNIGHT, SYLVA TO FRANKLIN BRANTLEY
MCKNIGHT, TENNESSEE TO MALONE MCNAIRY
MCKNIGHT, W. M. TO MISS T. N. BETHELL 12-23-1868 (12-25-1868)
MCKNIGHT, WILLIAM W. TO MISS ELIZABETH SUTTON 7-5-1849 (NO RETURN)
MCLAIN, E. J. TO JOHN C. PETY
MCLIN, ALLICE M. TO J. E. RUCKER
MCMAHAN, J. T. TO MISS N. J. HIPP 10-17-1866 (10-18-1866)
MCMAHAN, L. J. TO A. W. PARKER
MCMAHAN, REBECCA ANN TO H. L. HARRELL
MCMICKLE, WILLIAM TO NANCY FORD 9-4-1838
MCMURRY, HATTIE E. TO R. A. MOORE
MCNABB, DILELAH TO J. S. ODOM
MCNAIRY, MALONE TO TENNESSEE MCKNIGHT 1-10-1867
MCNEELY, SARAH TO BENJAMIN VINSON
MCPHEARSON, MARGARETT E. TO COMPTON ASHFORD
MCREAD, W. TO R. M. HOLLIS 7-14-1860 (NO RETURN)
MCWHEARTER, L. H. TO J. H. WALE
MEACE, NANCY MANERVA TO DANIEL JAMES
MEADOR, WM. T. TO NANCY LEACH 2-13-1840 (NO RETURN)
MEANIS, JOHN TO MILITA KERBY 5-14-1838 (6-10-1838)
MEANS, MELVINA TO P. D. CUMMINGS
MEANTS?, JAMES TO SUSAN A. MAYES? 11-30-1851 (12-1-1851)
MEARS, ELIJAH TO NANCY BAILY 4-22-1840 (4-24-1840)
MEARS, JAMES TO MRS. MARY C. TEDDER 11-14-1848
MEARS, JAMES TO NANCY ELKINS 7-2-1842 (7-3-1842)
MEARS, JOHN C. TO MISS FRANCES E. WHERRY 12-20-1866
MEARS, M. TO THOMAS TARWATER
MEARS, MARK TO MISS ELIZABETH HAILEY 7-1-1867 (7-3-1867)
MEARS, REBECCA TO JOEL THOMAS
MEARS, ROBERT R. TO R. J. WATTERS 11-2-1864 (11-3-1864)
MEARS, SARAH TO GEORGE W. BUCY
MEARS, THOMAS J. TO MISS ELISABETH ALEXANDER 12-30-1854
MEARS, W. T. TO EMLEY F. BRYSON 12-2-1871 (12-3-1871)
MEARS, WILLIAM TO MISS MARY S. WOOD 10-?-1870 (10-20-1870)
MEASEL, N. C. TO A. D. PATTON
MEDDOW, VINCENT TO MARYANN WHIT 12-24-1838 (NO RETURN)
MEDFORD, HENRY TO MISS MALINDA ----- 3-22-1856

MEDFORD, HENRY TO MISS MARY HARRIS 6-26-1844
MEDLOCK, THOMAS TO HARIETT FLETCHER 12-27-1871 (12-28-1871)
MEDOW, NANCY TO S. W. KNOX
MEEKS, J. W. TO MATILDA BURNETT 7-5-1873 (NO RETURN)
MEERS, GABRIEL TO MISS MARTHA BOLEN 8-2-1866 (EXECUTED--NO DATE)
MELLON, THOMAS J. TO SARAH KATHARINE TURNER 8-3-1853
MELTON, AILCY C. TO GREENFIELD MELTON
MELTON, ANN C. TO L. P. GOFF
MELTON, ANNE TO JOHN CUMMINS
MELTON, ANUL TO SARAH LVANER? 7-21-1851 (7-24-1851)
MELTON, BENJAMIN TO MISS MALISSA CAROLINE ELKINS 1-28-1846
MELTON, C. D. TO MISS MARY GIVENS 11-1-1866 (11-7-1866)
MELTON, CYTHIA AN TO HENRY CAMPBELL
MELTON, DILLARD TO MISS MARY JETTON 11-7-1855 (11-8-1855)
MELTON, E. J. TO CHARLES SHERLEY
MELTON, E. R. TO MISS SARAH CAMPBELL 7-31-1867 (8-1-1867)
MELTON, E. R. TO RACHEL A. SMITH 7-25-1860
MELTON, ELIAS R. TO MISS R. A. BAILEY 11-18-1858 (NO RETURN)
MELTON, ELISHA TO MISS EZZY GILLEY 8-23-1866
MELTON, ELIZA JANE TO JONATHAN G. STONE
MELTON, ELIZA TO CHARLES B. LANIER
MELTON, ELIZA TO DAVID EVANS
MELTON, ELIZABETH TO H. Y. TITTLE
MELTON, ELIZABETH TO J. M. MELTON
MELTON, ELYSIS R. TO MISS RUTHA A. BALY 11-18-1858
MELTON, EMALINE TO JAMES HIGGINS
MELTON, FRANCIS TO MISS JOSEPHINE GUNTER 4-10-1867 (4-11-1867)
MELTON, GEORGE G. TO MISS MARTHA E. WALKUP 1-16-1854 (1-17-1854)
MELTON, GREENFIELD TO MISS AILCY C. MELTON 1-8-1849
MELTON, H. P. TO MISS MARGARETCUMMINS 1-9-1867 (1-10-1867)
MELTON, HIGDON TO MISS LUCY NOKES 5-10-1867 (5-14-1867)
MELTON, J. A. TO MISS M. CUMMINS 10-28-1859 (NO RETURN)
MELTON, J. D. TO MISS MARTHA NEUGENT 1-7-1853
MELTON, J. H. TO MISS S. E. SULLINS 2-13-1860 (NO RETURN)
MELTON, J. M. TO MISS ELIZABETH MELTON 3-7-1857 (3-8-1857)
MELTON, JAMES M. TO MARY PENDLETON 7-8-1845 (7-10-1845)
MELTON, JANE CAROLINE TO JAMES BLAIR
MELTON, JO TO BENJ. SHERLEY
MELTON, JOEL D. TO MISS ELISABETH NEELY 4-21-1860
MELTON, JOEL D. TO MISS MARY J. WALKUP 3-4-1850 (3-5-1850)
MELTON, JOHN M. TO MISS HANAH D. TURNER 5-14-1870 (5-15-1870)
MELTON, JOHN TO MISS SARAHFINE WARREN 3-28-1867
MELTON, JOHN W. TO RUTHA BURGER 3-11-1842
MELTON, JONNATHAN TO SARAH J. MOORE 3-29-1873 (3-30-1873)
MELTON, JOSEPH TO MISS BIDDY SMITH 10-2-1841 (10-5-1841)
MELTON, LUKE TO MISS PARLEE POWELL 12-25-1868 (12-27-1868)
MELTON, M. J. TO TOLBERT F. SHIRLEY
MELTON, MARTHA E. TO WM. BAILEY
MELTON, MARTHA J. TO JAS. R. LANCE
MELTON, MARTHA TO JAMES GRIZZLE
MELTON, MARY E. TO JO B. HAWKINS
MELTON, MARY TO A. H. CUMMINGS
MELTON, MARY TO JOHN HAWKINS
MELTON, MATILDA J. TO TOLBERT SHERLY
MELTON, MENERVA TO MAN P. PURTAN
MELTON, NANCY J. TO FRANCIS HOLLANDSWORTH
MELTON, NANCY TO WILLIAM PITMAN
MELTON, POLLY TO ABRAHAM PARTEN
MELTON, POLLY TO WILFORD LITRELL
MELTON, POLLY TO WILLIAM GRIZLE

MELTON, RHODY TO JOHN HOLTERMAND
MELTON, RICHARD TO MALLISSA ASHFORD 7-24-1841 (7-25-1841)
MELTON, S. J. TO J. T. MOORE
MELTON, S. J. TO S. J. GIVENS
MELTON, SARAH A. TO DANIEL JETTON
MELTON, SARAH F. TO PLEASANT R. TURNER
MELTON, SARAH JANE TO BENJAMIN CUMMINGS
MELTON, SARAH TO H. N. POWELL
MELTON, SELINA TO BETHEL PARSLEY
MELTON, STACY TO BENGAMIN F. MAYO
MELTON, SUSAN TO WILLIAM POWELL
MELTON, W. S. TO MISS E. J. HOUSE 3-6-1866
MELTON, WILLIAM J. TO MISS MARY HENDRICKSON 1-4-1844 (NO RETURN)
MELTON, ZERUNA TO JOHN D. CAMPBELL
MERIT, ELIZABETH TO JOHN MCCABE
MERITT, MADISON TO MISS EASTER WILMOTH 9-8-1841 (9-9-1841)
MERPHEY, V. S. TO JOHN PHILIPS
MERRATT, JOSIAH TO MISS MARY Y. SMITH 12-6-1843 (NO RETURN)
MERRETT, NANCY TO J. B. DAVENPORT
MERRETT, PRESLEY TO ELIZABETH WIMBERLY 9-16-1865 (9-17-1865)
MERRIMAN, EWIN TO MISS NANCY SPURLOCK 4-23-1856
MERRIMAN, EZEKIEL TO ELIZABETH CAPPS 3-23-1839 (3-24-1839)
MERRIMAN, FILIA ANN TO MENROW SPERLOCK
MERRIMAN, MATILDA TO WILLIAM SULLIVAN
MERRIMAN, SARAH TO JOSIAH PITTS
MERRIMAN, THOMAS TO MAHALA FARLER 2-5-1844 (NO RETURN)
MERRIMON, THOMAS TO RODA CANTRELL 9-29-1869
MERRITT, CATHARINE TO THOMAS VAUGHN
MERRITT, HARMAN TO MISS NANCY SMITHSON 2-21-1849
MERRITT, JACKSON TO MISS MARRY WIMBERLY 7-2-1853 (NO RETURN)
MERRITT, JAMES M. TO MARY A. TURNER 12-27-1849 (1-9-1850)
MERRITT, JAMES TO MISS ELIZABETH WOOD 8-29-1867
MERRITT, MARY A. TO JOEL SMITH
MERRITT, MERRY ANN TO J. R. HENDRICKSON
MERRITT, NANCY TO J. B. DAVENPORT
MERRITT, NANCY TO PLESANT EDDING
MERRITT, SARAH TO J. B. LASITER
MERRITT, THOMAS TO MRS. MARY C. ELKINS 5-2-1871 (5-3-1871)
MERRITT, W. H. TO MISS MARY E. GILLEY 9-13-1869 (9-14-1869)
MERRITT, WILLIAM TO MISS SERVELLA SHITT 9-22-1866 (9-23-1866)
MESSICK, SARAH TO WASHINGTON WILLIAMS
METTON, J. D. TO MISS MARTHA T. NEUGENT 6-7-1853 (6-9-1853)
MICKEY, MARY TO JOHN LANDSDEN
MICKEY, MOSES TO MISS CYNTHA SUMMAR 7-27-1867 (7-30-1867)
MIDDLESTON, PATIENCE TO SAMUEL CARMON
MILER, WM. H. TO MISS ANNA E. CARMICHAEL 2-3-1870
MILES, MAHALA A. TO JAMES A. SMITHSON
MILES, ROBERT S. TO MISS MARGARETT HALL 5-20-1853 (5-24-1853)
MILES, TELFORD TO MISS RUTHA BARRETT 12-29-1853
MILIGAN, ELIZABETH TO T. M. GARMENT
MILLAR, SARRAH M. TO WM. H. LANCE
MILLER, BETHANY TO BERY WOMACK
MILLER, CAROLINE TO WM. PELHAM
MILLER, ELIHU J. TO MISS ELIZABETH LOWE 10-17-1845 (10-19-1845)
MILLER, JOSEPH TO MISS SUSAN BRAGG 1-19-1856 (EXECUTED--NO DATE).
MILLER, LANY TO ED LYONS
MILLER, RICHARD TO MISS MARGARET DENTON 1-12-1856 (1-13-1856)
MILLER, WILLIAM C. TO MISS ELVIRA L. D. SEAWELL 9-25-1841 (9-26-1841)
MILLER, WILLIAM C. TO MISS MARTHA BREWER 7-25-1852
MILLIGAN, DAVID T. TO ELIZABETH THOMPSON 4-13-1839 (5-9-1839)

MILLIGAN, ELIZABETH TO ALEXANDER JETTON
MILLIGAN, ELIZABETH TO IRA HOLLINGSWORTH
MILLIGAN, ELIZABETH TO JAMES A. MORGAN
MILLIGAN, GEORGE W. TO LUCY HIGGINS 3-4-1869
MILLIGAN, J. P. TO CAMELEE LITTLE 2-25-1865 (NO RETURN)
MILLIGAN, JACK TO SUSAN TITTLE 2-26-1845
MILLIGAN, JAMES C. TO MISS CYNTHIA VASSER 12-19-1840 (11?-18-1840)
MILLIGAN, JOEL TO PENNEY PEDIGO 6-18-1838 (6-20-1838)
MILLIGAN, JOHN P. TO MARY J. BRYSON 3-22-1873 (3-23-1873)
MILLIGAN, JOHN TO DORCAS CRABTREE 4-5-1839 (4-21-1839)
MILLIGAN, JOHN TO MARTHA A. ODOM 7-5-1871 (NO RETURN)
MILLIGAN, JOHN TO MISS CATHARINE LANCE 6-2-1870 (6-8-1870)
MILLIGAN, JULIE A. TO WILLIAM COLLINS
MILLIGAN, M. B. TO FRANCES POWELL 2-17-1872 (2-18-1872)
MILLIGAN, MARIAH TO GEORGE MANFRES
MILLIGAN, NANCY TO JESSEE PATRICK
MILLIGAN, PARALEE TO J. S. ODOM
MILLIGAN, RUTHY TO RICHARD ASHFORD
MILLIGAN, W. H. TO MISS ALSENA E. SUMMAR 7-26-1866 (8-2-1866)
MILLIKIAN, ALBERT G. TO MISS SARAH GAITHER 2-26-1846
MILLIKIN, A. G. TO MISS L. E. BYFORD 6-21-1866
MILLIKIN, ALBERT G. TO MISS MARY J. TENERSON 8-31-1854
MILLIKIN, ANNIE TO B. F. ELROD
MILLIKIN, JOHN TO MISS PARTHENY O. BYFORD 1-2-1854 (1-3-1854)
MILLIKIN, PARLEE TO A. M. BESS
MILLIKIN, PARTHANA TO JAMES FAULKAM
MILLIKIN, PARTHENA TO THOMAS BURCHETT
MILLSTEAD, JAMES TO LOUISA SULLINS 2-8-1854
MILLSTED, M. A. TO T. J. HUNT
MILTON, SANDY TO MISS SOPHA BARTON 12-7-1870 (12-15-1870)
MINGLE, CHRISTENY TO W. C. JONES
MINGLE, GEORGE TO MISS POLLY TRAVIS 11-26-1847
MINGLE, NANCY J. TO JAMES A. HOWETH
MINGLE, SARAH J. TO HENRY W. DEVENPORT
MINGLE, W. T. TO E. J. MCBROOM 7-26-1873 (7-27-1873)
MINGLE, WILLIAM J. TO MISS ALICE CATHEY 2-10-1851
MINTEN, J. G. TO MISS MARTHA JANE TRAVIS 12-14-1858
MITCHEL, DANIEL W. TO ELEANOR MCGLOCKLIN 6-18-1840
MITCHEL, E. H. TO MISS MARTHA A. YONG 10-24-1859 (NO RETURN)
MITCHEL, G. W. P. TO MISS E. C. BARRETT 10-2-1855 (10-4-1855)
MITCHEL, JAMES H. TO MISS ELIZABETH ELROD 11-20-1847
MITCHEL, JANE TO STEPHEN CHILDRESS
MITCHEL, N. A. TO G. P. RAINS
MITCHEL, NILE A. TO MISS ISSABELLA LANSLEY? 8-8-1850
MITCHEL, SUSAN TO THOS. J. HOOVER
MITCHEL, SYNTHA TO E. T. BRANDON
MITCHEL, THOS. P. TO MISS M. J. TEAGUE 7-15-1857 (7-21-1857)
MITCHELL, A. L. TO T. F. CARRACK
MITCHELL, ANDY TO MARY FERRELL 2-18-1873
MITCHELL, ANN E. TO J. H. GORDON
MITCHELL, CALLIE TO W. M. BRAGG
MITCHELL, D. W. TO MISS MARTHA A. GARDNER 8-26-1871
MITCHELL, ELIZABETH J. TO GEORGE S. STROUD
MITCHELL, GEO. TO MOLLIE GORDON 12-28-1871
MITCHELL, ISAAC S. TO MISS ELIZABETH S. COOK 12-31-1857
MITCHELL, J. T. TO MARY C. JARRATT 5-31-1872 (6-2-1872)
MITCHELL, JAMES A. TO MISS MARY S. GEORGE 9-19-1866 (9-20-1866)
MITCHELL, JOHN E. TO MISS E. A. GANDY 12-22-1857 (NO RETURN)
MITCHELL, JOHN F. TO MISS BETHENA WAMACK 11-17-1855
MITCHELL, JOHN N. TO MARY RIGSBY 12-22-1871

MITCHELL, MARIAH TO ANDERSON KEELE
MITCHELL, MARY J. TO GEORGE W. SMITH
MITCHELL, MATTIE TO SAMUEL THOMPSON
MITCHELL, MIRA A. TO ROBERT G. SMITH
MITCHELL, MOLLIE TO JOSEPH M. ELLISON
MITCHELL, NANCY A. TO D. B. YEARWOOD
MITCHELL, SARAH D. TO G. W. HOOSER
MITCHELL, SARAH J. TO WILLIAM H. MCFERRIN 11-8-1866
MOFITT, MAY TO ANDREW LOGUE
MOLLEN, J. C. TO JAMES C. POSTON
MOLLEY, ROBERT TO SUSAN GRIZZEL 4-17-1854 (5-4-1854)
MONGOMERY, SARAH JANE TO ROBERT HATFIELD
MOODY, CHARLES TO MISS MALINDA MORGAN 7-16-1870 (7-17-1870)
MOODY, JNO. TO MELVINA RICHERSON 8-14-1873
MOODY, JOHN TO SALLY HAMMONS 11-4-1865 (11-5-1865)
MOODY, M. E. TO G. W. PERRYMAN
MOODY, MARGARETT TO WILLIAM SMITH
MOODY, MARY MALINDA TO THORNTON HARP
MOODY, WILLIAM TO ELENDER BARRETT 10-4-1854
MOON, ALEXANDER TO MISS S. STROUD 7-24-1858 (7-26-1858)
MOON, CHARLOTA TO JOHN N. MCKNIGHT
MOON, CHARLTTE TO JACOB DAVIS
MOON, G. T. TO MISS S. J. KNOX 3-3-1856 (3-4-1856)
MOON, ISABELLA TO ELI B. BARRATT
MOON, JOHN TO MARTHA E. EDWARDS 2-1-1873 (2-2-1873)
MOON, JOHN TO MISS CHARITY EDWARDS 10-22-1855 (10-29-1855)
MOON, MARGARET TO SAMUEL A. DAVIS
MOON, MARTHA CAROLINE TO HIRAM WILSON
MOON, MARY F. TO M. S. SMITH
MOON, NANCY TO JOHN ROGERS
MOON, NANCY TO THOMAS CAMPBELL
MOON, NANCY TO WM. KING
MOON, SARAH TO CHARLY LAW
MOONAHAM, ROBERT TO M. A. MANIUS 12-20-1857
MOONYHAM, JOHN TO MISS ARRMANDA MAINES 12-11-1858 (12-12-1858)
MOORE, A. G. TO MISS MARTHA M. TRAVIS 1-20-1857
MOORE, ABNER TO MISS A. MCADAMS 5-27-1859 (EXECUTION NOT CLEAR)
MOORE, B. H. TO N. C. BOGLE 12-4-1873 (12-5-1873)
MOORE, BENJAMAN TO MISS NANCY ANN SAPP 1-12-1856 (1-13-1856)
MOORE, C. NANCY TO C. C. GUNTER
MOORE, DELILA TO JAMES W. FERRELL
MOORE, E. C. TO A. B. TAYLOR
MOORE, ELIZABETH J. TO SAMUEL A. SWOAPE
MOORE, ELVIRA TO J. J. TOBBERT
MOORE, FLORRENCE TO ALF BARTON
MOORE, FRANCES C. TO ALEXANDER SPARKS
MOORE, GEORGE W. TO JOSEPHINE HATCHINS 9-24-1868
MOORE, J. G. TO MISS BETTIE TAYLOR 12-15-1870
MOORE, J. T. TO S. J. MELTON 2-21-1872 (2-22-1872)
MOORE, JACOB TO LUCY F. SOAPE 2-3-1842
MOORE, JACOB TO N. J. AKERS 9-17-1872 (9-19-1872)
MOORE, JANE C. TO JAMES N. L. HARRIS
MOORE, JESSEE G. TO VIRGINIA P. TAYLOR 2-27-1865 (2-28-1865)
MOORE, JESSEE TO FRANCES L. HUTCHENS 9-2-1865 (NO RETURN)
MOORE, JOSE TO ANTHONY MARTIN
MOORE, JOSEPH TO SARAH LACKEY 10-8-1839
MOORE, JOSEPHINE TO JACKSON MARTIN
MOORE, L. B. TO MISS ELIZABETH ODOM 6-5-1843
MOORE, LOTTY TO DAVID DAVIS
MOORE, M. A. TO S. H. STEPHENS

MOORE, M. L. TO WM. B. BRYSON
MOORE, MARGARET TO J. B. DAVANPORT
MOORE, MARTHA E. TO JAMES J. GOWEN
MOORE, MARY J. TO WILLIAM C. STACY
MOORE, NANCY E. TO BENJAMIN SMITH
MOORE, NANCY ELEANOR TO WILLIAM R. HILL
MOORE, NANCY TO J. A. BRYSON
MOORE, NANCY TO JACKSON MAGON
MOORE, NANCY TO JAMES BELL
MOORE, PERMELA TO SAMUEL EADS
MOORE, R. A. TO MISS HATTIE E. MCMURRY 11-13-1872 (11-14-1872)
MOORE, R. J. TO C. T. LOWE
MOORE, ROBERT D. TO MISS HELAN ALEXANDER 2-1-1869 (2-4-1869)
MOORE, RUTH TO NIMROD SMITH
MOORE, SAMUEL A. TO MISS MARY BERKS 2-14-1848
MOORE, SAMUEL JR. TO MISS RUTH BRASHEARS 6-2-1845 (6-5-1845)
MOORE, SAMUEL TO MISS FRANCES ANN SMITH 5-15-1844 (5-18-1844)
MOORE, SARAH J. TO JONNATHAN MELTON
MOORE, SARAH TO ISHAM VANCE
MOORE, WM. A. T. TO MISS P. A. MCADOW 12-3-1859 (EXECUTED--NO DATE)
MOORE, WM. N. TO MISS LUCINDA BROWN 11-3-1857 (11-5-1857)
MOORE, ZACHARIAH T. TO MISS LAVINA C. HUTCHINS 5-14-1870 (5-15-1870)
MORE, HOWEL TO MISS MATILDA WOMMACS? 3-11-1852
MORE, MARY TO E. M. WHITT
MORGAN, ALEXANDER TO KATHARINE RODGERS 3-2-1839 (NO RETURN)
MORGAN, ALEXANDER TO MISS SARAH JANE PITTS 11-4-1869
MORGAN, ANDERSON TO MALINDA ALFORD 12-15-1865
MORGAN, CAROLINE TO WM. TENPERY
MORGAN, CATHARINE TO A. B. BARRATT
MORGAN, CYNTHIA TO WILLIAM DUKE
MORGAN, DELILA C. TO JAMES G. SMITH
MORGAN, ELIZABETH E. TO FELIX WHITT
MORGAN, ELIZABETH TO JOE A. KNOX
MORGAN, GORDON TO ARTA M. ELKINS 9-7-1838 (9-10-1838)
MORGAN, HUBBARD TO MISS MARY E. GAITHER 4-15-1869
MORGAN, J. S. TO MISS D. F. COX 8-19-1859 (NO RETURN)
MORGAN, JACKSON TO ELIZABETH MARES 10-7-1842
MORGAN, JACKSON TO MISS NANCY MORGAN 10-26-1844 (10-27-1844)
MORGAN, JACKSON TO NANCY HERIMAN 7-24-1839 (7-25-1839)
MORGAN, JAMES A. TO ELIZABETH MILLIGAN 10-2-1865
MORGAN, JAMES A. TO MISS SARAH E. REED 7-27-1870
MORGAN, LARENA TO AMOS CAMPBELL
MORGAN, LIDDIA TO WILLIAM SPEARS
MORGAN, LIDY E. TO W. E. YOUNG
MORGAN, LIZA E. TO DAVID VANCE
MORGAN, M. J. TO S. H. HARRIS
MORGAN, MALINDA TO CHARLES MOODY
MORGAN, NANCY TO JACKSON MORGAN
MORGAN, ROXANAH TO JOHN H. TODD
MORGAN, SARAH G. TO J. R. WALKER
MORGAN, SERECIA E. TO J. W. CAMPBELL
MORGAN, WESLEY A. TO MALINDA HAMMEN 11-26-1864 (11-27-1864)
MORGAN, WILLIAM TO ANNIS BARRETT 9-23-1865 (9-24-1865)
MORRETT, JOHN TO MISS SARAH JANE WHITT 1-15-185 (1-16-1853)
MORRIS, C. TO CAHAL HOLLANDSWORTH
MORRIS, CAROLINE TO JAMES R. GARAWAY
MORRIS, ELIZABETH TO C. D. MULLENIX
MORRIS, LEVI TO NANCY F. MATHIS 1-24-1873 (1-29-1873)
MORRIS, MARY M. TO DANIEL TRAVIS
MORRIS, MARY P. TO BLUFORD J. MULLINIX

MORRIS, SARAH TO C. H. HALL
MORRIS, WILLIAM TO TALITHA THOMPSON 5-29-1847
MOSES, R. R. TO MISS E. M. BERRETT 4-20-1857 (NO RETURN)
MOSEY, DORETHA TO N. J. BLUE
MOSS, CHARLES D. TO MISS JANE CUNNINGHAM 4-3-1859
MOSS, W. D. TO MARY ALFORD 1-24-1860 (NO RETURN)
MOTEN, MARGARETT TO JOHN BANKSTON
MULLENAX, MARY TO PRESLEY HIGGINS
MULLENIX, C. D. TO MISS ELIZABETH MORRIS 9-4-1871
MULLENS, JOSEPH TO NANCY ASHFORD 8-14-1838 (8-16-1838)
MULLENS, NANCY TO GEORGE ASHFORD
MULLICAN, ANTNEY TO MISS JOSEPHINE PRESTON 9-23-1867 (9-25-1867)
MULLIN, JOHN H. TO MISS MARGARET J. KEELE 10-15-1866
MULLINAX, JAMES S. TO MISS ELIZABETH E. POWELL 1-19-1850 (1-23-1850)
MULLINGAX, SARAH E. TO G. W. BOGLE
MULLINIX, BLUFORD J. TO MISS MARY P. MORRIS 2-1-1867 (2-3-1867)
MULLINS, DANIEL C. TO JANE MULLINS 7-20-1839 (7-25-1839)
MULLINS, DAVID TO LEAH COVINGTON 5-28-1840 (6-4-1840)
MULLINS, DOSUNE TO MARY CATHEY 2-26-1840 (2-16?-1840)
MULLINS, DOZIER TO MISS ADALINE SUTTON 4-26-1844
MULLINS, FRANCES E. TO JESSEE MCBROOM
MULLINS, HENRY B. TO MISS JANETTE CANTRELL 2-16-1847
MULLINS, J. B. TO R. E. YOUNG 7-13-1860 (EXECUTED--NO DATE)
MULLINS, J. H. TO N. J. PHILLIPS 10-11-1872 (10-13-1872)
MULLINS, JAMES B. TO MISS MARTHA E. YOUNG 9-24-1866
MULLINS, JANE TO DANIEL C. MULLINS
MULLINS, JANE TO JOHN YOUNG
MULLINS, JOHN A. TO MISS MARGARETT J. BEESON 10-17-1847 (10-18-1847)
MULLINS, JOHN W. TO MISS HANNAH C. SAPP 6-15?-1845 (6-20-1845)
MULLINS, JULIA ANN TO JOHN A. WILLIAMS
MULLINS, JULIA TO JAMES M. EVANS
MULLINS, LOUISA TO HENRY COX
MULLINS, LUCINDA TO STEPHEN CANTRELL
MULLINS, MAHALA TO THOMAS VAUGHAN
MULLINS, MARGRET TO WILLIAM DENTON
MULLINS, MARTHA TO WILLIAM ARVIN
MULLINS, MISS VINA JANE TO SAMUEL SPEARS
MULLINS, REBECCA TO T. J. THOMPSON
MULLINS, S. D. TO JULIE A. HAYS 12-24-1872 (12-25-1872)
MULLINS, SARAH TO SAMUEL YOUNG
MULLINS, W. H. TO MISS NANCY E. OWENS 8-26-1871 (8-27-1871)
MULLINS, WILLIAM S. TO MISS ELIZABETH CANTRELL 12-7-1848
MULLINS, WILLIAM TO SARAH ANN HAYS 7-7-1842 (7-8-1842)
MUNCEY, MCCASLIN TO TILDEY HAILEY 8-4-1855 (8-5-1855)
MUNCY, ELIZABETH TO JAMES A. ORRICK
MUNCY, ELIZABETH TO WM. R. EDDINGS
MUNCY, EMLEY TO M. H. MANUS
MUNCY, HESTER L. TO RISTON SMITHSON
MUNCY, SARAH TO L. D. H. WILSON
MUNY, MCCASLEN TO TILDY HOLY 8-3-1855 (RETURNS MISSING)
MUNY, SARAH TO WM. G. PENDLETON
MURFREE, I. N. B. TO MISS AMERICA GIVINS 2-6-1869 (2-7-1869)
MURFREE, MARY E. TO M. B. GILLEY
MURFREY, B. F. TO MISS ELIZA DENNIS 8-2-1849
MURFREY, LUCRETIA TO ADEN HOLLINSWORTH
MURFREY, ROBERT S. TO MISS SARAH JANE FARRELL 10-3-1845 (NO RETURN)
MURFREY, SALLY ANN TO JOSHUA VASSER
MURPHREY, W. G. TO MISS PRUDY SPURLOCK 2-28-1866 (3-2-1866)
MURPHY, J. D. TO NANCY A. HOLLINGSWORTH 12-17-1864 (12-21-1864)
MURPHY, ROBT. T. TO ALDONA DRIVER 7-30-1873 (NO RETURN)

MURPHY, ROBT. TO MISS CANDIS SMITH 4-12-1855 (RETURNS MISSING)
MURPHY, SARAH JANE TO SAMUEL YONG
MURRY, DAVIS B. TO MISS SARAH A. PINKERTON 3-28-1866 (3-29-1866)
NAPER, JOHN TO CARLINE SMITH (NO DATES--WITH SUMMER 1860 ENTRIES)
NEAL, LOU G. TO W. P. COTHRAN
NEALEY, MEDFORD C. TO MARY FRANCES SMITH 9-14-1865 (9-17-1865)
NEALY, MARY ANN TO WM. J. ROGERS
NEEL, T. M. TO SARAH E. MASON 8-24-1854
NEELEY, ELIGAH TO MISS SARAH E. HIGDON 6-10-1867
NEELEY, FRANKLIN TO OLLEY HOLLOWMAN 10-10-1865 (10-11-1865)
NEELEY, MARY TO DONALSON BARKER
NEELEY, NANCY E. TO H. HOLLANDSWORTH
NEELY, CAROLINE TO ROBERT BAILY
NEELY, ELISABETH TO JOEL D. MELTON
NEELY, ELIZABETH TO WILLIAM M. BAILEY
NEELY, HARRIET DELILA TO C. M. RANKHORN
NEELY, ISAAH TO MISS ELIZABETH EVON 1-12-1852
NEELY, ISAEAH TO MISS ANN CAPPS 4-20-1844 (4-24-1844)
NEELY, JOSEPH H. TO E. MATILDA HOLLIS 2-21-1860 (2-22-1860)
NEELY, L. A. TO R. W. NEELY
NEELY, N. L. TO MISS HARIETT D. ELKINS 3-30-1854
NEELY, R. E. TO H. R. ELKINS
NEELY, R. W. TO MISS L. A. NEELY 8-25-1859 (NO RETURN)
NEELY, SARAH A. TO BENJAMIN VINSON
NEELY, SARAH A. TO IRA HOLLINGSWORTH
NELSON, SAMUEL TO MARTHA MASSEY 12-22-1866 (12-27-1866)
NEUGENT, MARTHA T. TO J. D. METTON
NEUGENT, MARTHA TO J. D. MELTON
NEVAL, JOHN TO MISS MALISSA MCCAFFREY 3-1-1867
NEW, ALLEN TO HANNAH NEW 8-24-1865 (8-27-1865)
NEW, FANNY TO L. B. FRANKS
NEW, HANNAH TO ALLEN NEW
NEW, JOHN C. TO MARY E. ORRON 7-20-1865
NEW, MARIA TO JAMES TAYLOR
NEWBY, GEORGE TO FANNIE WOOD 1-16-1868
NEWBY, WILLIAM TO ELIZABETH PITMAN 10-7-1863 (NO RETURN)
NEWGENT, JUDAH TO JOHN J. SMITH
NICHOL, CYNTHIA C. TO JACKSON REED
NICHOL, J. W. TO MISS MARY R. HOLMS 12-19-1866 (12-20-1866)
NICHOL, J. Y. TO D. C. HOLLIS 12-6-1864
NICHOL, JOSEPH TO MISS SARAH KEELE 12-21-1847 (12-22-1847)
NICHOLS, DANIEL A. TO MISS SARAH M. VINSON 3-17-1857 (NO RETURN)
NICHOLS, ELIZA A. TO WILLIAM A. GIVENS
NICHOLS, INTHY ADALINE TO WM. J. WALKUP
NICHOLS, MARGARETT JANE TO JOHN WESTLEY PARKER
NICHOLS, PHEBA J. TO SAMUEL BERRETT
NICKELS, SARAH TO HENRY ROGERS
NIGHT, CALVIN TO MISS MARGARETT BOGLE 2-16-1857 (2-18-1857)
NIGHT, JOHN TO MISS SARAH M. HORRAL 2-26-1852
NIVENS, SARAH TO NEDHAM JARNAGIN
NOKES, JOHN TO MISS MARGARET HIGGINS 7-29-1870 (7-31-1870)
NOKES, LUCY TO HIGDON MELTON
NOKES, MARRY ANN TO T. J. THOMPSON
NOKES, NANCY TO WILLIAM BRASHEARS
NOKES, NANCY TO WM. SPURLOCK
NOKES, NELSON TO MISS FLORA ELAM 6-3-1843 (6-4-1843)
NOKES, WILLIAM B. TO MARY STONE 11-16-1839 (11-21-1839)
NORTHCUT, VISA E. TO GILES S. BONERS
NORTHCUTT, GEORGE E. TO MISS NANCY SCOTT 12-21-1867 (NO RETURN)
NORTHCUTT, WILLIAM TO CAROLINE TODD 12-25-1873

NUCKLES, MARY TO DANIEL REED
NUGAN, JOHN S. TO MISS MARGARET HOLLIS 9-20-1866
OCONNER, CAROLINE TO PLEASANT CHUMBY
OCONNER, JEREMIAH TO MARY HIGGINS 11-29-1848
ODAM, MANDY TO A. F. JAMES
ODEM, S. F. TO R. L. OWEN
ODOM, A. L. TO W. C. DILL
ODOM, ABRAHAM TO HANAH MCADOW 5-31-1867 (NO RETURN)
ODOM, ANN ELIZA TO JAMES W. ORAND
ODOM, ARMSTED J. TO ELIZA J. BOGLE 10-14-1847 (10-15-1847)
ODOM, C. C. TO LUCY OWEN 10-13-1855 (NO RETURN)
ODOM, CANTRELL B. TO MISS ELIZABETH OWEN 8-19-1847
ODOM, D. T. TO M. W. WILLARD
ODOM, ELIZABETH G. TO JAMES A. RAMSEY
ODOM, ELIZABETH TO L. B. MOORE
ODOM, F. E. TO H. C. VAUGHAN
ODOM, FANNY TO CHARLES DILLON
ODOM, HANAH J. TO J. A. WILLARD
ODOM, HANAH TO WILLIAM TEMBLETON
ODOM, HARRY TO MARY LUNDSDON 8-21-1865 (NO RETURN)
ODOM, J. H. TO A. E. BREWIES 10-23-1872 (10-25-1872)
ODOM, J. S. TO DILELAH MCNABB 10-12-1871 (10-16-1871)
ODOM, J. S. TO PARALEE MILLIGAN 12-26-1872
ODOM, JAMES W. TO MISS ELIZA L. OWEN 11-11-1866
ODOM, JOHN (COL) TO CINDA HANCOCK 4-12-1873 (NO RETURN)
ODOM, JOHN S. TO MISS JULIAN ODOM 11-10-1866 (11-28-1866)
ODOM, JUDA ANN TO CHARLES DILLON
ODOM, JUDEA ANN TO MOSES SNEED
ODOM, JULIAN TO JOHN F. ODOM
ODOM, L. A. TO WM. B. WILLARD
ODOM, LOUISA TO BERTON SUMMER
ODOM, M. M. TO MISS S. E. FLOYD 8-30-1871 (8-31-1871)
ODOM, MANDY TO A. J. JAMES
ODOM, MARGARET A. TO I. I. HAMMONS
ODOM, MARTHA A. TO JOHN MILLIGAN
ODOM, MARY E. TO W. B. SPARKS
ODOM, MARY L. TO R. L. OWEN
ODOM, MARY TO M. V. WILSON
ODOM, MARY TO WILLIAM C. PATRICK
ODOM, N. M. TO REEPES P. KELLY
ODOM, NANCY TO JOHN A. WILLARD
ODOM, NANNIE TO JOHN R. STONE
ODOM, R. L. TO MISS L. J. BREWIN? 8-5-1871 (8-6-1871)
ODOM, S. M. TO J. M. COUCH
ODOM, SAMUEL C. TO JOSEPHINE E. BOGLE 9-21-1872 (9-22-1872)
ODOM, SARAH L. TO J. C. FITE
OFFICER, ANN TO JESSEE THOMPSON
OFFICER, JAMES TO MARTHA MARTIN 2-1-1870 (2-2-1870)
OGLESBY, ADALINE TO PEYTON H. HAYES
OGLESBY, J. H. TO MISS R. J. CARUTHERS 2-24-1869 (2-25-1869)
OGLESBY, S. H. TO MISS MARGRETT SMITH 6-7-1871 (6-29-1871)
OLFORD, MARGRETT TO J. T. RODGERS
OLIVAR, THOMAS TO MARY FORD 2-19-1845
OLIVER, DELIA TO WILLIAM C. WOODALL
OLIVER, J. R. TO MISS E. C. MCFERRIN 12-21-1859 (NO RETURN)
OLIVER, JOHN H. TO MARY E. MCFERRIN 8-22-1865
ONEAL, E. G. TO MISS MAUD? AMERICA TINSLY 1-2-1860 (NO RETURN)
ONEEL, SARAH JANE TO ISHAM SIMMONS
ORAND, E. M. TO J. W. D. HOLLIS
ORAND, ELIZABETH TO EDWARD ELDER

ORAND, J. M. TO ELIZABETH TRIBBLE 2-19-1863 (NO RETURN)
ORAND, JAMES W. TO MISS ANN ELIZA ODOM 4-25-1849 (NO RETURN)
ORAND, MARGRETT M.? TO SAMUEL JONES
ORR, JOHN M. TO NANCY MATHEWS 11-4-1839 (NO RETURN)
ORRAN, MARY E. TO JOHN C. NEW
ORRAND, ANTHONY TO AMANDA HERRIMAN 12-21-1865 (LICENSE RETURNED NOT ENDORSED)
ORRAND, JOANNAH TO JONATHAN BRANDON
ORRAND, THOMAS A. TO MISS NANCY M. DAVENPORT 10-19-1867 (10-20-1867)
ORRICK, JAMES A. TO MISS ELIZABETH MUNCY 8-30-1866
OSBON, HARVEY TO N. L. TRAVIS 10-31-1864 (11-2-1864)
OSBORN, H. M. TO G. W. VAUGHN
OSMENT, JOSEPH L. TO MISS MARY HAWKINS 6-27-1866 (6-28-1866)
OSMENT, LUCINDA C. TO EDMUND PARKER
OSMENT, MARTHA J. TO HUGH EDDINGTON
OVERALL, AMERICA C. TO LEANDER JENNINGS
OVERALL, HORACE A. TO MISS CAROLINE OWEN 4-9-1850 (NO RETURN)
OWEN, A. H. TO ARCH MARKUM
OWEN, ABRAHAM TO MISS MALISSA BAILEY 12-26-1867
OWEN, ALFORD TO LUCINDA FUSTON 12-21-1855 (12-23-1855)
OWEN, CAROLINE TO HORACE A. OVERALL
OWEN, DRUCILLA TO WILLIAM B. COOPER
OWEN, ELBERT TO MISS MARY PARKER 9-23-1844 (9-24-1844)
OWEN, ELIZA L. TO JAMES W. ODOM
OWEN, ELIZABETH TO CANTRELL B. ODOM
OWEN, H. D. TO WM. BASHAM
OWEN, JEREMIAH J. TO MISS ALEATHY FINLEY 11-21-1851
OWEN, JOS. D. TO MARY AN FRANCIS 3-10-1864 (3-15-1864)
OWEN, LUCY TO C. C. ODOM
OWEN, MARY TO EZEKIEL REED
OWEN, MARY TO PETER RICKETS
OWEN, NANCY TO JOHN MARCUM
OWEN, R. L. TO MARY L. ODOM 9-13-1864 (9-14-1864)
OWEN, R. L. TO MISS S. F. ODEM 1-28-1852 (1-29-1852)
OWEN, S. E. H. TO MALISSA ADAMSON 9-18-1869 (9-19-1869)
OWEN, THOMAS TO MISS ELIZA BLANCET 2-2-1854
OWEN, WILLIAM B. TO E. N. CATHEY 4-5-1840
OWENBY, L. M. TO MISS K. J. SMITH 12-24-1867 (NO RETURN)
OWENS, A. G. TO A. E. GROOM 2-25-1873 (2-27-1873)
OWENS, CLAIBORNE TO MARY ANN BLANKS 12-31-1842 (1-1-1843)
OWENS, JEREMIAH J. TO EMALY TEAGUE 7-5-1842
OWENS, NANCY E. TO W. H. MULLINS
OWENSBY, LIZZIE N. TO J. L. TAYLOR
OWIN, SUSAN M. TO JAMES H. DOM
OWNBY, E. D. TO MISS SYNTHA E. KNOX 1-9-1868

PACE, ELIZABETH A. TO CREED HELMS
PACE, LEATHEY TO ROBERT PHILIPS
PACE, REBECCA TO GEORGE GANNON
PAGE, JOHN W. TO MISS FANNIE F. MCFERREN 8-21-1866 (8-23-1866)
PALLETT, G. W. D.? TO MISS NANCY E. ERVIN 10-25-1849
PARKE, JOHN TO MISS MARTHA CHERRY 2-25-1841
PARKER, A. W. TO L. J. MCMAHAN 12-18-1871 (12-24-1871)
PARKER, ADAM TO KATHARINE ADCOCK
PARKER, ANGELINE TO PLESANT COTHRAN
PARKER, BETSY ANN TO GIDAN STASY
PARKER, CAROLINE TO ALLEN SPRY
PARKER, CORNELIUS TO MISS CHARITY SAULS 10-28-1846 (10-29-1846)
PARKER, D. F. TO MISS MALVINA JACOBS 6-14-1853 (NO RETURN)
PARKER, EDMUND TO MISS LUCINDA C. OSMENT 9-23-1868 (9-24-1868)
PARKER, FRANKLIN TO DIANITIA CATHARINE INGLIS 4-3-1840 (4-6-1840)
PARKER, GEORGE TO MARY A. FINLEY 8-9-1865
PARKER, ISABELLA TO JOHN J. STACY
PARKER, J. E. TO MISS MARY J. R. RAINS 2-15-1870 (2-17-1870)
PARKER, JOHN A. TO MISS CATHARIN JANE FINLY 9-13-1856 (9-14-1856)
PARKER, JOHN TO ARRENEA BANKS 11-9-1854
PARKER, JOHN WESTLEY TO MISS MARGARETT JANE NICHOLS 6-24-1847
PARKER, JULY ANN TO JAMES JASPER WOMACK
PARKER, LEWIS TO MISS M. A. RIGSBY 2-3-1859 (NO RETURN)
PARKER, LORENZO D. TO MISS JANE WEBBER 11-5-1840 (NO RETURN)
PARKER, MARY ANN TO EDWARD ESTES
PARKER, MARY J. TO WM. L. ERSRY
PARKER, MARY TO ELBERT OWEN
PARKER, MARY TO J. M. BRAXTON
PARKER, NANCY TO JOHN DUKE
PARKER, NATHANIEL TO MISS MALISSA TUCKER 9-3-1868
PARKER, REBECCA TO GEORGE SPRY
PARKER, SAMUEL F. TO MISS MARGARET PEYTON 4-24-1866 (4-25-1866)
PARKER, SARAH ELIZABETH TO WILLIAM SPRY
PARKER, SARAH L. A. TO THOMAS READY
PARKER, SILAS TO MISS FANNIE BROWN 4-9-1867 (4-11-1867)
PARKER, THOMAS TO MISS EASTER CANTRELL 1-4-1849
PARKER, THOMAS TO SARAH WILLIAMS 11-19-1852 (11-23-1852)
PARKER, VIOLET TO WILLIAM WISER
PARKERSON, J. F. TO MISS S. A. PATTERSON 8-27-1870 (8-29-1870)
PARRETT, HYRAM TO MISS D. C. BOWEN 9-9-1870 (9-11-1870)
PARRIS, HARRIET TO J. P. ELKINS
PARRIS, HARRIETT J. TO J. P. ELKINS
PARRIS, J. B. JR. TO CAROLINE BOGLE 7-22-1872
PARRIS, J. B. TO MISS M. J. ELKINS 8-13-1859 (NO RETURN)
PARRIS, J. R. TO MISS BETTIE LOGAN 7-25-1866
PARSLEY, BETHEL TO SELINA MELTON 12-26-1871 (12-28-1871)
PARSLEY, BRICE TO NANCY DANIEL 8-16-1838
PARSLEY, JAMES TO MANERVIA DAVIS 3-1-1838
PARTEN, ABRAHAM TO MISS POLLY MELTON 5-3-1849
PARTEN, HENRY TO MISS NANCY DAVENPORT 4-3-1860
PARTEN, JOHN L. TO MISS SUSAN STARR 2-15-1849
PARTEN, WILLIAM H. TO MISS RUTH YOUNG 1-26-1847 (1-27-1847)
PARTIN, ELIZA TO HENRY ENOS
PARTON, CHARLOTTE TO JOHN TUBB
PARTON, ELIZABETH TO JOHN H. RICHARDSON
PARTON, HENRY TO ELIZABETH WALLS 5-3-1864
PARTON, JOHN TO L. N. HART 2-2-1872 (2-4-1872)
PARTON, NANCY A. TO SAMPSON J. KING
PARTON, SALINDA TO WM. YOUNG

PASCAL, THOMAS TO MISS MALISA PORTERFIELD 5-3-1853
PASCHAL, N. T. TO SALLIE E. CARNAHAN 5-14-1873 (NO RETURN)
PATEN, MONFORD TO MISS NANCY J. BRAGG 8-17-1850 (8-18-1850)
PATERSON, EMILY H. TO W. L. FOSTER
PATRICK, JESSE TO MISS NANCY MILLIGAN 12-25-1848 (12-28-1848)
PATRICK, JESSEE TO MISS J. S. H. COX 11-27-1858 (11-30-1858)
PATRICK, LAURA ANN TO JACOB A. KELLY
PATRICK, LOCKY J. TO JOHN HIGGANS
PATRICK, MARY A. TO NELSON JOHNSON
PATRICK, MARY ANN TO ELIJAH MANUS
PATRICK, ROBERT TO CYNTHIA VASSER 7-4-1842 (7-14-1842)
PATRICK, WILLIAM C. TO MISS MARY ODOM 6-13-1844
PATTEN, J. A. TO MISS M. C. ROBERTS 11-9-1865
PATTERSON, ANN TO WILLIAM DENBY
PATTERSON, EMMA TO DREWERY PEARCEY
PATTERSON, ENOCH TO MISS THANEY KERSEY 7-26-1845 (7-27-1845)
PATTERSON, FRANCES TO WILLIAM BLANTON
PATTERSON, J. C. TO MISS MARY COPE 12-21-1870 (12-22-1870)
PATTERSON, J. M. TO NANCY M. RAMSEY 3-13-1872 (3-14-1872)
PATTERSON, JOHN TO SUSAN SELLARS 9-1-1841 (9-2-1841)
PATTERSON, MARTHA TO ALEXANDER PORTER
PATTERSON, MARY C. TO WM. H. RUSSELL
PATTERSON, NANCY TO MILTON WARD
PATTERSON, R. W. TO MISS LOUISA GOAD 2-11-1847
PATTERSON, ROBERT TO MISS CAROLINE BURGER 5-12-1841 (5-13-1841)
PATTERSON, S. A. TO J. F. PARKERSON
PATTERSON, SUSAN TO WM. CAMPBLE
PATTON, A. D. TO N. C. MEASEL 7-12-1873 (NO RETURN)
PATTON, CAROLINE M. TO ASA SPANGLER
PATTON, DAVID M. TO MISS JANE MCGILL 7-20-1848
PATTON, DAVID TO MARY HALE 3-13-1860
PATTON, ELIZABETH TO DAVID G. BRANDON
PATTON, HARRIETT TO JOHN GORDON
PATTON, JOHN TO POLLY WIMBERLEY 10-15-1849 (10-17-1849)
PATTON, KATHARINE TO JAMES BRADFORD
PATTON, MARGARET F. TO JAMES LAMBERTH
PATTON, MARGARET TO JAMES MCELROY
PATTON, MARY ANN TO JOHN JAMES MCELROY
PATTON, MARY S. TO JAMES H. REED
PATTON, MARY TO JONES WATSON
PATTON, MATTIE J. TO B. A. KING
PATTON, NANCY ELEANOR TO THOMAS W. HORN
PATTON, ROBERT H. TO FRANCES M. LOWE 11-20-1844 (11-21-1844)
PATTON, TEMPA TO SAMUEL TEMPLETON
PATTRICK, MARY E. TO E. G. FERRELL
PATTRICK, PINEY TO J. D. SUMMAR
PATY, H. A. TO JOHN A. FITE
PAUL, CLENDENEN TO SARAH L. ESPEY 9-18-1871 (9-21-1871)
PAYNE, ELIZA TO WILLIAM EDWARDS
PEALER, KATHARINE A. TO GEORGE KING
PEALER, KING TO MARY ANDERSON 2-25-1840
PEALER, LENY? TO MISS MARTHA ANDERSON 3-8-1845 (3-9-1845)
PEALER, PAGE TO MISS MILLEY CHERRY 7-28-1846 (7-30-1846)
PEALER, SALLY TO WILLIAM KING
PEARCE, MALINDA J. TO H. M. BOGLE
PEARCEY, DREWERY TO EMMA PATTERSON 11-8-1871 (NO RETURN)
PEARSON, R. C. TO MISS C. N. SIMMAN 11-16-1870
PEARSON, RICHARD TO JANE BROWN 7-9-1863 (NO RETURN)
PEARSON, THOMAS TO MALINDA T. WHITE 8-31-1842
PEAY, R. A. TO J. R. KNOX

PEAY, RUFUS D. TO MARTHA J. HARRIS 8-2-1864 (8-3-1864)
PEAY, TIENDOLPHUS TO MISS J. R. WALKUP 1-16-1867
PEDEN, JAMES TO MISS SARAH WHITELEY 12-27-1845
PEDIGO, PENNEY TO JOEL MILLIGAN
PEDIGO, SARAH TO HENRY DEVENPORT
PEDON, AMANDA TO J. C. CAMPBELL
PEDON, E. A. TO J. J. HARRIS
PEDON, M. J. TO H. G. DEVENPORT
PEDON, MARY J. TO JESSEE RICHARDS
PEDON, SARAH TO DANIEL BURKE
PEEDON, ELISAR TO RICHARD VANCE
PEELER, MARY A. TO W. J. CLARK
PEERCE, JAMES TO MALINDA JONES 2-26-1863 (NO RETURN)
PELHAM, ELIZABETH C. TO JACOB M. LEMONS
PELHAM, LEVI TO MISS MARTHA DANIEL 1-25-1847 (2-3-1847)
PELHAM, MARY J. TO H. W. WILSON
PELHAM, WM. TO MISS CAROLINE MILLER 1-8-1853 (1-9-1853)
PEMELTON, THOS. TO ARMINDA JACOBS 7-9-1863 (NO RETURN)
PENDERGRASS, MARY TO ALEXANDER RATLEY
PENDLETON, BENJAMIN TO MARY HIGGINS 3-14-1840 (3-15-1840)
PENDLETON, BENJAMIN TO MISS AELISA MCADOW 1-26-1848
PENDLETON, ELISABETH TO HENRY ELAM
PENDLETON, ELIZABETH TO WILLIAM SPARKS
PENDLETON, H. TO MISS MARY A. HALEY 6-1-1858 (6-2-1858)
PENDLETON, JOHN JR. TO MISS LUCINDA WEST 8-9-1847
PENDLETON, JOHN L. TO MISS MARY E. LYNN 9-26-1867 (NO RETURN)
PENDLETON, MARY ANN TO JOHN W. PERRY
PENDLETON, MARY TO JAMES M. MELTON
PENDLETON, MELINDA TO CHARLES WEST
PENDLETON, RACHEL TO H. S. BOWERS
PENDLETON, SAMUEL TO MARY THOMAS 12-21-1842
PENDLETON, SARAH TO FRANCIS BOWERS
PENDLETON, SARAH TO J. H. PRATOR
PENDLETON, STACY C. TO BENJAMIN A. STONE
PENDLETON, THOMAS D. TO MISS ELIZABETH SHEPHERD 8-3-1849 (8-5-1849)
PENDLETON, W. G. TO L. G. DUNCAN 10-10-1871 (NO RETURN)
PENDLETON, WILLIAM T. TO MISS MARY ELIZABETH FERRELL 8-8-1867 (8-11-1867)
PENDLETON, WM. G. TO MISS SARAH MUNY 6-9-1855 (6-10-1855)
PENY, JAMES P. TO ELIZA HIGGINS 3-12-1840
PEOPLES, JACK TO FANNY REEVES 8-13-1853
PEOPLES, JENNIE TO SAM DANIEL
PEOPLES, JOHN TO MISS JUDIE VAUGHN 1-7-1871 (1-12-1871)
PEOPLES, MARTHA TO J. D. WRIGHT
PERCELL, NANCY P. TO E. J. JACO
PERRY, ALBERT TO MISS LOUISA SULLIVAN 2-3-1841 (2-4-1841)
PERRY, CATHARINE TO JOSEPH ST. JOHN
PERRY, ED TO H. J. CRESON 1-11-1872
PERRY, EDMOND TO MISS MARY COLLINS 1-31-1858
PERRY, HENRY R. TO SALLY ANN HANEE? 2-2-1842 (2-6-1842)
PERRY, J. H. TO MISS ROCINDA WALKUP 9-7-1871
PERRY, JENNIE TO THOS. CAMPBELL
PERRY, JOHN W. TO MARY ANN PENDLETON 1-19-1842
PERRY, MALISA TO HENRY CRAIN
PERRY, MARTHA E. TO JOHN SISSOM
PERRY, MOSES TO ELIZABETH GREAR 7-19-1865 (NO RETURN)
PERRY, N. O. TO MISS MAHALA GAITHER 2-5-1867 (SOLEMNIZED, DATE OMITTED)
PERRY, NATHANIEL TO MISS LETTICIA LUSTER 6-14-1841
PERRYMAN, G. W. TO MISS M. E. MOODY 11-29-1859 (NO RETURN)
PETRILL, MARTHA TO ARNOLD COPLAND
PETTUS, J. A. TO MISS M. A. ROBERTS 12-9-1867 (12-10-1867)

PETTY, ASEAH TO J. J. CRAFT
PETTY, CAROLINE TO PHILIP HARRIS
PETTY, EASTHER TO JOEL HOPKINS
PETTY, ELIZA A. TO FLEMING W. HALL
PETTY, ELIZABETH ANN TO JAMES WILLIAMS
PETTY, G. A. TO MISS MARY SMITH 1-14-1856 (2-3-1856)
PETTY, JAMES A. TO MARGARET E. BRANDON 12-2-1865 (12-3-1865)
PETTY, JAMES TO FRANCES HARRIS 9-18-1865 (9-21-1865)
PETTY, JAMES TO MISS ANNIS PEYTON 4-19-1845 (4-20-1845)
PETTY, JOHN TO MISS E. J. MCLAIN 11-19-1853 (11-20-1853)
PETTY, MARIAR F. TO WM. H. DAVIS
PETTY, MARTHA TO JAMES P. MCCLAIN
PETTY, MARY TO JAMES HILL
PETTY, MICAGAH TO MARY CUNNINGHAM 9-28-1855 (9-29-1855)
PETTY, NANCY ANN TO WM. PHILIPS
PETTY, NANNIE D. TO T. Y. DAVIS
PETTY, SOPHY TO JAMES JETTON
PETTY, WILLIAM E. TO MISS HESSIE ANN CRAFT 8-14-1866 (8-15-1866)
PETTY, WILLIAM E. TO MISS RUTH RHEA 11-10-1847 (11-11-1847)
PEYDAN, NANCY TO JOHN BURK
PEYDEN, BARBARA A. TO W. S. DAVENPORT
PEYDON, JOSEPH TO SUSAN A. RICHARDS 9-22-1854
PEYTON, ANNIS TO JAMES PETTY
PEYTON, MARGARET TO SAMUEL F. PARKER
PHALON, E. H. TO MISS FRANCES E. DILLON 9-11-1865 (9-12-1865)
PHILIPS, BENJAMIN H. F. TO ELIZABETH CHURCH 9-24-1842
PHILIPS, DAVID H. TO MARGARETT BRALLEY 9-10-1842 (9-11-1842)
PHILIPS, ELIZABETH TO RICHARD BARRATT
PHILIPS, HANEY TO PATTON FARLER
PHILIPS, HUGH B. TO MISS MARY L. E. PRATOR 8-3-1867 (8-6-1867)
PHILIPS, JAMES TO ELIZABETH TURNER 11-27-1849
PHILIPS, JOHN TO V. S. MERPHEY 3-8-1855
PHILIPS, MARGARETT TO NATHAN T. WOODS
PHILIPS, MARTHA TO BENJAMIN F. WOODS
PHILIPS, MARY ANN TO WM. G. SUMNER
PHILIPS, MARY TO DAVID TODD
PHILIPS, NANCY A. TO JAMES GLAZEBROOKS
PHILIPS, ROBERT TO LEATHEY PACE 12-10-1839
PHILIPS, SAMUEL R. TO SARAH A. BRALLEY 2-3-1843 (2-5-1843)
PHILIPS, SAMUEL TO MISS UNICE E. TABOUR 7-17-1848 (NO RETURN)
PHILIPS, SARAH TO LEWIS MAXEY
PHILIPS, SETH TO MISS MARTHA SHIPES 3-19-1855 (NO RETURN)
PHILIPS, WM. C. TO NANCY EDWARD 5-23-1859 (EXECUTION NOT CLEAR)
PHILIPS, WM. C. TO SARAH S. HOLLAND 11-13-1854 (11-17-1854)
PHILIPS, WM. TO MISS NANCY ANN PETTY 12-7-1853 (12-8-1853)
PHILLIPPS, JANIE TO W. D. HOUSE
PHILLIPS, CAROLINE TO N. C. C. WOOD
PHILLIPS, E. M. TO M. J. BLANTON 1-26-1872 (1-28-1872)
PHILLIPS, ELIZABETH TO GEORGE ST. JOHN
PHILLIPS, ELIZABETH TO JOHN T. JOHNSON
PHILLIPS, J. C. TO M. P. GOOD 12-15-1871 (12-24-1871)
PHILLIPS, N. J. TO J. H. MULLINS
PHILLIPS, WILLIAM TO M. V. WARREN 4-13-1858
PHINS?, WM. M. TO MISS SARAH AUSTON 10-9-1857 (10-10-1857)
PINKERTON, MARY TO GEORGE DANIEL
PINKERTON, SARAH A. TO DAVIS B. MURRY
PITARD, ELIZABETH TO JOHN HAYS
PITARD, ROWANN TO JOHN HAYS
PITARD, SARAH JANE TO D. F. BRAGG
PITMAN, AMANDY TO T. F. WEST

PITMAN, DISA TO JAMES M. GUNTER
PITMAN, ELIZABETH TO WILLIAM NEWBY
PITMAN, J. N. M. TO G. M. WILSON 9-9-1872 (9-11-1872)
PITMAN, SARAH AN TO VINCENT CAMPBELL
PITMAN, STANFORD TO LUCY ANN ELKINS 12-25-1866
PITMAN, THOS. M. TO MISS MARTHA LEFEVER 8-21-1852 (8-22-1852)
PITMAN, WILLIAM TO MISS EASTER L. FORD 6-27-1849
PITMAN, WILLIAM TO MISS NANCY MELTON 5-11-1844 (5-12-1844)
PITT, REUBEN TO MISS MARY A. BYFORD 11-26-1855 (11-27-1855)
PITTARD, JAS. L. TO B. F. TENPENNY 7-28-1860 (7-29-1860)
PITTARD, MARY L. TO JOSEPH W. TENPENNY
PITTERED, P. H. TO MISS S. M. WEATHERFORD 9-4-1867
PITTMAN, ELIZABETH TO GEORGE ST. JOHN
PITTS, JAMES TO EMALINE SPURLOCK 10-17-1862 (NO RETURN)
PITTS, JOSIAH TO SARAH MERRIMAN 9-13-1843
PITTS, LUCINDA TO MICHAEL GRIGGS
PITTS, MANDY M. TO SAMUEL BOWEN
PITTS, SARAH JANE TO ALEXANDER MORGAN
POFF, CHARLES TO MISS MARTHA GOODING 12-16-1841
POFF, MARY ANN TO JAMES REED
POLLETT, ELIZABETH TO MEREDITH ACRES
POLOCK, DANIEL M. TO MARY ANN GOOD 11-29-1865 (11-30-1865)
POLOCK, ELIZABETH ANN TO JAMES W. BRYANT
POND, SARAH TO JOHN TRAVIS
POPE, MARK A. TO MELISSA HADLEY 2-24-1840 (2-26-1840)
PORTER, ALEXANDER TO MISS MARTHA PATTERSON 12-26-1866
PORTER, SOLOM TO MARGRETT BURKETT 5-17-1872
PORTERFIELD, LEONADES F. TO MISS SEPTIMA F. WITHERSPOON 11-29-1843 (11-30-1843)
PORTERFIELD, MALISA TO THOMAS PASCAL
PORTERFIELD, MARGARET TO LEMUEL A. REED
PORTERFIELD, MARIAH E. TO JOHN FISHER
PORTERFIELD, MARY TO DANIEL TRAVIS
PORTERFIELD, P. C. TO MILTON E. WATTS
PORTERFIELD, SAMUEL G. TO MISS MARY SUMMAR 3-7-1848 (3-9-1848)
POSTON, JAMES C. TO MISS J. C. MOLLEN 6-16-1852 (6-18-1852)
POTERFIELD, M. M. TO S. N. MCELROY
POTERFIELD, MARY E. TO WILLIAM SULLIVAN
POWEL, JOHN TO REBECCA FANEN 3-26-1864 (3-27-1864)
POWEL, PEYTON TO MISS PARLEE WOOD 7-18-1866
POWEL, SARAH TO ROBERT HANKINS
POWELL, ELIZABETH E. TO JAMES S. MULLINAX
POWELL, FRANCES TO M. B. MILLIGAN
POWELL, H. N. TO SARAH MELTON 12-16-1856 (12-18-1856)
POWELL, JAMES TO MISS LUCY REEVES 9-5-1850 (9-8-1850)
POWELL, NANCY TO THOS. KIRBY
POWELL, PARLEE TO LUKE MELTON
POWELL, RHODA TO WM. C. SMITHSON
POWELL, THOMAS TO RACHEL GEORGE 8-29-1872
POWELL, WILLIAM TO MISS SUSAN MELTON 9-5-1846 (9-6-1846)
POWELL, WM. TO LIZZIE BRAGG 6-11-1873 (6-12-1873)
POWELL, ZANIE A. TO ALFORD LEDBETTER
PRATER, ARCH TO PARALEE SANDERS 4-7-1873
PRATER, C. L. TO LUCINDA ELKINS 7-17-1873 (NO RETURN)
PRATER, DAVID M. TO NANCY MAXEY 12-6-1865 (12-7-1865)
PRATER, JAMES TO MISS MARGARETT E. ELKINS 2-18-1850
PRATER, JOHN TO MISS ELIZA DARBERY 3-4-1871 (3-5-1871)
PRATER, KESSIAH TO NATHAN WOODS
PRATER, M. M. TO MISS LIZA JANE EKENS 12-1-1856 (NO RETURN)
PRATER, MARTHA C. TO CHARLES FARLY
PRATER, MARY ELIZABETH TO THOS. DILLARD PRATER

PRATER, MATTIE A. TO W. W. GRAY
PRATER, THOMAS M. TO MISS LETTY FARLEY 10-26-1846
PRATER, THOS. DILLARD TO MISS MARY ELIZABETH PRATER 11-1-1859 (NO RETURN)
PRATER, WILLIAM C. TO DELILA STANFIELD 2-17-1843
PRATOR, BENJAMIN P. TO ELIZABETH A. WARREN 3-9-1839 (3-10-1839)
PRATOR, CLAYTON TO MISS K. J. SULLIVAN 7-7-1866 (EXECUTED--DATE OMITTED)
PRATOR, ELIZA J. TO ANDREW J. WOODS
PRATOR, G. D. TO MISS M. F. WOODS 6-2-1869 (6-6-1869)
PRATOR, J. C. TO MISS KATHARINE KERTZ 12-3-1856 (NO RETURN)
PRATOR, J. H. TO MISS SARAH PENDLETON 2-22-1869 (2-25-1869)
PRATOR, M. E. TO WILLIAM BASSHAM
PRATOR, M. J. TO J. F. DUKIN
PRATOR, MARCUS TO MISS RHAMY DURRETT 1-3-1855 (1-4-1855)
PRATOR, MARY L. E. TO HUGH B. PHILIPS
PRATOR, NANCY E. TO PATTON FOWLAR
PRATOR, T. E. TO MISS M. E. INGLIS 8-12-1867 (NO RETURN)
PRATOR, W. R. J. TO MISS TEBIPHA FARLEY 1-22-1855
PRESTON, E. C. TO MISS ELIZABETH TENPENNY 12-16-1856 (NO RETURN)
PRESTON, ELI TO MISS POLLY WALLS 11-12-1841 (11-14-1841)
PRESTON, ELIZABETH TO WARD BARRATT
PRESTON, FRANCES C. TO W. B. CUMMINS
PRESTON, H. L. TO T? T? C. DRAKE 9-7-1865
PRESTON, JAMES TO ELIZABETH YOUNG 9-11-1865
PRESTON, JAMES TO MARY YOUNG 8-2-1865
PRESTON, JOHN F. TO MISS PARLEE STONE 12-22-1847
PRESTON, JOHN SR. TO MISS JANE GILLEY 1-11-1851
PRESTON, JOHN TO MALISA RIGSBY 12-26-1872 (12-27-1872)
PRESTON, JOSEPH TO SALLY LUSTER 7-2-1838 (7-3-1838)
PRESTON, JOSEPHINE TO ANTNEY MULLICAN
PRESTON, JOSIE TO WM. P. DAVIS
PRESTON, LUCINDA TO WILLIAM TEASLEY
PRESTON, MARTHA E. TO JAMES H. YOUNG
PRESTON, MARTHA J. TO SAM B. DAVENPORT
PRESTON, NANCY E. TO WM. H. YOUNG
PRESTON, REBECCA L. TO D. P. HARRIS
PRESTON, REBECCA TO GEO. DAVENPORT
PRESTON, REBECCA TO THOMAS TEASLEY
PRESTON, SALLIE TO JOSEPH BAILEY
PRESTON, SAMUEL TO SARAH JANE FOSTER 5-27-1850 (6-8-1850)
PRESTON, SARAH E. TO J. F. SCOTT
PRESTON, SARAH TO HENRY M. T. WALLS
PRESTON, THOMAS TO MISS ELIZA RIGSBY 1-22-1845 (1-23-1845)
PRESTON, WILLIAM JR. TO MISS JANE RIGSBY 6-29-1850 (6-30-1850)
PRESTON, WM. L. TO SUSAN FITSPATRICK 10-17-1871 (10-18-1871)
PRICE, JAMES M. TO MISS MARY ANN SMITH 1-5-1847
PRICE, NANCY TO ELIJAH HOPKINS
PRICE, PETER TO MISS MARTHA F. ESSARY 1-12-1850
PRICE, WILLIAM TO MISS ELIZABETH CLEMENTS 11-19-1844
PRIM, THOMAS N. TO MISS MARGARETT HENDERSON 12-6-1855
PRIME, JOHN C. TO MISS A. J. GUNTER 8-25-1853 (NO RETURN)
PRIOR, SARAH TO JOHN W. BAKER
PUCKET, NARCISSA TO JAMES GUY
PUCKETT C. S. TO MISS M. CLEAIR SAND 8-30-1853
PUMPHREY, MATTHEW T. TO MARGARET HOLT 8-1-1838 (8-2-1838)
PURL, SARRAH TO A. THOMPSON
PURTAN, MAN P. TO MISS MENERVA MELTON 3-26-1857
QUALLS, JULIANN TO W. M. LITTLE
QUARLES, J. T. TO MISS IDIE BETHEL 11-25-1872 (NO RETURN)
QUARLES, WM. TO DARKUS J. STANEY 2-18-1873 (NO RETURN)
RAGLAND, WILLIAM J. TO MISS RUTH HICKS 9-29-1847 (9-26?-1847)

RAINS, DELPHIA TO WILLIAM CUMMINGS
RAINS, G. P. TO MISS N. A. MITCHEL 9-30-1858 (10-?-1858)
RAINS, JAMES B. TO MISS S. J. STANS 9-30-1852 (10-9-1852)
RAINS, JOHN TO MISS MARY WEBBER 9-12-1850 (9-22-1850)
RAINS, MARY J. R. TO J. E. PARKER
RAINS, N. E. TO F. M. HOPE
RAINS, R. D. TO W. B. D. DUNCAN
RAINS, RHODA TO ROBERT BAILEY
RALSTON, DAVID N. TO ISSABELLA A. MCKNIGHT 9-10-1842 (9-15-1842)
RAMSEY, CAROLINE TO JOHN ARMSTRONG
RAMSEY, ELIZABETH TO WILLIAM W. GUNTER
RAMSEY, JAMES A. TO MISS ELIZABETH G. ODOM 12-27-1845 (12-28-1845)
RAMSEY, LUTHUR S. TO MISS J. M. GRAHAM 6-2-1855 (6-3-1855)
RAMSEY, NANCY M. TO J. M. PATTERSON
RAMSEY, R. M. TO E. C. HANCOCK 1-18-1860 (NO RETURN)
RANEY, ELIZA TO THOMAS FORD
RANKHORN, C. M. TO MISS HARRIET DELILA NEELY 2-25-1867
RATLEY, ALEXANDER TO MISS MARY PENDERGRASS 8-14-1866 (8-15-1866)
RATLY, MALISA TO JAMES UNDERWOOD
RAWLENS, MARY TO J. A. COUGHANOUR
RAWLINGS, ANDREW TO GENINNIA GRIMES 3-30-1872 (3-31-1872)
RAWLINGS, MANERVY TO WM. BRAWLEY
READ, JAMES TO MISS RUTHA RICHARDS 10-4-1851 (10-?-1851)
READY, AARON TO MARGARET HEMMAN 2-24-1865
READY, C. C. TO MISS MARY A. ALEXANDER 8-14-1871 (8-15-1871)
READY, CALLIE TO CHARLES ELLEDGE
READY, ELIAS ALEXANDER TO MISS SARAH MCEWIN 8-7-1848
READY, EMELINE TO J. F. REED
READY, FRANKLIN TO ZELPHA GAITHER 8-26-1865 (9-3-1865)
READY, JAMES M. TO MISS SARAH C. GANNON 6-13-1867
READY, JOHN S. TO MISS MAHALY T. BRYSON 7-27-1871
READY, M. E. TO W. T. KEATON
READY, SHOPHIA TO JOHN HERRIMON
READY, THOMAS TO MISS SARAH L. A. PARKER 2-16-1850 (NO RETURN)
READY, WILLIAM TO MARTHA ELIZABETH WILLARD 10-12-1848
REAGAN, R. A. TO MARY J. MCFERIN 11-28-1864 (11-29-1864)
REAVES, A. H. TO MISS M. J. BURGER 1-1-1853 (1-4-1853)
REDDY, MIRAM TO JOHN BYRN
REED, AMANDA TO JORDAN BLACNETT
REED, AMANDY TO J. E. DENTON
REED, D. B. TO MISS MALISSA FANN 11-29-1847 (11-30-1847)
REED, DANIEL TO MARY NUCKLES 8-9-1842 (8-14-1842)
REED, DAVID TO ELIZABETH HAILY 9-12-1838
REED, ELEAZOR TO GRISSY BEATY 10-17-1840
REED, ESTHER TO JAMES GIBSON
REED, EZEKIEL TO MISS MARY OWEN 5-20-1871 (5-21-1871)
REED, GEORGE TO MISS SARAH SOAPE 6-16-1848 (6-17-1848)
REED, H. B. TO MISS MALISSA J. SAFFLE 9-25-1867 (9-26-1867)
REED, HUGH TO MISS MARY ANN LAMBUTH 5-15-1848 (5-17-1848)
REED, J. F. TO MISS EMELINE READY 7-22-1858 (NO RETURN)
REED, J. I. TO M. J. MCCLAIN 3-22-1873 (3-23-1873)
REED, J. R. TO NANCY E. WILLIAMS 10-20-1873 (10-21-1873)
REED, JACKSON TO MISS CYNTHIA C. NICHOL 11-12-1850
REED, JAMES H. TO MISS MARY S. PATTON 8-30-1867 (9-1-1867)
REED, JAMES TO MARY ANN POFF 1-6-1840 (1-19-1840)
REED, JAMES TO MISS MARY LASETER 2-17-1869 (5-18-1869)
REED, JANE TO E. K. THOMAS
REED, JANE TO JOHN CARUTHERS
REED, JOHN H. TO MISS NANCY A. EDWARDS 6-25-1859 (NO RETURN)

REED, JOHN TO MISS ELIZABETH LAMBERT 2-14-1850
REED, LEMUEL A. TO MARGARET PORTERFIELD 4-16-1840
REED, LUCY TO W. C. TOLBERT
REED, LUKE TO ELIZA M. SAFFLE 8-22-1872
REED, LYDIA A. TO THOMAS WAMMACK
REED, MALISSA C. TO THOMAS J. BUSEY
REED, MARTHA TO DANIEL VANCE
REED, MARY E. TO JAMES N. JOHNSON
REED, PENEY TO HARVEY HAMILTON
REED, SARAH E. TO JAMES A. MORGAN
REED, SARAH TO JONNATHAN BRANDON
REED, WILLIAM M. TO MISS MARY JANE STACY 11-2-1867 (11-3-1867)
REED, WILLIAM TO JEMIMA FANN 10-4-1838
REEVES, FANNY TO JACK PEOPLES
REEVES, LUCY JANE TO JAMES POWELL
REEVES, MARY ANN TO JOHN HERRIMAN
REEVES, SALENA TO MATHEW DERMIS
REEVES, SALINA TO JAMES LEDBETTER
REID, ALFORD TO MISS MARRY J. YONG 9-28-1854
RETTON, E. TO WM. C. LOWIS
REYNOLDS, ADALINE D. TO DAVID MCDANIEL
REYNOLDS, JOHN A. TO MISS MARTHA M. WILKERSON 4-15-1852
REYNOLDS, JOHN TO MARGT. ELIZA WEATHERSPOON 12-23-1839 (12-24-1839)
REYNOLDS, MARGARETT TO WILLIAM BONDS
REYNOLDS, NANCY TO JAMES MCDANIEL
REYNOLDS, WILLIAM TO MISS MARY S. WITHERSPOON 12-23-1845 (12-24-1845)
RHEA, ABAGAIL TO GEORGE HALEY
RHEA, BETSY TO DAVID SPANGLER
RHEA, ELEANOR TO MORDECAI M. DUKE
RHEA, RUTH TO WILLIAM E. PETTY
RICH, WILLIAM TO ELEANOR COX 2-26-1845 (2-27-1845)
RICHARDS, JESSE TO MISS KATHARINE VANCE 9-16-1847
RICHARDS, JESSEE TO MARY J. PEDON 12-1-1873
RICHARDS, JESSEE TO MRS. SARAH J. BUCY 1-17-1871
RICHARDS, MANDY TO WM. BOWEN
RICHARDS, NANCY A. TO JOB BURKETT
RICHARDS, REBECCA TO JAMES TENPENNY
RICHARDS, RUTHA TO JAMES READ
RICHARDS, SUSAN A. TO JOSEPH PEYDON
RICHARDSON, AGNESS TO JOHN BOWLIN
RICHARDSON, BRICE M. TO CAROLINE FANN 4-15-1840 (4-14?-1840)
RICHARDSON, EMILY M. TO WILLIAM J. HARRIS
RICHARDSON, JOHN L. TO ELIZABETH PARTON 10-26-1865 (10-27-1865)
RICHARDSON, LUCY TO ELI HILL
RICHARDSON, MAY TO MISS MARTHA A. SMITH 8-6-1866
RICHARDSON, ROXANAH TO HENRY JONES
RICHARDSON, SUSAN TO WM. SUMMAR
RICHERSON, DREW TO MISS RENIAH UNDERWOOD 8-21-1858 (8-22-1858)
RICHERSON, FRANKLIN TO MISS C. BURK 6-11-1859 (NO RETURN)
RICHERSON, MELVINA TO JNO. MOODY
RICHERSON, SERGE D. TO MISS E. D. UNDERWOOD 5-12-1858 (5-13-1858)
RICHERSON, WM. G. TO MISS NANCY L. SUTHERN 9-27-1855
RICKETS, PETER TO MARY OWEN 11-4-1862 (NO RETURN)
RICKETS, ROBERT S. TO MISS NARCISSA JIMERSON 11-2-1859 (NO RETURN)
RIDENER, L. W. TO MISS P. E. WATSON 7-28-1871
RIDEOUT, ELLA TO HUNTER HARPER
RIDEOUT, EVALINE TO AMBROSE HARRIS
RIDEOUT, JOHNSON TO ELLER JETTON 12-28-1868 (12-29-1869?)
RIDEOUT, MANCA TO WILLIAM FERRELL
RIGBY, ELIZABETH ANN TO JOHN GILLEY

RIGGBY, ALMAND TO MISS R. J. SULLIVAN 7-12-1854 (7-16-1854)
RIGSBY, BAILAM TO MISS SALLIE GIVENS 10-2-1869 (10-3-1869)
RIGSBY, CAROLINE TO J. M. BURKETT
RIGSBY, ELIZA TO THOMAS PRESTON
RIGSBY, FRANCES A. TO J. B. FERRELL
RIGSBY, J. A. TO MISS SARAH LITTLE 8-7-1858 (8-8-1858)
RIGSBY, JANE TO BAZEL ASHFORD
RIGSBY, JANE TO WILLIAM PRESTON
RIGSBY, JOHN K. TO SARAH DAVIS 12-25-1844 (12-26-1844)
RIGSBY, L. L. L. TO G. W. UNDERHILL
RIGSBY, M. A. TO LEWIS PARKER
RIGSBY, M. J. TO THOMAS VINSON
RIGSBY, MALIND C. TO J. J. C. CAPSHAW
RIGSBY, MALISA TO JOHN PRESTON
RIGSBY, MARTHA J. TO THOMAS J. VINSON
RIGSBY, MARTHA TO VINSON BLANTON
RIGSBY, MARY E. TO D. S. FORD
RIGSBY, MARY E. TO R. L. HIGGINS
RIGSBY, MARY TO JOHN N. MITCHELL
RIGSBY, NELSON TO M. J. HEARNDON 1-2-1873
RIGSBY, ROBERT TO BA--- JONES 9-15-1860
RIGSBY, SALLY TO JOSIAH FUSTON
RIGSBY, THOMAS TO MARGARET YOUNG 10-9-1852 (10-10-1852)
RIGSBY, THOMAS TO MISS JANE YOUNG 1-12-1855 (1-14-1855)
RIGSBY, WILLIAM T. TO MISS MARTHA TUTTLE 11-29-1849
RIGSBY, WM. TO SARAH A. YOUNG 4-18-1872
RIGSLY, RUTHEY TO JOHN DAVIS
RING, ELIZABETH TO THOMAS HOLT
RING, JOHN TO POLLY HANEY 12-25-1841
RING, LAYFAYETT TO MISS EMLA CAMPELL 12-22-1852 (12-23-1852)
RING, M. E. TO W. B. HAILEY
RING, MISS NANCY ANN TO NOAH SAINE
RING, WILLIAM TO MISS NANCY ESPY 9-4-1846 (9-6-1846)
RING, WM. TO MISS M. C. WHITEFIELD 9-20-1854 (9-21-1854)
RITCH, ELIZABETH TO JAMES GRINDSTAFF
RITCH, JAMES O. TO MISS ELVIRA F. HALE 12-4-1867 (12-8-1867)
RITCH, RUFUS TO MISS JOSIE KENNEDY 2-21-1871 (2-23-1871)
RITCHEY, GEORGE TO MISS HARRIET C. GILLEY 12-10-1866 (12-12-1866)
ROBERSON, FOSTER M. TO MISS MARTHA DAVENPORT 12-22-1869 (12-26-1869)
ROBERSON, JOSEPHINE TO K. T. BRANDON
ROBERSON, LAHAMA E. TO JAMES BRAGG
ROBERSON, MARY P. TO THOMAS D. BRAGG
ROBERSON, PHENEY TO GEORGE W. SADLER
ROBERSON, ROBERT TO SUSAN WOODS 1-2-1869 (1-3-1869)
ROBERSON, SAMUEL TO TENNIE EWING 7-17-1872 (NO RETURN)
ROBERSON, W. M. TO MISS SARAH SUMMER 8-28-1859 (NO RETURN)
ROBERTS, E. TO JAMES TITTLE
ROBERTS, ELIZABETH TO GEORGE TAYLOR
ROBERTS, M. A. TO J. A. PETTUS
ROBERTS, M. C. TO J. A. PATTEN
ROBERTS, MELBERRY TO MARTIN MCCULLOCH
ROBERTS, SARAH JANE TO WILLIAM WADE
ROBERTS, THOMAS J. TO MISS NANCY C. LEIGH 11-22-1869 (11-25-1869)
ROBERTS, THOMAS TO MISS NANCY C. SPRY 5-4-1866 (NO RETURN)
ROBERTSON, S. W. TO SALATHA J. HIGDON 7-4-1854 (7-5-1854)
ROBINSON, AMANDA TO LEWIS E. W. WITHERSPOON
ROBINSON, JACOB TO ELIZABETH WIMBLEY 12-29-1855 (NO RETURN)
ROBINSON, JOSEPH TO R. M. BOGLE 11-4-1854 (11-5-1854)
ROBINSON, JOSEPH W. TO REIA M. BOYLE 11-4-1854 (11-5-1854)
ROBINSON, R. S. TO MISS MARY ST. JOHN 1-10-1856

ROBINSON, SUFFRONA TO MARTIN S. HOOVER
ROBINSON, VINA A. TO ROBERT GORDON
ROBINSON, WILLIAM M. TO MISS IZA EVALINE SUMMERS 5-27-1850 (NO RETURN)
RODGERS, J. T. TO MARGRETT OLFORD 12-6-1871 (12-16-1871)
RODGERS, JOHN TO MISS JANE MCCLAIN 4-8-1858
RODGERS, KATHARINE TO ALEXANDER MORGAN
RODGERS, RAMZEL H. TO MISS EASTER S. MCKNIGHT 5-2-1844 (NO RETURN)
RODGERS, WILLIAM TO MISS EMILY MARIAH BUSH 12-16-1867 (12-17-1867)
RODGERS, ZION TO STACY J. RUSSELL 9-6-1863 (NO RETURN)
ROEMINES, ELEANOR TO WILLIAM WOMACK
ROGERS, ARY URSULA TO JOHN BOWEN
ROGERS, ELIZABETH TO J. CUNINGHAM
ROGERS, HENRY TO MISS SARAH NICKELS 3-10-1853 (3-13-1853)
ROGERS, JAMES TO MISS ELIZABETH ALFORD 8-11-1856 (8-12-1856)
ROGERS, JOHN JR. TO MISS CINTHIA DAVIS 6-6-1845
ROGERS, JOHN JR. TO MISS POLLY BULLING? 6-17-1846
ROGERS, JOHN TO NANCY MOON 6-11-1842 (6-12-1842)
ROGERS, LEANAH TO WILLIAM O. CONNER
ROGERS, WILBERN TO MISS MAHULDA BULLEN 1-4-1847 (1-10-1847)
ROGERS, WM. J. TO MISS MARY ANN NEALY 5-27-1857 (NO RETURN)
ROGERS, ZILPHA TO LEWIS DAVIS
ROMINE, JEREMIAH TO MISS ELIZABETH SELAH EMERY 8-4-1848 (8-8-1848)
ROOD, C. C. TO MRS. POLLY SMITH 12-6-1847
ROSS, JAMES TO MISS ABAGALE WHITTAMORE 3-5-1866 (3-15-1866)
ROSS, JAMES TO MISS DISA SPANGLER 4-10-1848 (4-11-1848)
ROSS, WILLIAM S. TO MISS MARY E. BUSH 10-30-1867
ROTTY, JACKSON TO MISS MARRY ANN WHITFIELD 5-21-1853 (5-22-1853)
ROUGHTON, JAMES TO MISS MARTHA B. HALPAYNE 1-24-1848
RUCKER, AMANDA M. TO JOHN H. STEWART
RUCKER, ELIZABETH C. TO ROBERT N. JUSTICE
RUCKER, GOODLOE TO HENRY RUSHING
RUCKER, J. E. TO MISS ALLICE M. MCLIN 12-7-1869 (12-8-1869)
RUCKER, JAMES TO JANE RUCKER 11-29-1867 (12-30-1867)
RUCKER, JANE TO JAMES RUCKER
RUCKER, JOHN E. TO MISS LUCINDA A. STEWART 11-1-1866
RUCKER, L. TO RUBEN MCKNIGHT
RUCKER, MARIAH S. TO DANIEL F. WEEDON
RUSHING, AL? TO MISS CATHERINE LYONS 10-15-1870
RUSHING, ELLEN TO SI YORK
RUSHING, EMILY TO HENRY BARNES
RUSHING, FRANK TO MISS DOSIA BARNES 3-10-1871
RUSHING, H. B. TO MISS PRUDIE KITTRELL 3-2-1870
RUSHING, HENRY TO GOODLOE RUCKER 8-24-1865 (8-27-1865)
RUSHING, JOHN R. TO MISS TENNIE L. BETHELL 1-31-1866
RUSHING, MARTHA TO L. W. WILLIAMS
RUSHING, MATHA TO W. A. CATHCART
RUSSEL, M. W. TO BARTHENA J. BOREN 1-28-1864 (1-31-1864)
RUSSELL, STACY J. TO ZION RODGERS
RUSSELL, WM. H. TO MARY C. PATTERSON 4-30-1864
SADLER, GEORGE W. TO PHENEY ROBERSON 11-20-1839
SAFFLE, ELIZA M. TO LUKE REED
SAFFLE, M. A. TO J. H. LASETER
SAFFLE, MALISSA J. TO H. B. REED
SAFFLE, W. A. TO MISS M. L. C. GAITHER 1-22-1868 (1-23-1868)
SAGELY, B. L. TO NANCY TODD 12-21-1872 (12-29-1872)
SAGELY, MARIAH ELVINA TO WILLIAM JEFFERSON ARNOLD
SAGELY, MARY ANN TO WILLIAM BYNUM
SAGELY, NANCY ELEANOR TO SAMUEL W. GRAY
SAINE, NOAH TO MISS NANCY ANN RING 9-8-1840 (9-9-1840)
SAND, M. CLEAIR TO C. S. PUCKETT

SAND, MARTHA FRANCES TO A. O. ALEXANDER
SANDERS, PARALEE TO ARCH PRATER
SANDERS, SARAH T. TO JOHN A. WOOD
SANDERS, SARRAH A. TO WM. T. TODD
SANFORD, THOMAS B. TO MRS. ELIZABETH R. TAYLOR 2-14-1849 (2-15-1848?)
SAPP, E. S. TO A. M. CRANE
SAPP, HANNAH C. TO JOHN W. MULLINS
SAPP, JANE TO JOHN BARRETT
SAPP, MARTHA E. TO SAMUEL GANNON
SAPP, NANCY ANN TO BENJAMIN MOORE
SAPP, POLLY TO LARKIN HAMMON
SATINE, LAURA TO G. W. WEBB
SAULS, CAROLINE TO GRUNDY FANN
SAULS, CHARITY E. TO JAMES BOGLE
SAULS, CHARITY TO CORNELIUS PARKER
SAULS, DAVID TO MISS JULIANN DUGGIN 3-21-1859 (NO RETURN)
SAULS, HENRY TO MARTHA L. COOPER 10-6-1869 (10-10-1869)
SAULS, JOHN H. TO ELIZA JANE GAITHER 8-27-1846
SAULS, NANCY TO ABNER D. ALEXANDER
SAULS, RHODA TO THOMAS TEDDER
SAULS, RUTH TO G. W. HARRIS
SAULS, WILLIAM TO MARTHA BOGLE 12-8-1842
SAWLES?, J. D. TO MISS S. E. BEADON 11-5-1870 (11-7-1870)
SCISSAM, MILLEY E. TO G. W. SPRY
SCOTT, CATHARINE TO CARTER GOINS
SCOTT, H. A. TO NANNIE SHELTON 8-14-1872
SCOTT, HENRY TO MISS MARY WILSON 10-3-1846
SCOTT, J. F. TO SARAH E. PRESTON 12-30-1865 (12-31-1865)
SCOTT, JULY ANN D. TO JOHN N. WOMACK
SCOTT, MARRY ANN TO GRANVILL TODD
SCOTT, MARY ANN TO BENJAMIN WILSON
SCOTT, MARY E. TO L. T. DUNCAN
SCOTT, NANCY TO GEORGE E. NORTHCUTT
SCOTT, SAM TO MISS NANCY BOGLE 12-26-1870
SEAL, JOHN TO MISS MARY WOODSIDE 2-13-1868
SEAL, SARAH JANE TO NEWTON SHEARLY
SEAL, THURSEY A. TO BENJAMIN WILSON JR.
SEALES, MARTHA E. TO SAMUEL A. HOPKINS
SEALS, JAMES TO MISS MARTHA A. BALEY 4-12-1871
SEALS, MARTHA A. TO H. B. MARKER
SEAT, NANCY M. TO ROBERT WAMACK
SEATES, ALESALA TO WILLIAM H. COX
SEAWELL, ELVIRA L. D. TO WILLIAM C. MILLER
SEAWELL, FRANCIS M. TO ABAGAIL BATES 1-5-1842
SEAWELL, SUSAN C. TO JAMES T. HENDERSON
SEE, ANDREW TO NANCY M. BOGLE 7-21-1864 (NO RETURN)
SELLARS, JORDAN B. TO ELIZA CURTIS 6-26-1840 (6-28-1840)
SELLARS, MALISSA TO JOHN HANCOCK
SELLARS, SALINA TO MARTIN BROWN
SELLARS, SUSAN TO JOHN PATTERSON
SESSIN, C. I. TO WM. HILL
SEWELL, EMERSON TO MISS PATSEY WAMACK 8-3-1867 (8-4-1867)
SHACKLETT, JOHN L. TO MISS LOU BATES 12-13-1866 (12-14-1866)
SHEARLY, NEWTON TO SARAH JANE SEAL 9-26-1855 (RETURNS MISSING)
SHELLEY, DIADEMA TO JOHN E. SMITH
SHELTON, HENRY TO TABITHA SMITH 8-22-1872
SHELTON, MARGRET W. TO JACOB W. JEWELL
SHELTON, NANNIE TO H. A. SCOTT
SHELTON, THOMAS W. TO MISS LOUISA J. BYNUM 12-21-1869
SHEPHERD, ELIZABETH TO THOMAS D. PENDLETON

SHERES, JANE TO WM. BRANDON
SHERLEY, BENJ. TO MISS JO MELTON 1-12-1871
SHERLEY, CHARLES TO MISS E. J. MELTON 1-30-1852 (2-2-1852)
SHERLEY, EMILY TO DAVID DELANG
SHERLEY, JANE TO G. D. HICKS
SHERLEY, LUKE TO MISS LOUISA KEEL 2-24-1859
SHERLEY, M. J. TO W. W. WITTY
SHERLY, TOLBERT TO MATILDA J. MELTON 9-21-1852 (9-22-1852)
SHEROD, JOHN A. TO MISS EMALINE CHERRY 9-20-1855
SHERREL, URIAH TO NANCY SIMPSON 8-28-1865
SHIPES, MARTHA TO SETH PHILIPS
SHIRLEY, ALFRED TO MISS SARAH N. BAILEY 1-30-1866
SHIRLEY, JOHN W. TO MISS MARGARET E. BAILY 12-28-1859 (NO RETURN)
SHIRLEY, LUK TO MISS LOUISA KELL 2-21-1859 (2-24-1859)
SHIRLEY, TOLBERT F. TO MISS M. J. MELTON 9-21-1852 (9-22-1852)
SHOELFORD, MARY E. TO H. A. WILY
SHOEMATE, SALENDA TO JOHN STAR
SHORES, JANE TO JOHN LEIGH
SHURLOCK, WILLIAM TO MISS MARINDA FERRELL 4-28-1848 (4-30-1848)
SILVERTOOTH, ELIZABETH TO EDMOND COVINGTON
SIMMAN, C. N. TO R. C. PEARSON
SIMMONS, BARBRARY TO JEFFERSON STANFIELD
SIMMONS, ISHAM TO MISS KATHARINE TOLIVAR 1-5-1849
SIMMONS, ISHAM TO MISS SARAH JANE ONEEL 4-10-1844
SIMMONS, J. TO LUCINDA LEWIS 10-30-1864 (10-31-1864)
SIMMONS, JAMES TO MISS MATILDA J. BYFORD 9-11-1868 (9-12-1868)
SIMMONS, JANE TO R. D. GOODWIN
SIMMONS, JESE TO ELIZA A. DUNCAN 12-22-1865 (12-24-1865)
SIMMONS, MARY E. TO LEANDER BYFORD
SIMMONS, WILLIAM TO PURITY LASATER 1-24-1842 (1-25-1842)
SIMMS, M. T. TO MISS MARGARET J. MCADOW 1-14-1867 (NO RETURN)
SIMPSON, ANDREW S. TO MISS ELENOR FINLY 1-1-1857 (NO RETURN)
SIMPSON, CINTHY TO JOHN WEBBER
SIMPSON, DAVID TO L. N. TOLBERT 12-23-1871 (12-24-1871)
SIMPSON, DAVIS E. TO MARY E. STACY 5-13-1853
SIMPSON, ISAAC T. TO MISS MELINDA C. STEPHENS 10-10-1848
SIMPSON, JAMES TO MISS ELIZABETH M. TROLLINGER 2-4-1847
SIMPSON, JANE TO JOSEPH A. BALTIMORE
SIMPSON, JOANAH F. TO JOHN H. HOLLIS
SIMPSON, JOHN A. TO MISS MARGARET CHERRY 9-11-1845 (10-12-1845)
SIMPSON, LIDEY TO HARVY A. GANNON
SIMPSON, LOUISA JANE TO JOSEPHUS TINLEY
SIMPSON, MARTHA A. TO JESSE B. BRANDON
SIMPSON, MARTHA J. TO THOS. G. MCGUIRE
SIMPSON, MARY ELIZABETH TO PHILIP J. BALTIMORE
SIMPSON, NANCY TO URIAH SHERREL
SIMPSON, OLIVE TO ABRAHAM GOODING
SIMPSON, P. M. TO MARY T. WILLIAMS 9-4-1872 (NO RETURN)
SIMPSON, PETER TO MISS NITHA A. GANNON 2-26-1848 (2-27-1848)
SIMPSON, R. TO A. T. BRANDON
SINGLETON, H. D. TO MISS S. J. WARREN 9-2-1868
SISSAM, LISA A. TO PETER B. DUNCAN
SISSOM, CALVIN TO MISS MARTHA TODD 10-14-1870 (10-20-1870)
SISSOM, DELILA C. TO ISAIAH COOPER
SISSOM, EMALINE TO N. J. S. LYON
SISSOM, H. A. TO SARAH E. COOPER 9-6-1872 (9-13-1872)
SISSOM, ISAH TO ANNA HEATHCOCK 11-22-1864 (12-1-1864)
SISSOM, JESSE TO MILISA JANE ANGLES 10-13-1838 (NO RETURN)
SISSOM, JOHN TO MARTHA E. PERRY 2-3-1863 (2-11-1863)
SISSOM, JOSEPH H. TO MISS LUANNA J. FORD 10-15-1870 (10-16-1870)

SISSOM, MARY A. TO JAMES W. COO-EN
SISSOM, REBECCA TO J. C. JERNIGAN
SISSOM, SARAH E. TO THOMAS J. COOPER
SISSOM, SARAH TO BENJAMIN F. CRESON
SISSOM, SARAH TO RICHARD JERNIGAN
SISSOM, THOMAS TO REBECCA WEBBER 11-14-1848
SISSOM, W. J. TO E. A. TINDEL 12-27-1871
SISSOM, WILLIAM TO MISS SARAH WEBBER 6-5-1844 (6-6-1844)
SISSOM, WM. J. TO MISS PERMELIA J. TOLBERT 12-14-1869 (NO RETURN)
SISSOME, JAMES TO MISS NANCY SISSOME 11-17-1858
SISSOME, NANCY TO JAMES SISSOM
SKURLOCK, LUCINDA TO ALEXANDER BRASHEARS
SLENDLY, SARAH TO M. D. L. COOPER
SLONE, RUTH TO NIMROD SMITH
SMITH, A. B. TO M. E. STONE 11-9-1871
SMITH, A. M. TO S. S. BRYSON 11-18-1873 (NO RETURN)
SMITH, ADALINE TO BEVERLY WILLARD
SMITH, ALBERT TO ELIZABETH MCKNIGHT 8-21-1865 (8-26-1865)
SMITH, ANDREW TO MISS KATHARINE ST. JOHN 9-5-1849
SMITH, ANN F. TO WARREN DAVENPORT
SMITH, BENJAMIN TO MISS NANCY E. MOORE 3-6-1848 (NO RETURN)
SMITH, BIDDY TO JOSEPH MELTON
SMITH, CANDIS TO ROBT. MURPHY
SMITH, CARLINE TO JOHN NAPER
SMITH, CAROLINE TO JAMES H. WOOD
SMITH, CASSINDA TO JAMES G. MASON
SMITH, COPEN TO ELLEN LEWELLEN 10-30-1865
SMITH, E. N. TO WM. J. ADAMS
SMITH, ELIZA TO GEO. DANIEL
SMITH, ELIZABETH TO DILLARD L. GAMON
SMITH, ELIZABETH TO JOHN G. KNOX
SMITH, EMELINE TO JAMES ALLEN
SMITH, FERIBA TO JOHN BROWN
SMITH, FRANCES ANN TO SAMUEL MOORE
SMITH, G. O. TO ELIZABETH ANDREWS 1-7-1851 (NO RETURN)
SMITH, GEORGE W. TO MARY J. MITCHELL 9-20-1864 (NO RETURN)
SMITH, GREENBERRY TO MISS POLLY BARRATT 9-26-1848 (10-5-1848)
SMITH, HENRY TO MANERVA SULLIVAN 7-26-1842
SMITH, ISAAC TO CALIDONIA ELKINS 5-18-1864
SMITH, ISABELA TO JOHN WILLIAMS
SMITH, J. B. TO FRANCES E. LOWE 4-26-1873 (4-27-1873)
SMITH, J. C. TO MISS ELIZABETH A. FAGAN 1-26-1849 (1-28-1849)
SMITH, JAMES G. TO MISS DELILA C. MORGAN 1-17-1866 (1-18-1866)
SMITH, JANE TO THOMAS C. ASHWORTH
SMITH, JAS. I. TO M. J. ST. JOHN 12-10-1859
SMITH, JESSE TO MISS MELISSA FANN 7-13-1847 (RETURNED BY GROOM NOT EXECUTED)
SMITH, JOEL TO MISS MARY A. MERRITT 9-4-1866
SMITH, JOHN E. TO MISS DIADEMA SHELLEY 1-12-1841 (1-14-1841)
SMITH, JOHN J. TO MRS. JUDAH NEWGENT 5-10-1848 (5-11-1848)
SMITH, JOHN R. TO MISS BARBARY DERRYBERRY 11-6-1850 (RETURNED--NO ENDORSEMENT)
SMITH, JOHN TO MISS BARBARY THOMPSON 7-10-1845
SMITH, JOHN TO MISS POLLY SULLINS 7-13-1850
SMITH, JOSEPH F. TO MISS ANNE F. JONES 11-13-1846
SMITH, JOSEPH TO MISS LUCINDA HILL 2-20-1849 (2-22-1849)
SMITH, JOSEPHINE A. TO SOLOMON SPICER
SMITH, K. J. TO L. M. OWENBY
SMITH, LIZZIE TO THOS. CARTER
SMITH, LORENZO D. TO MISS MARTHA JANE CROW 2-26-1846
SMITH, M. D. TO MISS SALLIE M. WEEDON 3-24-1869 (3-25-1869)
SMITH, M. E. TO A. M. GOODLOE

SMITH, M. S. TO MARY F. MOON 2-7-1873 (2-8-1873)
SMITH, MARGRETT TO S. H. OGLESBY
SMITH, MARTHA A. TO MAY RICHARDSON
SMITH, MARY ANN TO JAMES M. PRICE
SMITH, MARY FRANCES TO MEDFORD C. NEALEY
SMITH, MARY L. TO WILBURN H. WALLACE
SMITH, MARY TO ABRAM MCCRARY
SMITH, MARY TO BENJAMIN J. HAYS
SMITH, MARY TO G. A. PETTY
SMITH, MARY Y. TO JOSIAH MERRATT
SMITH, MOSES A. TO MISS NANCY SMITH 10-8-1846
SMITH, NANCY TO MOSES A. SMITH
SMITH, NANCY TO WILLIAM SMITH
SMITH, NEIL H. TO MISS FANNY E. DAVENPORT 12-21-1847 (12-22-1847)
SMITH, NIMROD TO RUTH MOORE 2-26-1860 (NO RETURN)
SMITH, NIMROD TO RUTH SLONE 2-6-1860 (NO RETURN)
SMITH, O. J. TO J. M. BRANDON
SMITH, POLLY ANN TO DANIEL BOGLE
SMITH, POLLY TO C. C. GOOD
SMITH, RACHEL A. TO E. R. MELTON
SMITH, ROBERT G. TO MISS MIRA A. MITCHELL 12-11-1867 (12-12-1867)
SMITH, S. C. TO C. F. BETHELL
SMITH, S. J. TO T. G. JAMISON
SMITH, SARAH TO JOHN DAVENPORT
SMITH, SARAH TO W. F. ADAMS
SMITH, SARRAH J. TO G. G. C. GRIMES
SMITH, SOPHIA ANN TO JOHN B. BOYD
SMITH, SUSAN L. TO JAMES T. TAYLOR
SMITH, T. B. TO MARY BALY 6-20-1860
SMITH, TABITHA TO HENRY SHELTON
SMITH, THOMAS TO JOSEPHINE FOWLER 11-12-1862 (NO RETURN)
SMITH, WILLIAM A. TO MISS ELIZA TENNESSEE GOWEN BARRETT 12-28-1866 (1-2-1867)
SMITH, WILLIAM H. TO MISS MARGARETT E. MCKNIGHT 12-23-1846 (12-25-1846)
SMITH, WILLIAM J. TO MISS MARTHA C. MARSHALL 7-26-1850 (NO RETURN)
SMITH, WILLIAM TO MISS MARGARETT H. MOODY 1-19-1860
SMITH, WILLIAM TO MISS NANCY SMITH 7-25-1845 (7-27-1845)
SMITH, WM. TO MARY FORD 5-13-1864 (5-15-1864)
SMITH, ZACHARIAH TO SUSAN C. LANSDEN 11-9-1844 (NO RETURN)
SMITHM, W. J. TO MISS FRANCES FINLEY 6-30-1866 (7-1-1866)
SMITHSEN, WM. C. TO MISS RHODA POWELL 1-24-1857 (NO RETURN)
SMITHSON, H. TO MISS SARAH BRAGG 10-2-1855 (10-4-1855)
SMITHSON, JAMES A. TO MISS MAHALA A. MILES 2-11-1847
SMITHSON, JAMES TO PATSY HUTCHINS 6-3-1840 (6-4-1840)
SMITHSON, JOHN M. F. TO SARAH E. BOREN 10-7-1868 (10-11-1868)
SMITHSON, JOSHUA C. TO MISS LUCY P. BANK 10-17-1854
SMITHSON, LAVISA J. TO A. F. WILSON
SMITHSON, NANCY TO HARMAN MERRITT
SMITHSON, RISTON TO MISS HESTER MUNCY 11-4-1870 (11-6-1870)
SMITHSON, SARAH J. TO ROBT. S. KIRBY
SMITHSON, WILLIAM C. TO MISS LUAN KERSEY 12-21-1849 (12-23-1849)
SMOOT, ARTHUR N. TO MISS SARAH GOODING 8-23-1850 (8-25-1850)
SNEED, MOSE TO PATSEY GRIMETT 3-14-1872
SNEED, MOSES TO JUDEA ANN ODOM 12-28-1867
SNEED, T. H. TO G. FANN
SNELLING, A. M. P. TO JOSEPH Y. BOGLE
SNIPES, C. W. TO MISS MAYN HOLLIS 12-25-1851
SNOW, SAMUEL TO ALSE ADAMSON 1-18-1870
SOAP, GORGE W. TO NANCY C. UNDERWOOD 6-3-1852
SOAPE, ELIZABETH ANN TO JAMES HARDY BYFORD
SOAPE, LUCY F. TO JACOB MOORE

SOAPE, SARAH TO GEORGE REED
SOAPE, WILLIAM C. TO MISS MARGARETT E. MCCASLIN 8-3-1848
SOAPE, ZENOBIA E. TO ROBERT M. FOSTER
SOUTHERLAND, ARCHIBALD TO MARY LAWSON 11-1-1842
SOUTHERLAND, POLLY TO ROBERT GILSON
SOUTHERLAND, RACHAEL TO THOMAS L. GREEAR
SOUTHERN, JEMIMA TO RICHARD D. GIBSON
SOWELL, SARAH JANE TO DAVID TUCKER
SOWELL, WILLIAM F. TO DOSIA E. ELKINS 3-20-1867
SPANGLER, ABIGAIL TO JESSE G. WHITAMORE
SPANGLER, ASA TO MISS CAROLINE M. PATTON 7-15-1843 (7-16-1843)
SPANGLER, DAVID TO MISS BETSY RHEA 2-24-1848 (NO RETURN)
SPANGLER, DISA TO JAMES ROSS
SPANGLER, MARY E. TO JOEL BREWER
SPANGLER, MILLY TO JOHN SWANER
SPANGLER, N. D. TO A. H. ST. JOHN
SPANGLER, SAMUEL TO MISS TABITHA WHITAMORE 10-14-1841
SPANGLER, SAMUL TO LETHIE J. BANKS 11-29-1855
SPANGLER, SARAH A. TO F. A. ST. JOHN
SPARKS, ALEXANDER TO MISS FRANCES C. MOORE 9-18-1868
SPARKS, MARY F. TO JAMES T. DOUGLAS
SPARKS, W. B. TO MISS MARY E. ODOM 1-6-1858 (1-7-1858)
SPARKS, WILLIAM TO MISS ELIZABETH PENDLETON 5-11-1866 (NO RETURN)
SPATTON, NATHAN TO SINIA E. LASITER 9-4-1868
SPEARS, GEO. M. TO MARY E. WOOD 12-22-1873
SPEARS, SAMUEL TO MISS VINA JANE MULLINS 7-11-1840 (7-13-1840)
SPEARS, WILLIAM TO LIDDIA MORGAN 6-7-1838
SPERLOCK, MENROW TO MISS FILIA ANN MERRIMAN 12-23-1856 (12-24-1856)
SPICER, EMMA TO J. W. TODD
SPICER, HENRY TO MISS SALLY HOLYFIELD 6-14-1841
SPICER, JOSEPH A. TO ELIZABETH HOLLAND 1-13-1863 (NO RETURN)
SPICER, SOLOMON TO DELITHA HATFIELD 2-6-1840
SPICER, SOLOMON TO JOSEPHINE A. SMITH 8-19-1865
SPICER, WM. TO ELIZA MCDOUGLE 12-20-1872 (12-22-1872)
SPIELLE, R. S. TO MISS FRANCES M. KENNADY 6-15-1856 (6-16-1856)
SPIZER, WILLIAM TO NANCY ANNE YOUNGBLOOD 6-17-1840 (6-18-1840)
SPRADLIN, ELMIRA C. TO WILLIAM C. HATFIELD
SPRAY, J. M. TO MISS SARAH BURT 8-23?-1852 (NO RETURN)
SPREY, ELIZABETH TO CHARLES O. TARLOW
SPRY, ALLEN TO MISS CAROLINE PARKER 1-21-1858 (NO RETURN)
SPRY, ELIZABETH TO CHARLES TABOUR
SPRY, G. W. TO MISS MILLEY E. SCISSAM 12-21-1854
SPRY, GEORGE TO REBECCA PARKER 9-14-1865 (9-15-1865)
SPRY, H. A. TO DENNIS WILLIAMS
SPRY, ISABELLA TO THOS. WILLIAMS
SPRY, MARY M. TO WILLIAM C. ASHLY
SPRY, NANCY C. TO ALBERT E. HALL
SPRY, NANCY C. TO THOMAS ROBERTS
SPRY, WILLIAM TO MISS SARAH ELIZABETH PARKER 3-23-1850 (3-31-1850)
SPURLOCK, A. T. TO T. L. BOGLE
SPURLOCK, C. J. F. TO C. P. BRAMER
SPURLOCK, ELISABETH TO G. R. CAMPBELL
SPURLOCK, ELIZABETH TO STERLING B. HERRIMAN
SPURLOCK, EMALINE TO JAMES PITTS
SPURLOCK, H. C. TO NANCY HERREMAN 4-23-1840
SPURLOCK, J. B. TO MISS ANGELINE SULLERS 10-19-1857
SPURLOCK, JOHN A. TO MISS MARY FERRELL 12-27-1849 (NO RETURN)
SPURLOCK, JOSEPH TO MALISSA O. CARMICHAEL 5-3-1865 (5-4-1865)
SPURLOCK, JOSEPH TO MISS IBBIA WEBB 1-18-1870
SPURLOCK, JOSEPH TO MISS MARY A. VANDAGRIFF 9-14-1859

SPURLOCK, JOSIAH JR. TO MISS ELMIRA HOWARD 5-28-1846
SPURLOCK, JULIAN TO OSIAS D. BRIM
SPURLOCK, MARIAH D. TO HARBERT H. SULLIVAN
SPURLOCK, NANCY TO EWIN MERRIMAN
SPURLOCK, PAMELIA A. TO DANIEL FORD
SPURLOCK, PRUDY TO W. G. MURPHREY
SPURLOCK, S. A. TO WILLIAM C. MASON
SPURLOCK, SARAH TO JOHN FERRELL
SPURLOCK, WM. TO NANCY W? NOKES 7-31-1873 (8-1-173)
ST. CLAIR, BENJAMIN TO M. A. HALL 8-30-1865 (8-31-1865)
ST. JOHN E. M. TO MISS JANE STONE 12-29-1852
ST. JOHN, GEORGE TO ELIZABETH STANDBY 7-13-1839
ST. JOHN, A. H. TO N. D. SPANGLER 1-31-1872 (NO RETURN)
ST. JOHN, ELIZA TO JNO. T. TODD
ST. JOHN, EMALINE J. TO JOHN S. HERRYMAN
ST. JOHN, F. A. TO SARAH A. SPANGLER 12-21-1864 (NO RETURN)
ST. JOHN, FLOYD TO MATILDA CUMINS 3-8-1849
ST. JOHN, GEORGE TO ELIZABETH PITTMAN 8-2-1842 (8-4-1842)
ST. JOHN, GEORGE TO MISS ELIZABETH PHILLIPS 1-8-1870 (NO RETURN)
ST. JOHN, GEORGE TO MISS R. KIRBY 11-27-1855
ST. JOHN, H. J. TO MISS BUENAVISTA STONE 9-11-1867
ST. JOHN, HARMON TO MISS MARTHA JANE BATES 4-29-1846 (4-30-1846)
ST. JOHN, J. W. TO M. J. ESPY 12-16-1872 (12-22-1872)
ST. JOHN, JOHN TO MISS E. KIRK 8-31-1859 (NO RETURN)
ST. JOHN, JOHN TO UPHEY EDWARDS 1-29-1857
ST. JOHN, JOSEPH TO MISS CATHARINE PERRY 1-11-1866
ST. JOHN, KATHARINE TO ANDREW SMITH
ST. JOHN, M. E. TO MARTHA H. WOOD 10-30-1862
ST. JOHN, M. J. TO JAS. I. SMITH
ST. JOHN, MALISA TO GUNTER MCDOUGLE
ST. JOHN, MARGARET J. TO JOHN W. MCDOUGAL
ST. JOHN, MARTHER TO JAMES FERREL
ST. JOHN, MARY L. TO JAMES E. WARD
ST. JOHN, MARY TO R. S. ROBINSON
ST. JOHN, SUTTY TO JOHN MCDOUGLE
ST. JOHN, W. T. TO SARAH ANN B. WHITFIELD 7-28-1866 (EXECUTED-NO DATE)
ST. JOHNS, MARRY C. TO ALVIN BATES
STACEY, MARY TO LEE OZBURN
STACY, ABRAM H. TO MISS ISABELLA A. HOLT 9-24-1869 (10-3-1869)
STACY, ADLINE TO HUGH COWTHRON
STACY, BENJAMIN L. TO MISS PEGGY JANE MAXEY 7-4-1846 (7-5-1846)
STACY, ELIZABETH N. TO G. W. WIMBERLEY
STACY, ELIZABETH TO C. H. WILLIAMS
STACY, EMELINE TO BLACKBURN HOLT
STACY, JAMES F. TO MISS MARY ELIZABETH LASATER 3-30-1846
STACY, JOHN A. TO MISS MARY ELIZABETH JANE BYNUM 4-4-1868 (4-5-1868)
STACY, JOHN J. TO MISS ISABELLA PARKER 10-19-1841 (10-20-1841)
STACY, JOHN W. TO MISS LUCINDA GOODING 7-12-1848
STACY, JOSEPH TO MISS E. J. ----- 9-3-1855 (9-4-1855)
STACY, LUCINDA TO WM. BYNUM
STACY, MARY E. TO DAVIS E. SIMPSON
STACY, MARY JANE TO WILLIAM M. REED
STACY, REBECCA TO ALEXANDER J. MCCULLOUGH
STACY, SAMUEL H. TO MISS POLLY HAITHCOCK 11-19-1866
STACY, SARAH ADALINE TO JOHN BROWN
STACY, SARAH E. TO WM. H. EDWARDS
STACY, SUSAN A. TO W. J. BUSH
STACY, SUSANAH TO SAML. P. GANNON
STACY, SUSANNA TO WM. S. BRYANT
STACY, W. J. TO MISS MARY J. WILSON 9-12-1871 (9-17-1871)

STACY, WILLIAM C. TO MISS MARY J. MOORE 8-17-1869
STACY, WILLIAM D. TO MISS LUCY M. HOLLIS 7-7-1841 (7-13-1841)
STAFFORD, CHARLOTTE TO ELIAS VERNON
STAFFORD, MARY A. TO JAMES M. BASHAM
STAMPER, JAMES TO REBECCA C. BELL 12-2-1865 (12-3-1865)
STANDBY, ELIZABETH TO GEORGE ST. JOHN
STANDLY, ANGALINE TO ROBERT CATHEY
STANDLY, ELIZABETH TO STEPHEN P. CHILDRESS
STANDLY, T. TO MISS JANE SUMMER 12-26-1853 (12-27-1853)
STANFIELD, DELILA TO WILLIAM C. PRATER
STANFIELD, JEFFERSON TO BARBRARY SIMMONS 2-15-1842
STANFIELD, PARLEE TO WILLIAM GOODING
STANLEY, DARKUS J. TO WM. QUARLES
STANLEY, ELIZA TO WM. C. DAVENPORT
STANLEY, SUSAN C. TO JOHN H. GANN
STANLY, MARTH TO ROBERT GANN
STANLY, MORT TO REBECCA DAVIS 6-24-1873 (NO RETURN)
STANLY, ROBERT M. TO CHRISTENA COX 2-18-1865 (2-21-1865)
STANLY, SUSAN C. TO ANDY DAVIS
STANS, S. J. TO JAMES B. RAINS
STANTON, REBECCA TO ISAIAH BAINE
STAR, JOHN TO MISS SALENDA SHOEMATE 6-26-1843 (6-28-1843)
STAR, SARAH TO AARON HUTCHINS
STARR, JANE TO WILLIAM HULEHENS
STARR, JOHN TO MISS SALLIE ANN VAUGHAN 8-2-1867 (8-3-1867)
STARR, JOSEPHINE TO ROBERT L. SULLINS
STARR, NANCY TO WILLIAM WILDMAN
STARR, RUTHY TO REESE HAMMONS
STARR, SUSAN TO JOHN L. PARTEN
STASY, GIDAN TO MISS BETSY ANN PARKER 9-17-1870 (9-18-1870)
STATOM, HENRY V. TO CYRENE C. HAZLEWOOD 9-7-1865
STATTS, WM. TO MISS HARRIETT C. JONES 5-9-1856 (NO RETURN)
STEPHEN, MARY J. TO JAMES M. TARPLY
STEPHEN, R. K. TO MISS MARRY J. GEORGE 8-22-1855 (RETURNS MISSING)
STEPHENS, ARTALIA P. TO JOSEPH D. MCKNIGHT
STEPHENS, BENJ. TO MARY TAYLOR 11-22-1873 (11-23-1873)
STEPHENS, BENJ. TO MISS ANN WOOD 8-3-1871
STEPHENS, H. G. TO MISS TENNESSEE BYRNS 12-13-1869 (12-15-1869)
STEPHENS, J. W. TO MISS AMANDA S. HIGGINS 1-12-1869 (1-20-1869)
STEPHENS, JAMES H. TO MISS MARTHA R. COOK 1-13-1870
STEPHENS, JOHN TO NANCY MCBROOM 9-22-1865 (11-19-1865)
STEPHENS, M. J. TO JOSEPH DILLEN
STEPHENS, MARRY TO G. W. CRANK
STEPHENS, MARTHA F. TO JOHN L. BREWER
STEPHENS, MELINDA C. TO ISAAC T. SIMPSON
STEPHENS, S. H. TO MISS M. A. MOORE 12-21-1867 (12-22-1867)
STEPHENS, S. J. A. TO JOHN STONE
STEPHENS, SIMEON D. TO MISS CHARLOTTE CAROLL 12-7-1848
STEWART, CAROLINE TO GEORGE KITTRELL
STEWART, ELIZABETH TO SPEAKER HOLLAND
STEWART, ISABELA JANE TO JOHN B. JETTON
STEWART, JAMES TO MISS FRANCES TAYLOR 10-21-1858
STEWART, JOHN H. TO AMANDA M. RUCKER 12-7-1865
STEWART, LUCINDA A. TO JOHN E. RUCKER
STEWART, MATTIE TO J. H. THROW
STEWART, ROBERT M. TO SARAH C. WALKER 12-10-1839 (12-12-1839)
STINE, W. G. TO MISS JULINA CUMINS 12-14-1859 (NO RETURN)
STONE, BENJAMIN A. TO MISS STACY C. PENDLETON 7-16-1845 (7-17-1845)
STONE, BUENAVISTA TO H. J. ST. JOHN
STONE, BUENAVISTA TO WM. B. WILCHER

STONE, ELIZABETH TO JAMES M. EVANS
STONE, FLORA M. TO REGNEER H. MASON
STONE, HENRY D. TO MANERVA LORANCE 3-6-1865 (3-8-1865)
STONE, ISSABELLA TO ROBERT BAILEY
STONE, JANE TO E. M. ST. JOHN
STONE, JANE TO JAMES SUMMER
STONE, JOHN R. TO MISS NANNIE ODOM 11-14-1866
STONE, JOHN TO S. J. A. STEPHENS 6-30-1872
STONE, JOHN W. TO MISS ELIZABETH SULLIVAN 5-28-1850
STONE, JOHN W. TO SARAH E. JETTON 11-6-1845
STONE, JONATHAN G. TO MISS ELIZA JANE MELTON 10-26-1848
STONE, JOSAPHINE TO W. J. WHITE
STONE, M. E. TO A. B. SMITH
STONE, MARGARET A. TO PORTER FOSTER
STONE, MARY TO JOHN N. BAILY
STONE, MARY TO WILLIAM B. NOKES
STONE, NANCY ANN TO EDMUND BARTON
STONE, NANCY TO JOHN W. BARRY
STONE, NORVENA TO WATSON J. DELANY
STONE, PARLEE TO JOHN F. PRESTON
STONE, RUTH A. TO DILLARD BAILEY
STONE, SARAH TO A. M. WEEDON
STONE, THOS. D. TO MISS NANCY M. BOGLE 2-11-1871 (2-12-1871)
STONE, WILLIAM J. TO MISS POLLY ANN FOSTER 2-15-1849
STOR, MARY TO C. C. EVANS
STORY, W. J. TO MISS Z. A. WEST 10-20-1859
STRAND, MIRIAH TO JNO. E. KING
STRONG, JULIE TO HARDY DAVENPORT
STROUD, BARCELONA TO J. M. HOOVER
STROUD, GEORGE S. TO MISS ELIZABETH J. MITCHELL 11-12-1857
STROUD, JESSEE TO MISS ELIZABETH BANKS 8-7-1858 (NO RETURN)
STROUD, S. TO ALEXANDER MOON
SULLEN, MARGARET TO PHILIP COOPER
SULLENS, ALEXANDER TO ELIZABETH HICKENBOTTAM 10-25-1852
SULLENS, ALEXANDER TO MISS ELIZABETH HICKEMBOTTOM 10-25-1852
SULLENS, JAMES TO MISS HARRETT BARNES 7-20-1852 (7-21-1852)
SULLENS, M. TO C. FERRELL
SULLENS, MARGARET TO PHILIP COOPER
SULLENS, RICHMOND TO MISS LUCINDA WOMACK 9-18-1849
SULLENS, SUSAN TO ROBERT W. HIGGANS
SULLENS, SUSAN TO WILLIAM LEDBETTER
SULLENS, WILLIAM TO MRS. DOVE CUMMINS 3-18-1849
SULLERS, ANGELINE TO J. B. SPURLOCK
SULLINS, JOHN J. TO MISS NANCY BUNCH 5-1-1869
SULLINS, LOUISA TO JAMES MILLSTEAD
SULLINS, MATILDA TO ISAH CONLEY
SULLINS, POLLY TO JOHN SMITH
SULLINS, ROBERT L. TO MISS JOSEPHINE STARR 5-26-1866
SULLINS, S. E. TO J. H. MELTON
SULLINS, SAMUEL TO MISS RUTH FERRELL 10-1-1867 (10-3-1867)
SULLINS, SUSANAH TO ENOCH FERRELL
SULLINS, V. A. TO N. C. CONLEY
SULLINS, ZACRIAH TO MISS MARGARETT ----- 10-26-1854 (NO RETURN)
SULLIVAN, A. E. TO N. J. BURKE
SULLIVAN, ANDREW TO FRANCES BRAGG 2-25-1845
SULLIVAN, ANN E. TO JOHN A. DODD
SULLIVAN, CASWELL TO ELIZABETH HOUSE 1-8-1845 (1-9-1845)
SULLIVAN, DOVE TO WARREN CUMMINGS
SULLIVAN, DRUCILLA TO JOHN ALFORD
SULLIVAN, ELIZABETH TO JOHN W. STONE

SULLIVAN, ELVIRA TO PLEASANT GUNTHER
SULLIVAN, HAMEY TO ALBERT DODD
SULLIVAN, HARBERT H. TO MISS MARIAH D. SPURLOCK 7-25-1849
SULLIVAN, JAMES T. TO MISS NANCY E. MCBROOM 1-18-1871 (1-19-1871)
SULLIVAN, JANE TO WILLIAM HOUSE
SULLIVAN, JOHN R. TO MRS. NANCY BROWN 3-5-1850
SULLIVAN, K. J. TO CLAYTON PRATOR
SULLIVAN, L. C. TO JAMES CARTER
SULLIVAN, LAURA ANN TO ANDREW J. BAILEY
SULLIVAN, LOUISA TO ALBERT PERRY
SULLIVAN, LUCINDA TO MALACKI CUMMINGS
SULLIVAN, MAHAMA TO J. MCALEXANDER
SULLIVAN, MANERVA TO HENRY SMITH
SULLIVAN, MARTHY A. TO R. S. LAFEVERS
SULLIVAN, MARY A. TO DAVID TENPENNY
SULLIVAN, MARY E. TO CALVIN C. BRANON
SULLIVAN, MARY TO W. G. FERRELL
SULLIVAN, MINTY TO A. O. WALKUP
SULLIVAN, NANCY RUTH TO GEORGE W. THURSTON
SULLIVAN, R. F. TO MISS ISABELLA FALKENBERY 11-29-1866
SULLIVAN, R. J. TO ALMAND RIGGBY
SULLIVAN, REBECCAH TO ARTHUR WARREN
SULLIVAN, SAMUEL C. TO MANERVA BAILEY 6-30-1842
SULLIVAN, T. C. TO E. FINLY 9-25-1860 (NO RETURN)
SULLIVAN, T. G. TO MRS. MATILDA B. BARRY 7-26-1869 (7-27-1869)
SULLIVAN, THOMAS G. TO MARGARETT BRAGG 9-6-1842
SULLIVAN, TILDY TO JOHN HIBDON
SULLIVAN, W. H. TO M. L. FERRELL 3-7-1872
SULLIVAN, WILLIAM A. TO MISS JOANNA GANNON 7-18-1867
SULLIVAN, WILLIAM L. TO MISS DEMARIES E. DODD 1-17-1866 (1-18-1866)
SULLIVAN, WILLIAM L. TO MISS MATILDA TEASLEY 10-30-1841 (10-31-1841)
SULLIVAN, WILLIAM TO MARY E. POTERFIELD 7-27-1865 (7-28-1865)
SULLIVAN, WILLIAM TO MISS MATILDA MERRIMAN 8-13-1847 (8-18-1847)
SULLIVAN, WM. H. TO MISS RACHEL A. TEAGUE 11-19-1857
SULLIVAN, ZACHARIAH TO MISS MARY E. HERRYMAN 1-24-1867
SUMARS, MISA TO FRANCIS WILLARD
SUMER, CINDY L. TO J. J. BREYSON
SUMERS, SARAH TO WILLIAM BOGLE
SUMMAR, ALSENA E. TO W. H. MILLIGAN
SUMMAR, BALDY H. TO MISS POLLY BLAIR 11-4-1844 (11-5-1844)
SUMMAR, BERTON TO LOUISA SUMMAR 1-1-1870 (NO RETURN)
SUMMAR, C. R. TO J. C. MCADOO
SUMMAR, CANTRELL B. TO MRS. MARY BRANDON 11-21-1844
SUMMAR, CYNTHA TO MOSES MICKEY
SUMMAR, ELIJAH TO EUNICY SUMMAR 10-17-1844
SUMMAR, ELIZABETH TO ARMSTED FRANCIS
SUMMAR, ELIZABETH TO JAMES VANCE
SUMMAR, EUNICY TO ELIJAH SUMMAR
SUMMAR, EUNICY TO RICHARD TENPENNY
SUMMAR, EVERT TO MARY M. WITHERSPOON 11-22-1838
SUMMAR, J. C. TO MISS SUSAN WARREN 3-18-1870 (NO RETURN)
SUMMAR, J. D. TO MISS PINEY PATTRICK 10-15-1867
SUMMAR, J. N. TO MISS SARAH E. DONNELL 3-15-1867
SUMMAR, LAVISA TO C. C. FRANCIS
SUMMAR, LOUISA TO BERTON SUMMAR
SUMMAR, MARTHA J. TO JAMES W. CANTRELL
SUMMAR, MARY LAVISA TO WILLIAM VICKERS
SUMMAR, MARY TO SAMUEL G. PORTERFIELD
SUMMAR, MILLEY TO SAMUEL MATHEWS
SUMMAR, NANCY TO JOSHUA VASSER JR.

SUMMAR, T. D. TO MISS MARY J. HARRIS 8-8-1866 (9-2-1866)
SUMMAR, WM. TO MISS SUSAN RICHARDSON 1-14-1871 (1-15-1871)
SUMMAR, Z. T. TO MISS PARTHENA BRYSON 1-28-1869
SUMMARS, MARY TO CORNELIUS BRANDON
SUMMER, B. D. TO MISS ELIZABETH BRYSON 11-22-1857 (11-20?-1857)
SUMMER, BERTON TO LOUISA ODOM 8-21-1865 (NO RETURN)
SUMMER, ELIZABETH TO M. A. WILLARD
SUMMER, JACOB L. TO MISS SARRAH J. WILLSON 8-25-1857 (NO RETURN)
SUMMER, JAMES TO JANE STONE 8-14-1872 (8-18-1872)
SUMMER, JANE TO T. STANDLY
SUMMER, MARTHA N. TO JOSEPH WILLIAMS
SUMMER, P. E. TO J. D. TRAVIS
SUMMER, PITSON TO W. R. DAVENFORT
SUMMER, SARAH E. TO THOS. N. LOW
SUMMER, SARAH TO W. M. ROBERSON
SUMMER, W. A. TO WILLIAM BLANK
SUMMERS, ----- TO ROBERT BRYSON
SUMMERS, AMANDA J. TO JOHN N. HILL
SUMMERS, AMANDA J. TO P. G. COOPER
SUMMERS, IZA EVALINE TO WILLIAM M. ROBINSON
SUMMERS, J. A. TO MISS SARAH E. MCGILL 12-3-1867
SUMMERS, JAMES TO MISS MARTHA E. LEWIS 12-4?-1854 (12-7-1854)
SUMMERS, M. A. TO T. J. BROWN
SUMMERS, NANCY E. TO R. W. TARPLEY
SUMMERS, SARAH TO ARTHUR WORLEY
SUMMERS, SUSAN TO J. C. YOUNG
SUMMERS, TERESA TO FELLING M. YOUNG
SUMNAR, L. J. TO M. C. FRANCIS
SUMNAR, LOUISA TO JOHN T. VARDEL
SUMNAR, TELITHA TO WILLIAM WILLARD
SUMNAR, W. H. TO LUCIND WILSON 3-3-1863 (NO RETURN)
SUMNER, WM. G. TO MISS MARY ANN PHILIPS 4-22-1858
SUTHERN, NANCY L. TO WM. G. RICHERSON
SUTTEN, LAVENDER TO MISS JULENA (PELENA?) KIRBY 3-15-1856 (3-16-1856)
SUTTON, ADALINE TO DOZIER MULLINS
SUTTON, ELIZABETH TO WILLIAM W. MCKNIGHT
SUTTON, MARGARETT JANE TO DANIEL FITE
SUTTON, MARY TO ALEXANDER TASSEY
SWANER, JOHN TO MISS MILLY SPANGLER 3-11-1852 (3-16-1852)
SWOAPE, SAMUEL A. TO MISS ELIZABETH J. MOORE 4-20-1865
TABOUR, CHARLES TO ELIZABETH SPRY 7-18-1853 (7-19-1853)
TABOUR, NATHAN C. TO NANCY ANN LASATER 2-26-1845
TABOUR, UNICE E. TO SAMUEL PHILIPS
TACKETT, JOHN O. TO MISS KATHARINE FOSTER 5-29-1843
TAIT, SUSAN TO NORMAN WINNET
TALLEY, W. R. TO MISS HENRIETTA W. VINSON 6-30-1866 (7-19-1866)
TALLY, RICHARD TO CAROLINE CHUMLY 10-6-1862 (10-7-1862)
TARLETON?, SUSAN TO MAT DENNIS
TARLOW, CHARLES TO ELIZABETH SPREY 7-18-1853
TARLTON, JAMES W. TO JULY GALAHARE 12-9-1857 (12-10-1857)
TARPLEY, R. W. TO MISS NANCY E. SUMMERS 1-8-1870 (1-11-1870)
TARPLY, JAMES M. TO MISS MARY J. STEPHEN 5-12-1866 (NO RETURN)
TARWATER, THOMAS TO M. MEARS 10-13-1853 (10-14-1853)
TASSEY, ALEXANDER TO MARY SUTTON 5-7-1840
TASSEY, BETTIE JANE TO J. M. C. ALEXANDER
TASSIE, E. W. TO SARAH E. GRIZZEL 1-2-1873
TATE, ALEXANDER TO MISS NANCY CAMPBELL 10-8-1846 (NO RETURN)
TATE, AMANDA TO EDMUND H. TAYLOR
TATE, HANNAH EMALINE TO JOHN DIXSON MCEWEN
TATE, JACOB B. TO MISS ELIZABETH KERSEY 12-30-1851 (1-3-1852)

TATE, JOHN A. TO MALISA A. FERRELL 8-31-1872 (9-1-1872)
TATUM, A. C. TO MISS ELIZA MCADOW 12-30-1850
TATUM, M. E. TO T. E. HAYES
TATUM, R. F. TO MISS M. E. BETHELL 2-6-1867 (2-7-1867)
TAYLOR, A. B. TO MISS E. C. MOORE 10-28-1867 (10-29-1867)
TAYLOR, AGNES TO ALLEN TAYLOR
TAYLOR, AGNESS TO HENRY CANNON
TAYLOR, ALLEN TO AGNES TAYLOR 8-21-1867 (9-3-1865)
TAYLOR, BARRY K. TO MISS MARTHA COOPER 2-3-1851 (2-7-1851)
TAYLOR, BETTIE TO J. G. MOORE
TAYLOR, EDMUND H. TO MISS AMANDA TATE 8-25-1868
TAYLOR, ELIZABETH R. TO THOMAS B. SANFORD
TAYLOR, ELIZABETH TO ELIGAH ANDERSON
TAYLOR, ELVIRA TO WASHINGTON FUGETT
TAYLOR, FRANCES A. TO R. M. WILLIAM
TAYLOR, FRANCES TO JAMES STEWART
TAYLOR, GEORGE L. TO MISS JANE ANDERSON 11-2-1846
TAYLOR, GEORGE TO ELIZABETH ROBERTS 8-28-1865
TAYLOR, GEORGE TO SUSAN TAYLOR 8-26-1865
TAYLOR, J. G. TO JANE P. FINLEY 3-7-1872
TAYLOR, J. L. TO LIZZIE N. OWENSBY 10-14-1873 (10-16-1873)
TAYLOR, J. L. TO R. J. MCCULLOUGH 11-9-1871 (11-12-1871)
TAYLOR, J. R. TO MISS MALISSA MANUS 9-1-1870
TAYLOR, JAMES D. TO MISS MARTHA FERRELL 11-28-1870 (12-1-1870)
TAYLOR, JAMES T. TO MISS SUSAN L. SMITH 8-16-1855
TAYLOR, JAMES TO MARIA NEW 9-1-1865 (6-1-1865?)
TAYLOR, JAMES TO MISS ELIZABETH R. WHARTON 1-21-1847 (1-26-1847)
TAYLOR, JOHN M. TO MANERVA ANN MCBROOM 7-18-1865
TAYLOR, JULIA TO JORDON FERREL
TAYLOR, MARTHA L. TO WILLIAM W. ANDERSON
TAYLOR, MARTHA TO SAMUEL WEBB
TAYLOR, MARY JANE TO JOSEPH M. D. CATES
TAYLOR, MARY TO BENJ. STEPHENS
TAYLOR, NANCY TO GEORGE W. WOODERAL
TAYLOR, NATHANIEL M. TO MISS MARY HENDERSON? 8-25-1841 (8-26-1841)
TAYLOR, RICHARD TO NELLY BRASHEARS (LISTED AS ALLEY ON CTF) 5-9-1845
TAYLOR, S. E. TO T. G. COTTER
TAYLOR, SARAH TO JERDON THOMPSON
TAYLOR, SUSAN TO GEORGE TAYLOR
TAYLOR, VIRGINIA P. TO JESSEE G. MOORE
TAYLOR, W. N. TO MISS MARY CATES 8-26-1869
TAYLOR, WESLEY TO MARY BARTON 8-28-1865 (9-3-1865)
TEAGUE, EMALY TO JEREMIAH J. OWENS
TEAGUE, M. J. TO THOS. P. MITCHEL
TEAGUE, RACHEL A. TO WM. H. SULLIVAN
TEAGUE, ROXIE TO ANDREW ENGLISH
TEAGUE, SARAH A. TO JOHN H. CARNAHAN
TEAGUE, W. A. TO MISS SARAH P. THOMAS 3-16-1868 (3-17-1868)
TEASLEY, MATILDA TO WILLIAM L. SULLIVAN
TEASLEY, THOMAS TO MISS REBECCA PRESTON 4-13-1841 (4-18-1841)
TEASLEY, WILLIAM TO LUCINDA PRESTON 12-23-1841
TEDDER, D. H. TO SARAH A. FANN 7-31-1872
TEDDER, ELEANOR TO BENJAMIN W. WEST
TEDDER, JOHN L. TO MISS JEMIMA TUCKER 8-3-1866
TEDDER, MARY C. TO JAMES MEARS
TEDDER, MARY TO DANIEL TRAVIS
TEDDER, MELVINA TO J. M. DAVENPORT
TEDDER, SARAH TO J. T. DABBS
TEDDER, THOMAS TO MISS RHODA SAULS 3-26-1846
TEDFORD, MARY M. TO D. D. WARNACK

TEEPLES, ELIZABETH TO LIBE JOHNSON
TEMBLETON, WILLIAM TO MISS HANAH ODOM 7-24-1867
TEMPLETON, SAMUEL TO MISS TEMPA PATTON 3-16-1852
TENERSON, MARY J. TO ALBERT G. MILLIKIN
TENNISON, ELIZABETH TO JAMES TODD
TENNYSON, M. A. TO J. A. WALKUP
TENPENNY, ALFRED TO MISS FRANCES HAYS 10-18-1848
TENPENNY, B. F. TO JAS. L. PITTARD
TENPENNY, CHARLENY TO ALEXANDER D. MCBROOM
TENPENNY, DANIEL JR. TO MISS MARY JANE GAITHER 9-12-1844
TENPENNY, DANIEL TO N. J. T. ALEXANDER 2-20-1872
TENPENNY, DAVID TO MARY A. SULLIVAN 9-21-1865
TENPENNY, E. J. TO MARGARET TODD 12-16-1865 (12-17-1865)
TENPENNY, ELIZABETH TO E. C. PRESTON
TENPENNY, FRANCES TO MILES B. GEORGE
TENPENNY, JAMES TO MISS MARGART BURRY? 9-17-1859 (NO RETURN)
TENPENNY, JAMES TO MISS REBECCA RICHARD 7-27-1844
TENPENNY, JANE TO J. H. HOLLIS
TENPENNY, JOHN TO JANE BARTON 12-23-1869 (NO RETURN)
TENPENNY, JOHN TO MISS M. P. ALEXANDER 11-3-1853
TENPENNY, JOSEPH W. TO MISS MARY L. PITTARD 8-16-1859 (NO RETURN)
TENPENNY, JULIAN TO JAMES P. DUBOISE
TENPENNY, MARIAH TO JESSEE A. TODD
TENPENNY, MARY J. TO ALFORD VASSER
TENPENNY, MARYANN TO ISAAC MCBORREN
TENPENNY, RICHARD JR. TO MISS EUNICY SUMMAR 7-19-1847 (7-20-1847)
TENPENNY, RICHARD TO MISS NANCEY H. COOK 8-31-1871
TENPENNY, SAMUEL A. TO SARAH E. LEMMONS 11-23-1871
TENPENNY, SARAH TO ANDERSON VANCE
TENPERY, WM. TO MISS CAROLINE MORGAN 7-27-1858
TEPLES, MALVIRA TO E. D. MANIS
TERNER, ISAAC TO SARRAH S. VANE 3-28-1855 (3-29-1855)
THEIRS, ISAAC TO MARY JONES 8-4-1853 (NO RETURN)
THOMAS, A. D. TO T. G. CURLEE
THOMAS, A. TO MARIAH BUSH 10-11-1860 (NO RETURN)
THOMAS, AMANDA E. TO WILLIAM C. LEECH
THOMAS, DANIEL TO MISS MARY FARLER 8-1-1844
THOMAS, DILE TO ISHAM THOMAS
THOMAS, E. K. TO MISS JANE REED 4-13-1850 (NO RETURN)
THOMAS, EMA M. TO JOHN B. JOHNSON
THOMAS, EMALIZA TO JOSEPH MCEWIN
THOMAS, HENRY N. TO MISS MARY A. GOOD 10-12-1848
THOMAS, ISHAM TO DILE THOMAS 3-5-1866 (4-10-1866)
THOMAS, J. F. TO MISS HARRIET MACLAN 3-10-1859 (NO RETURN)
THOMAS, J. W. TO MISS M. E. DAVIS 4-4-1870 (4-7-1870)
THOMAS, JAMES N. TO MISS ELIZABETH WIMBERLEY 7-20-1844 (7-21-1844)
THOMAS, JANE TO THOMAS MANUS
THOMAS, JOEL TO MISS C. C. HIBDON 10-19-1859 (NO RETURN)
THOMAS, JOEL TO REBECCA MEARS 2-26-1873
THOMAS, JOHN A. TO MILLIA ALDRIDGE 10-2-1838
THOMAS, JUNE TO JOHN TODD
THOMAS, MARGARETT TO JACOB MARCUIS
THOMAS, MARY TO BENJ. UNDERWOOD
THOMAS, MARY TO JONNATHAN YOUNGBLOOD
THOMAS, MARY TO SAMUEL PENDLETON
THOMAS, NELSON Z? TO MARGARETT WIMBERLEY 2-8-1843
THOMAS, REZEN F. TO MISS ELEANOR WINNETT 2-28-1866 (3-1-1866)
THOMAS, S? F. TO HARRIET MACLIN 3-10-1859 (NO RETURN)
THOMAS, SAMUEL TO SARAH THOMAS 8-26-1865 (8-27-1865)
THOMAS, SARAH F. TO SILAS ELKINS

THOMAS, SARAH M. TO ISAAC N. JOHNSON
THOMAS, SARAH P. TO W. A. TEAGUE
THOMAS, SARAH TO JAMES M. KNIGHT
THOMAS, SARAH TO JOHN JEFFERSON FARLEY
THOMAS, SARAH TO SAMUEL THOMAS
THOMAS, WILLIAM TO MISS C. ELKINS 12-24-1857
THOMAS, WILLIAM TO MISS MARY C. MCCABE 8-25-1870 (NO RETURN)
THOMAS, WILLIAM TO ROXANNA WILLIAMS 8-9-1865 (8-8-1865) (SIC)
THOMAS, ZACHARIAH TO MISS ISSABELLA TRAVIS 10-8-1850
THOMASON, J. A. TO MISS S. T. BOWEN 11-10-1870 (11-11-1870)
THOMPSON, A. TO MISS SARRAH PURL 2-13-1838 (NO RETURN)
THOMPSON, ALLEN TO MARIAH BUSH 6-7-1860 (NO RETURN)
THOMPSON, BARBARY TO JOHN SMITH
THOMPSON, CAROLINE TO FRANKLIN CHURCH
THOMPSON, DANIEL TO SARAH BLACK 8-23-1865 (8-28-1865)
THOMPSON, DIANNA TO LEROY WORLEY
THOMPSON, ELIZABETH A. TO E. J. WOOD
THOMPSON, ELIZABETH TO DAVID T. MILLIGAN
THOMPSON, F. G. TO MARTHA J. COOPER 2-20-1854
THOMPSON, F. TO MISS SARAH YONG 8-10-1853 (NO RETURN)
THOMPSON, GIDEON TO MARGARETT ANN ESTES 12-26-1844
THOMPSON, HUGH L. TO MISS ANN E. HERRELL 4-13-1844 (4-14-1844)
THOMPSON, JAMES A. TO MARGARET TOWY? 11-9-1865 (EXECUTED--NO DATE)
THOMPSON, JAMES A. TO MISS MARGARET YOUNG 11-9-1865
THOMPSON, JERDON TO SARAH TAYLOR 1-20-1872
THOMPSON, JESSEE TO ANN OFFICER 10-17-1871
THOMPSON, JIM TO MALISA MARTIN 12-18-1872
THOMPSON, JOHN B. TO MISS NANCY M. EWING 2-13-1866 (2-14-1866)
THOMPSON, M. J. TO J. L. LANCE
THOMPSON, MARTHA ANN TO JOHN COOPER
THOMPSON, MATTIE Z. TO JOHN P. HARE
THOMPSON, NANCY TO WOODSON UNDERWOOD
THOMPSON, PARILEE V. TO WM. YOUNGBLOOD
THOMPSON, SAMUEL TO MATTIE MITCHELL 7-30-1868
THOMPSON, SARAH C. TO FRANKLIN COLEMAN
THOMPSON, T. J. TO MISS MARY ANN NOKES 2-2-1855 (2-2-1854?)
THOMPSON, T. J. TO MISS REBECCA MULLINS 2-15-1866 (2-18-1866)
THOMPSON, TALITHA TO WILLIAM MORRIS
THOMPSON, TAYLOR TO MISS SARAH E. ALMON 6-10-1868 (6-11-1868)
THOMPSON, W. D. T. TO MISS HARRIET C. GOOD 12-23-1869 (RETURNED NOT EXECUTED)
THOMPSON, WILLIAM TO LEVISA WORLEY 7-24-1840 (7-26-1840)
THOMPSON, WILLIAM TO MISS PAULINA HOLLIS 7-31-1845
THOMPSON, WM. TO MISS SARAH S. CATHY 10-10-1856
THROW, J. H. TO MISS MATTIE STEWART 11-17-1870
THROWER, FANNY TO JOHN JOURDAN
THURSTON, G. W. TO ANNALIZA FINLEY 11-17-1873
THURSTON, GEORGE W. TO MISS NANCY RUTH SULLIVAN 2-2-1851
TILFORD, NICHOLAS C. TO JULIA Y. GOWEN 4-25-1842 (4-26-1842)
TINDEL, E. A. TO W. J. SISSOM
TINLEY, JOSEPHUS TO MISS LOUISA JANE SIMPSON 1-19-1848
TINSLY, MAUD? AMERICA TO E. G. ONEAL
TITLE, SALENA TO JOHN DIRTING
TITTLE, ADAM JR. TO MISS JULIA ANN HENDERSON 1-4-1851 (1-5-1851)
TITTLE, ADAM TO MISS CINTHIA GANN 5-2-1846 (5-3-1846)
TITTLE, BARBARY ANN TO ISAAC HIGGINS
TITTLE, ELIZABETH TO AMOS GILLY
TITTLE, H. Y. TO MISS ELIZABETH MELTON 8-19-1870 (8-21-1870)
TITTLE, JAMES TO MISS E. ROBERTS 9-29-1854 (NO RETURN)
TITTLE, JOHN TO MISS SARAH ANN ELKINS 12-22-1853
TITTLE, JULIA ANN TO JOHN D. ELKINS

TITTLE, SAMUEL TO MISS LOCKY JANE HIGGINS 6-15-1857 (6-21-1857)
TITTLE, SARAH A. TO J. M. HERNDON
TITTLE, SELINA TO HENRY S. DUGGON
TITTLE, SUSAN TO JACK MILLIGAN
TOBBERT, J. J. TO ELVIRA MOORE 5-16-1864 (NO RETURN)
TODD, ALICE E. TO J. L. HOLLIS
TODD, ALMARINDA TO AVANDER FREEMAN
TODD, CAROLINE TO WILLIAM NORTHCUTT
TODD, DAVID TO MARY PHILIPS 7-1-1865 (7-8-1865)
TODD, DILLARD TO SARAH GANNON 10-29-1873
TODD, E. J. TO Z. BUSH
TODD, ELIZA J. TO JOHN W. MCDOUGAL
TODD, ELIZABETH TO JOHN HOLLIS
TODD, ELIZABETH TO JOHN TODD
TODD, GRANVILL TO MISS MARRY ANN SCOTT 12-15-1852
TODD, HYRAM TO HENRIETTA ESPEY 8-13-1840
TODD, ISABELLA TO JAMES GOODING
TODD, J. H. TO MISS M. E. BELL 5-18-1860 (5-20-1860)
TODD, J. W. TO EMMA SPICER 11-25-1865
TODD, JAMES H. TO MISS CORNELIA A. MCCABE 11-1-1866
TODD, JAMES JR. TO MISS ELIZABETH TENNISON 10-4-1845 (10-5-1845)
TODD, JAMES S. TO MISS JEMIMA COX 10-17-1846
TODD, JANE TO ISAAC HOOVER
TODD, JEMIMA M. TO JAMES W. FORD
TODD, JESSE TO MISS MARY F. GIVENS 3-14-1845 (3-16-1845)
TODD, JESSEE A. TO MARIAH TENPENNY 10-11-1862 (10-12-1862)
TODD, JNO. T. TO ELIZA ST. JOHN 8-8-1873
TODD, JOHN H. TO MISS ROXANAH MORGAN 5-15-1868 (5-17-1868)
TODD, JOHN R. TO MISS LAVISA BLANSETT 1-29-1853 (1-30-1853)
TODD, JOHN TO JUNE THOMAS 12-2-1868 (NO RETURN)
TODD, JOHN TO MISS ELIZABETH TODD 10-9-1866
TODD, L. A. TO MISS SALLIE A. BYNUM 2-28-1867 (3-3-1867)
TODD, L. J. TO J. F. MCKNABB
TODD, LEVI TO MARY VARDELLE 1-13-1841
TODD, LOCKY JANE TO GEORGE R. BOGLE
TODD, LOCKY JANE TO MARK L. YOUNG
TODD, M. E. TO J. A. BRANDON
TODD, M. F. TO MISS MALEDA CROUGHONOUR 5-12-1856 (5-13-1856)
TODD, M. T. TO J. M. LORANCE
TODD, MARGARET TO E. J. TENPENNY
TODD, MARGARETT TO WALTER WILSON
TODD, MARGRET TO G. B. GOOD *Good*
TODD, MARTHA C. TO T. B. JONES
TODD, MARTHA J. TO ISAAC N. LEMMONS
TODD, MARTHA TO CALVIN SISSOM
TODD, MARY J. TO BENGAMIN F. HOOVER
TODD, MICAJAH TO SUSANNAH COX 8-22-1838
TODD, MILTON TO MISS RACHAEL C. BODKINS 11-10-1845
TODD, MOLLIE TO FRANK LYONS
TODD, NANCY J. TO WILLIAM A. KNOX
TODD, NANCY P. TO JOSEPH P. HARPER
TODD, NANCY TO B. L. SAGELY
TODD, RANSON TO MATISA DUNCAN 11-20-1852 (11-21-1852)
TODD, REBECCA JANE TO ANDREW J. JERNIGAN
TODD, ROBERT TO MISS JANE BEVERLY 1-17-1859 (NO RETURN)
TODD, S. E. TO M. W. LAWRENCE
TODD, SARAH J. TO HENRY L. BUSH
TODD, SARAH TO JAMES A. MCCABE
TODD, SARAH TO JAMES WINNETT
TODD, SARAH TO THOMAS COOPER

TODD, SUE TO WILLIAM J. TODD
TODD, T. M. TO MISS MARY J. W. WILSON 2-28-1866 (3-1-1866)
TODD, W. L. TO MISS MARY J. MCCABE 9-9-1869
TODD, WALTER L. TO MARGARET ELKINS 6-15-1865
TODD, WILLIAM F. TO MISS JULIAN BRAGG 1-13-1868 (1-14-1868)
TODD, WILLIAM J. TO SUE TODD 11-22-1873 (11-23-1873)
TODD, WILSON TO MARY J. BARNES 10-20-1860 (NO RETURN)
TODD, WM. C. TO E. C. COUGHANOUR 9-17-1863 (9-20-1863)
TODD, WM. T. TO MISS SARRAH A. SANDERS 12-21-1854
TODD, WM. TO SARAH EWELL 6-18-1839 (6-21-1839)
TOLBERT, ELIZABETH B. TO M. A. KENNEDY
TOLBERT, JULY A. TO B. I. BYNUM
TOLBERT, L. J. TO ELIZABETH BYNUM 1-1-1866 (1-4-1866)
TOLBERT, L. N. TO DAVID SIMPSON
TOLBERT, P. J. TO W. J. ARNOLD
TOLBERT, PARLEE TO G. C. BURKES
TOLBERT, PERMELIA J. TO WM. J. SISSOM
TOLBERT, W. C. TO LUCY REED 5-8-1863 (NO RETURN)
TOLIVAR, KATHARINE TO ISHAM SIMMONS
TOWY?, MARGARET TO JAMES A. THOMPSON
TRAVERS, MARY TO ZACHARIAH WARREN
TRAVIS, DANIEL TO MARY TEDDER 5-19-1842
TRAVIS, DANIEL TO MISS MARY M. MORRIS 2-10-1871
TRAVIS, DANIEL TO MISS MARY PORTERFIELD 12-30-1856
TRAVIS, FRANKLIN TO MARTHA CROSS 6-15-1839 (NO RETURN)
TRAVIS, ISSABELLA TO ZACHARIAH THOMAS
TRAVIS, J. C. TO L. HOLEMANE
TRAVIS, JAMES TO MALINDA COULTER 10-29-1842
TRAVIS, JAMES TO MISS MARTHA CRAFT 2-29-1852 (NO RETURN)
TRAVIS, JAMES W. TO MISS CYNTHA JANE WHARRY 11-1-1848 (NO RETURN)
TRAVIS, JOHN A. TO NEOMI ALEXANDER 12-30-1863 (12-31-1863)
TRAVIS, JOHN TO MISS SARAH POND 10-14-1858
TRAVIS, MARTHA JANE TO J. G. MINTEN
TRAVIS, MARTHA M. TO J. G. MOORE
TRAVIS, MARY J. TO J. C. HAYS
TRAVIS, N. L. TO HARVY OSBON
TRAVIS, POLLY TO GEORGE MINGLE
TRAVIS, RIDY E. TO JOHN P. GANNON
TRAVIS, S. D. TO MISS SARAH J. LARANCE 12-29-1859 (NO RETURN)
TRAVIS, S. D. TO MRS. S. J. TRAVIS 12-13-1870
TRAVIS, S. J. TO S. D. TRAVIS
TRAVIS, SARAH M. TO JAMES A. KEELE?
TRAVIS, SOLOMON TO MINNERVA HOLT 1-16-1840
TRAVIS, WM. H. TO CATHARINE VANCE 12-26-1839
TRIBBABLE, TENNIE TO ALEX BARNES
TRIBBLE, ELIZABETH TO J. M. ORAND
TRIGG, AMANDA TO WILLIS BUSH
TRIMBLE, AARON TO MARY ANN MCKNIGHT 2-17-1866
TROLLINGER, ELIZABETH M. TO JAMES SIMPSON
TROLLINGER, MATILDA TO WILLIAM J. HALL
TROTT, HENRY TO HANNAH A. MAJORS 2-15-1842
TROTT, MARTHA ANN TO JAMES O. GEORGE
TUBB, JOHN TO MISS CHARLOTTE PARTON 1-31-1867
TUCKER, DAVID TO SARAH JANE SOWELL 2-17-1844 (2-19-1844)
TUCKER, JACK TO ELIZABETH KERBY 9-26-1872
TUCKER, JACKSON TO MISS LIZY BRAGG 5-9-1852
TUCKER, JAMES M. TO MISS MARY R. ESQUE 11-2-1850 (11-3-1850)
TUCKER, JEMIMA TO JOHN L. TEDDER
TUCKER, JOHN TO MISS ELIZA ISSABELLA CROSS 10-19-1848
TUCKER, KATHARINE TO WILSON GAITHER

TUCKER, LUCRETIA TO ANDERSON DAVIS
TUCKER, MALISSA TO NATHANIEL PARKER
TUCKER, PINKNEY TO MISS MARY HERRIMAN 5-23-1870 (5-26-1870)
TUCKER, SAMUEL TO JULIE Q. FANN 8-12-1872 (8-13-1872)
TUCKER, SARAH TO RANSOM P. HARRIS
TULLEY, HARRIET TO JAMES DONNELL
TURNER, C. A. TO JESSE WARRICK
TURNER, ELIZABETH TO JAMES PHILIPS
TURNER, G. T. TO MISS MARY E. EDWARDS 9-18-1869 (9-19-1869)
TURNER, HANAH D. TO JOHN M. MELTON
TURNER, J. E. TO MISS SUSAN ELLEDGE 12-24-1870 (12-25-1870)
TURNER, J. R. TO MISS M. P. HANCOCK 2-22-1858 (NO RETURN)
TURNER, JNO. E. TO SARAH E. ELLEDGE 11-26-1873
TURNER, M. E. TO G. W. YOUNGBLOOD
TURNER, M. E. TO S. A. BREWER
TURNER, M. M. C. TO JAMES W. BRIEN
TURNER, MARTHA TO ALEXANDER ADAMS
TURNER, MARY A. TO JAMES M. MERRITT
TURNER, NANCY TO JONATHAN A. CRAFT
TURNER, PLEASANT R. TO MISS SARAH F. MELTON 9-27-1869 (9-28-1869)
TURNER, SARAH KATHARINE TO THOMAS J. MELLON
TURNER, W. H. TO MISS M. J. BAILEY 9-29-1858
TURNEY, NANCY E. TO JOHN KEATON
TURNEY, PETER S. TO MISS ELIZA A. HANCOCK 12-11-1869 (12-12-1869)
TURNHEN?, JOHN TO M. P. ALEXANDER 11-3-1853
TUTTLE, MARTHA TO WILLIAM T. RIGSBY
TYREE, WILLIAM H. TO MISS ANGIE BATTON 11-19-1869 (11-24-1869)
UNDERHILL, A. E. TO NANCY HUTCHERSON 8-24-1865 (8-27-1865)
UNDERHILL, G. W. TO L. L. RIGSBY 2-22-1873 (2-26-1873
UNDERHILL, GEORGE W. TO MISS AMANDA T. FORD 6-13-1868 (6-14-1868)
UNDERWOOD, BENJ. TO MARY THOMAS 12-2-1872 (12-6-1872)
UNDERWOOD, E. D. TO SERGE D. ROBINSON
UNDERWOOD, ELIZABETH TO MARTIN UNDERWOOD
UNDERWOOD, JACOB TO POLLY MCBRIDE 6-8-1840
UNDERWOOD, JAMES TO MISS MALISA RATLY 10-1-1853 (10-2-1853)
UNDERWOOD, JOSEPH TO R. C. ISAM 8-27-1860 (8-29-1860)
UNDERWOOD, MARK L. TO MISS MARTHA WORLEY 7-23-1868 (7-26-1868)
UNDERWOOD, MARTIN TO ELIZABETH UNDERWOOD 9-19-1865
UNDERWOOD, MARY TO ARTHUR WORLEY
UNDERWOOD, MARY TO DAVID LAMBERT
UNDERWOOD, NANCY C. TO GORGE W. SOAP
UNDERWOOD, RENIAH? TO DREW RICHERSON
UNDERWOOD, THOMAS TO MARY HERRAL 12-27-1853 (12-28-1853)
UNDERWOOD, WOODSON TO NANCY THOMPSON 3-23-1865 (NO RETURN)
URSERY, SARRAH TO J. M. YOUNG
USSELTON, ELIZABETH TO JOHN HORN
VALENTINE, MARY TO J. W. BARRETT
VANCE, ANDERSON TO SARAH TENPENNY 1-27-1870
VANCE, CATHARINE TO WM. H. TRAVIS
VANCE, D. B. TO MISS BETTIE BREWER 11-22-1868 (11-23-1868)
VANCE, DANIEL TO MISS MARTHA REED 12-3-1857
VANCE, DAVID TO LIZA E. MORGAN 8-4-1864
VANCE, E. R. TO G. W. GARMAN
VANCE, ELIZA J. TO J. T. MASON
VANCE, ELIZA TO ALFRED VASSER
VANCE, ISHAM TO MISS SARAH MOORE 5-29-1866
VANCE, JAMES TO MISS ELIZABETH SUMMAR 2-8-1866
VANCE, KATHARINE TO JESSE RICHARDS
VANCE, RICHARD TO ELISAR PEEDON 1-6-1863
VANCE, SAMUEL TO MISS SARAH ANN ELLEDGE 11-13-1841 (11-14-1841)

VANCE, SARAH TO R. O. WALCUP
VANCE, THOMAS TO MISS MAHALA ARMSTRONG 2-14-1867
VANDAGRIFF, CHRISTOPHER TO ELIZA VIARS 1-19-1842 (1-2-1843)
VANDAGRIFF, JOHN TO MISS JANE MCGEE 4-28-1854 (NO RETURN)
VANDAGRIFF, MARY A. TO JOSEPH SPURLOCK
VANDAGRIFF, MARY JANE TO M. G. ELKINS
VANDAGRIFF, NANCY TO THOMAS J. WILLIAMS
VANDAGRIFF, RICHARD TO MISS MALINDA FRANCIS 12-22-1858
VANDAGRIFF, WILLIAM TO LUCINDA WILLIAMS 1-12-1843
VANDAGRIFFE, MARY TO CHARLES W. HOLLINSWORTH
VANDAGRIPH, LUCINDA TO PINKNEY JONES
VANDEGRIFF, MELVINA TO THOMAS J. WILLIAMS
VANDERGRIFF, ALEXANDER TO ALAMENTA KING 3-20-1838 (3-27-1838)
VANDERGRIFF, M. J. TO A. L. HANCOCK
VANDERGRIFF, MARION TO MISS SUSAN CAMPBELL 7-16-1859 (NO RETURN)
VANDERGRIFF, W. J. TO RHODA CAMPBELL 11-23-1865
VANDERGRIFF, WILLIAM TO PHEBE DILLIAN 12-13-1838
VANE, MARY A. TO MATHEW J. BRANDON
VANE, SARRAH S. TO ISAAC TERNER
VANHOOZER, W. J. TO MISS M. J. GILLEY 2-7-1870 (2-8-1870)
VARDEL, JOHN T. TO LOUISA SUMNAR 9-18-1863 (NO RETURN)
VARDELLE, MARY TO LEVI TODD
VASSER, ALFORD TO MISS MARY J. TENPENNY 3-4-1871
VASSER, ALFRED TO MISS ELIZA VANCE 7-29-1868
VASSER, ANNEY TO BRAZELL BORREN
VASSER, CASWELL TO MISS MARY JANE WEST 9-3-1850 (9-30-1850)
VASSER, CYNTHIA TO JAMES C. MILLIGAN
VASSER, CYNTHIA TO ROBERT PATRICK
VASSER, ELIZABETH J. TO A. J. YOUNGBLOOD
VASSER, JAMES TO MISS SARAH JANE MAGLOCKLIN 10-17-1849 (NO RETURN)
VASSER, JOSHUA JR. TO MISS SALLY SUMMAR 10-3-1844 (9?-3-1844)
VASSER, JOSHUA TO MISS SALLY ANN MURFREY 6-3-1847 (NO RETURN)
VASSER, W. J. TO MISS NANCY A. E. FREEMAN 3-6-1871 (3-7-1871)
VASSER, WILLIAM TO MISS LUCINDA ----- 5-3-1852 (5-4-1852)
VASSER, WILLIAM TO MISS MARIAH ARNOLD 11-29-1854 (11-30-1854)
VAUGHAN, H. C. TO F. E. ODOM 1-30-1864 (NO RETURN)
VAUGHAN, J. C. TO MISS L. B. WHERRY 12-18-1853 (12-19-1853)
VAUGHAN, SALLIE ANN TO JOHN STARR
VAUGHAN, THOMAS TO MAHALA MULLINS 4-28-1842
VAUGHN, G. W. TO H. M. OSBORN 5-5-1860 (5-9-1860)
VAUGHN, JUDIE TO JOHN PEOPLES
VAUGHN, MARTHA TO PINKNEY ARNETT
VAUGHN, THOMAS TO MISS CATHARINE MERRITT 12-2-1868
VERNON, ELIAS TO CHARLOTTE STAFFORD 10-16-1868
VIARS, ELIZA TO CHRISTOPHER VANDAGRIFF
VICKERS, R. L. TO MISS M. J. BERRYHILL 8-3-1871 (8-4-1871)
VICKERS, WILLIAM TO MISS MARY LAVISA SUMMAR 7-27-1869 (NO RETURN)
VINSON, BENJAMIN TO MISS SARAH A. NEELY 3-15-1854
VINSON, BENJAMIN TO SARAH MCNEELY 3-15-1854
VINSON, BETTIE TO JOHN HOLLANDSWORTH
VINSON, D. B. TO LIZZIE HOLLANDSWORTH 6-13-1872
VINSON, HENRIETTA W. TO W. R. TALLEY
VINSON, JAMES TO FRANCES MARKUM 9-19-1872
VINSON, LUIZA TO MARLING YONG
VINSON, MARY TO NATHAN BARRETT
VINSON, ROBERT TO MISS FRANCES L. BARRETT 12-2-1869
VINSON, SARAH M. TO DANIEL A. NICHOLS
VINSON, SARAH TO JOHN W. BARRETT
VINSON, THOMAS J. TO MISS MARTHA J. RIGSBY 10-16-1869 (NO RETURN)
VINSON, THOMAS TO M. J. RIGSBY 1-21-1872

VINSON, URSULA ANN TO SAMUEL BOWEN
VOSSER?, WM. TO MISS LUCINDA JONRAN 5-3-1852 (5-4-1852)
WADE, ELIZABETH TO PETER F. FRANKLIN
WADE, WILLIAM TO SARRAH JANE ROBERTS 7-14-1855 (RETURNS MISSING)
WADE, WM. TO MISS MARTHA ANN JONES 2-5-1855 (6-5-1855)
WALCUP, R. O. TO SARAH VANCE (NO DATES--WITH SUMMER 1860 ENTRIES)
WALDON, R. E. TO A. BONN
WALE, CELISA JANE TO H. B. HALL
WALE, J. H. TO JANE BLANTON 5-29-1860
WALE, J. H. TO L. H. MCWHEARTER 11-23-1872 (11-24-1872)
WALKER, J. R. TO SARAH G. MORGAN 9-1-1865 (9-3-1865)
WALKER, JEREMIAH C. TO MISS JUDAH F. GILLEY 8-5-1844 (8-25-1844)
WALKER, LEONARD TO NANCY M. ADAMSON 9-12-1842 (NO RETURN)
WALKER, SARAH C. TO ROBERT M. STEWART
WALKER, W. W. TO MISS L. G. WOOD 3-30-1866 (NO RETURN)
WALKER, W. W. TO MISS L. G. WOOD 3-30-1866 (4-1-1866)
WALKUP, A. O. TO MISS MINTY SULLIVAN 10-9-1855
WALKUP, E. N. TO MISS MARGARETT HIGGINS 12-27-1852 (12-25-1852) (SIC)
WALKUP, EMILY E. TO D. L. ELKINS
WALKUP, J. A. TO MISS M. A. TENNYSON 1-5-1859 (1-6-1859)
WALKUP, J. R. TO TIENDOLPHUS PEAY
WALKUP, J. W. TO M. A. YOUNG 10-9-1872 (NO RETURN)
WALKUP, M. F. TO S. M. YOURIE
WALKUP, MARTHA E. TO GEORGE G. MELTON
WALKUP, MARY J. TO JOEL D. MELTON
WALKUP, ROCINDA TO J. H. PERRY
WALKUP, WILLIAM TO MARYANN HOLLIS 9-8-1838 (9-9-1838)
WALKUP, WM. J. TO MISS INTHY ADALINE NICHOLS 8-23-1853 (8-24-1853)
WALLACE, A. M. TO S. C. WALLACE 10-27-1857
WALLACE, JAMES TO MARTHA COGWELL 7-21-1840
WALLACE, S. C. TO A. M. WALLACE
WALLACE, WILBURN H. TO MARY L. SMITH 10-2-1872 (10-3-1872)
WALLACE, WILLIAM TO MISS MILLIA WILLIAMS 3-28-1870 (NO RETURN)
WALLIS, S. R. TO S. A. WARREN
WALLS, CAROLINE TO JAMES G. CONLY
WALLS, DANIEL TO ELIZABETH CONNELLY 12-6-1849
WALLS, DANIEL TO MISS DOVY CINLY 11-12-1859 (NO RETURN)
WALLS, DOVEY TO PATTON FARLEY
WALLS, ELIZABETH TO HENRY PARTON
WALLS, HENRY M. T. TO MISS SARAH PRESTON 4-6-1848
WALLS, MARTHA TO WILLIS F. COUCH
WALLS, POLLY TO ELI PRESTON
WALTON, HENRY TO MISS E. WOODARD 11-9-1870 (11-10-1870)
WAMACH, ROBERT TO MISS NANCY M. SEAT 2-10-1853
WAMACK, AMANDA J. TO ELIGAH C. HIGGINS
WAMACK, BETHENA TO JOHN F. MITCHELL
WAMACK, J. S. TO MISS E. E. BOGLE 10-29-1857 (NO RETURN)
WAMACK, NANCY M. TO W. R. BOGLE
WAMACK, PATSEY TO EMMERSON SEWELL
WAMMACK, THOMAS TO LYDIA A. REED 7-10-1865 (7-12-1865)
WARD, CAROLINE TO J. G. ALEXANDER
WARD, JAMES E. TO MISS MARY L. ST. JOHN 8-2-1849 (8-3-1849)
WARD, M. S. TO MISS SARAH E. HODGES 8-17-1859
WARD, MILTON TO NANCY PATTERSON 12-24-1838 (NO RETURN)
WARD, NANCY A. TO JOSEPH H. BARRETT
WARE, SALLIE TO W. T. H. WHARTON
WARNACK, D. D. TO MARY M. TEDFORD 12-12-1865 (12-13-1865)
WARREN, ALEXANDER TO MISS NANCY ANN BARKLEY 1-6-1851 (1-7-1851)
WARREN, ARTHUR TO REBECCAH SULLIVAN 9-5-1839 (NO RETURN)
WARREN, BENJAMIN TO MISS MARRY CURDON 12-14-1852

WARREN, ELIZABETH A. TO BENJAMIN P. PRATOR
WARREN, ELVIRA TO ISAAC P. BLAIR
WARREN, J. W. TO MISS L. HALE 2-9-1856 (2-10-1856)
WARREN, JOHN TO MISS MARY E. BENSON 12-26-1846 (12-27-1846)
WARREN, M. V. TO WILLIAM J. PHILLIPS
WARREN, MARGARETTE ANN TO JOHN B. JUSTICE
WARREN, MARTHA TO RICHARD HANCOCK
WARREN, MARY FRANCES TO PRESTLY L. ADAMSON
WARREN, MARY TO B. H. HOLDER
WARREN, REBECCA J. TO SAMUL COOK
WARREN, S. A. TO S. R. WALLIS 3-13-1857 (3-15-1857)
WARREN, S. J. TO H. D. SINGLETON
WARREN, SARAHFINE TO JOHN MELTON
WARREN, SUSAN TO J. C. SUMMAR
WARREN, W. H. TO MISS SARRAH J. HERRALD 2-4-1857 (2-5-1857)
WARREN, ZACHARIAH TO MISS MARY TRAVERS 12-30-1843 (1-1-1844)
WARRICK, J. W. TO MISS LAVISA J. LYNN 8-20-1870 (NO RETURN)
WARRICK, JESSEE TO MRS. C. A. TURNER 10-2?-1870 (10-27-1870)
WATERS, CRAVIN TO MISS NANCY J. FARLEY 12-22-1870 (12-23-1870)
WATERS, DELITHA TO BENJAMIN FAULKENBERG
WATERS, EDWARD TO MISS TABITHA FARLER 8-3-1867 (8-4-1867)
WATERS, HENRY TO MISS CLEMENTINE HAILEY 2-27-1867 (SOLEMNIZED, DATE NOT FILLED IN)
WATKINS, EMANUEL TO MISS RACHAEL HARP 8-17-1843
WATSON, A. C. TO JOHN A. J. BROWN
WATSON, F. E. TO ALICE JUSTICE 12-30-1873
WATSON, G. M. D. TO MISS SARAH ELIZABETH WOODSIDE 7-29-1867 (7-30-1867)
WATSON, GENEVA TO C. A. COX
WATSON, JAMES N. TO MISS REBECCA MCALEXANDER 2-3-1848 (2-9-1848)
WATSON, JAMES TO M. E. WATSON 4-6-1869
WATSON, JOHN TO MARY WILSHER 10-31-1872 (NO RETURN)
WATSON, JONES TO MARY PATTON 9-25-1838 (9-26-1838)
WATSON, M. E. TO JAMES WATSON
WATSON, NANCY A. TO J. W. BULLEN
WATSON, NANCY A. TO J. W. BUTTER
WATSON, P. E. TO L. W. RIDENER
WATTERS, R. J. TO ROBERT R. MEARS
WATTS, MARY TO WILLIAM E. WITHERSPOON
WATTS, MILTON E. TO P. C. PORTERFIELD 8-31-1842 (9-1-1842)
WATTS, REBECCA E. TO WM. T. HILL
WEATHERFORD, S. M. TO P. H. PITTERED
WEATHERLY, JESSE TO NANCY MCKNIGHT 11-9-1867 (11-14-1867)
WEATHERSPOON, MARGT. ELIZA TO JOHN REYNOLDS
WEBB, ALSA TO MARY E. HIGGINS 9-25-1872 (9-29-1872)
WEBB, IBBIA TO JOSEPH SPURLOCK
WEBB, MAHALEY A. TO PATTRICK H. WEBB
WEBB, MARY E. TO L. B. MCFERIN
WEBB, PARLEE TO ISAAC WOOD
WEBB, PATTRICK H. TO MAHALEY A. WEBB 8-28-1865
WEBB, S. W. TO LAURA? SATINE 12-25-1851
WEBB, SAMANTHA TO JOHN BLEW
WEBB, SAMUEL TO MARTHA TAYLOR 9-2-1865 (9-4-1865)
WEBBER, BENJAMIN TO MARY ASHLEY 2-1-1864 (NO RETURN)
WEBBER, ELIZABETH TO RICHARD P. JOHNSON
WEBBER, ELIZABETH TO WILLIAM GRAY
WEBBER, F. M. TO FRANCES BRIANT 7-31-1865 (8-5-1865)
WEBBER, JANE ADALINE TO WILLIAM A. JAMISON
WEBBER, JANE TO LORENZO D. PARKER
WEBBER, JOHN A. TO MISS EFFA FINLEY 2-20-1846 (2-22-1846)
WEBBER, JOHN TO CINTHY SIMPSON 10-28-1852 (RETURN CROSSED OUT)
WEBBER, MARTHA L. TO WM. BYNUM

WEBBER, MARY TO JOHN RAINS
WEBBER, PHILLIP TO MISS ELISABETH WORLIEN? 2-14-1852 (NO RETURN)
WEBBER, POLLEY TO W. D. CAMPBELL
WEBBER, REBECCA TO THOMAS SISSOM
WEBBER, SARAH TO WILLIAM SISSOM
WEBBER, TENNESSEE P. TO JOSEPH H. WILLIAMS
WEEDAN, TENNESSEE E. TO A. N. FISHER
WEEDON, A. M. TO MISS SARAH STONE 4-11-1848 (NO RETURN)
WEEDON, A. M. TO PAULINA J. P. MATHEWS 3-27-1843 (3-30-1843)
WEEDON, DANIEL TO MARIAH S. RUCKER 6-6-1839 (NO RETURN)
WEEDON, J. P. TO W. J. WOOD
WEEDON, JO TO W. R. CAMPBELL
WEEDON, JOHN F. TO MARY JANE FERRELL 1-31-1843
WEEDON, JOHN F. TO MISS ELIZA ANN FERRELL 11-12-1849 (11-13-1849)
WEEDON, JOHN TO JULIA JETTON 10-8-1868 (11-22-1868)
WEEDON, JOHN TO JULIA JETTON 3-26-1867 (NO RETURN)
WEEDON, MARTHA E. TO JESSE BREWER
WEEDON, SALLIE M. TO M. D. SMITH
WEEDON, WESLEY TO VINA DEMENT 8-12-1872
WELCH, M. E. TO B. F. BARRET
WELLS, JOHN TO MRS. SARAH P. BROWN 4-11-1843
WEST, A. W. TO EMILY HARRIS 10-7-1863
WEST, A. W. TO MARTHA M. BRISON 6-26-1860 (NO RETURN)
WEST, BENJAMIN W. TO MISS ELEANOR TEDDER 9-28-1840 (9-29-1840)
WEST, CHARLES TO MISS MELINDA PENDLETON 10-7-1848
WEST, HENRY H. TO MISS ELISABETH CRAFT 6-29-1860 (7-1-1860)
WEST, JOHN A. TO RACHIEL COOPER 11-8-1860 (NO RETURN)
WEST, JOURDEN TO MISS PARALEE DAVIS 8-9-1858 (8-11-1858)
WEST, LUCINDA TO JOHN PENDLETON
WEST, MALINDA TO ALEX FINLY
WEST, MALISSA J. TO WILLIAM G. CARMICHAEL
WEST, MANERVA ANN TO SAMUEL B. ALLEN
WEST, MARY JANE TO CASWELL VASSER
WEST, NANCY E. TO J. W. LEWIS
WEST, S. A. TO J. H. YOUNGBLOOD
WEST, SALLY TO WILLIAM BRYSON
WEST, T. F. TO AMANDY PITMAN 6-10-1872
WEST, Z. A. TO W. J. STORY
WHARREY, LOUISA LAMIRA TO JONATHAN HALL
WHARRY, CYNTHA JANE TO JAMES W. TRAVIS
WHARRY, MALVINA ANN TO WILLIAM W. MCCULLOUGH
WHARTON, ELIZABETH R. TO JAMES TAYLOR
WHARTON, J. H. TO MISS M. H. WHEELER 2-1-1866
WHARTON, W. T. H. TO SALLIE WARE 3-28-1860 (3-29-1860)
WHEELER, ALICE S. TO J. W. CAMPBELL
WHEELER, EDNEY TO T. N. GRAHAM
WHEELER, M. H. TO J. H. WHARTON
WHEELER, N. T. TO MISS MARY BAIRD 11-10-1870
WHEELING, BENNETT TO MISS ELIZABETH BARRETT 12-19-1849 (12-20-1849)
WHEELING, JAMES M. TO ELIZABETH FRY 8-18-1852 (8-19-1852)
WHERRY, FRANCES E. TO JOHN C. MEARS
WHERRY, L. B. TO J. C. VAUGHAN
WHERRY, MARGARETT TO PRESTON HALL
WHIT, MISS MARTHA ANNE TO ANDREW J. COLWELL
WHITAMORE, ABAGALE TO JAMES ROSS
WHITAMORE, JESSE G. TO MISS ABIGAIL SPANGLER 12-21-1843 (12-24-1843)
WHITAMORE, TABITHA TO SAMUEL SPANGLER
WHITAMORE, WILLIAM TO MISS MARY ANN DUNCAN 1-10-1851 (1-12-1851)
WHITE, MALINDA T. TO THOMAS PEARSON
WHITE, W. J. TO MISS JOSAPHINE STONE 1-28-1851 (NO RETURN)

WHITEFIELD, M. C. TO WM. RING
WHITELEY, SARAH TO JAMES PEDEN
WHITFIELD, ELIZABETH A. TO W. E. WHITFIELD
WHITFIELD, HALY TO CARY JARNAGIN
WHITFIELD, MARRY ANN TO JACKSON ROTTY
WHITFIELD, MARY J. TO L. W. JERNIGAN
WHITFIELD, MATHEW TO MISS SARAH WHITFIELD 12-9-1851
WHITFIELD, SARAH ANN TO W. T. ST. JOHN
WHITFIELD, SARAH TO MATHEW WHITFIELD
WHITFIELD, W. E. TO ELIZABETH A. WHITFIELD 2-23-1854
WHITLOCK, E. B. TO MISS NANCY WILLSON 8-24-1852 (RETURNS MISSING)
WHITLOCK, JOHN TO SARAH BRAGG 10-24-1850
WHITT, BENJAMIN TO MISS SARAH YONG 8-10-1853
WHITT, E. M. TO MISS MARY MORE 7-6-1859 (NO RETURN)
WHITT, FELIX TO MISS ELIZABETH E. MORGAN 8-20-1846
WHITT, JONATHAN TO MISS NANCY COLWELL 8-4-1843
WHITT, MARYANN TO VINCENT MEDDOWS
WHITT, SARAH JANE TO JOHN MORRETT
WHITT, SERVELLA TO WILLIAM MERRITT
WHITTAMORE, NEWTON T. TO MISS MATILDA? BUSH 2-23-1866 (2-25-1866)
WHITTEMORE, SIMEON TO LOUISA F. HAYES 2-2-1860 (NO RETURN)
WHITTEMORE, WILLIAM B. TO MISS NANCY FINLEY 9-22-1866 (9-23-1866)
WHITTER, SAMUEL? TO MISS POLLY MAXEY 12-13-1869
WHORTON, THOMAS TO MISS ELIZABETH J. FERRELL 8-24-1870 (8-25-1870)
WHORTON, W. T. H. TO MISS B. L. KENNADY 1-24-1857 (NO RETURN)
WILCHER, DELILA E. TO JOHN E. BOGLE
WILCHER, J. A. TO MISS ELIZABETH C. CARTER 2-15-1868 (2-18-1868)
WILCHER, WM. B. TO MISS BUENAVISTA STONE 9-23-1869 (NO RETURN)
WILDMAN, WILLIAM TO MISS NANCY STARR 1-1-1847 (NO RETURN)
WILERFORD, JOHN TO FRANCES C. ELAM 7-28-1873 (7-31-1873)
WILEY, FRANCES ANN TO J. A. BAIRD
WILKERSON, MARTHA M. TO JOHN A. REYNOLDS
WILLARD, BEVERLY TO ADALINE SMITH 4-15-1863 (NO RETURN)
WILLARD, D. B. TO MISS MALISSA FRANCIS 1-23-1869 (1-24-1869)
WILLARD, FRANCIS TO MISA SUMARS 4-3-1865 (4-5-1865)
WILLARD, J. A. TO MISS HANAH J. ODOM 11-5-1857 (NO RETURN)
WILLARD, JOHN A. TO NANCY ODOM 11-21-1863 (11-22-1863)
WILLARD, M. A. TO ELIZABETH SUMMER 8-21-1864 (NO RETURN)
WILLARD, M. W. TO D. T. ODOM 11-16-1871 (11-19-1871)
WILLARD, MARTHA ELIZABETH TO WILLIAM READY
WILLARD, WILLIAM TO TELITHA SUMNAR 9-19-1842 (NO RETURN)
WILLARD, WM. B. TO L. A. ODOM 2-12-1864 (2-17-1864)
WILLIAM, DAVID TO REBECA FINLY 11-11-1851
WILLIAM, R. M. TO MISS FRANCES A. TAYLOR 9-15-1855 (RETURNS MISSING)
WILLIAMS, ANNIE TO J. W. MATHEWS
WILLIAMS, BENJAMIN TO RODA S. MCCULLOUGH 9-4-1865 (9-7-1865)
WILLIAMS, BERRY TO MISS CYRENA A. LEONARD 11-18-1847
WILLIAMS, C. H. TO MISS ELISABETH STACY 4-18-1857 (4-17?-1857)
WILLIAMS, DAVID TO MARY A. BROWN 9-21-1872 (9-22-1872)
WILLIAMS, DENNIS TO H. A. SPRY11-19-1873 (11-20-1873)
WILLIAMS, ELIZABETH TO NOAH DEAN
WILLIAMS, FRANCES TO L. P. BUSH
WILLIAMS, HARVEY T. TO MISS MARY C. HOLLIS 11-14-1848 (11-15-1848)
WILLIAMS, ISAAC TO MISS NANCY HAMLET 12-11-1851 (NO RETURN)
WILLIAMS, J. B. TO MISS MARY C. BYNUM 12-1-1868 (12-2-1868)
WILLIAMS, J. M. TO MISS A. A. DODD 10-22-1857
WILLIAMS, JAMES TO ELIZABETH ANN PETTY 1-30-1845 (NO RETURN)
WILLIAMS, JERUSHA TO JOHN W. HALEY
WILLIAMS, JESSE TO POLLY DUNCAN 9-22-1840
WILLIAMS, JOHN A. TO MISS JULIA ANN MULLINS 12-13-1849

WILLIAMS, JOHN B. TO MISS E. J. KERKLIN 11-23-1857
WILLIAMS, JOHN TO MISS ISABELA SMITH 12-1-1858
WILLIAMS, JOHN TO MISS TELITHA F. KUYKENDALL 2-21-1866 (2-23-1866)
WILLIAMS, JOSEPH H. TO MISS TENNESSEE P. WEBBER 12-2-1867 (12-10-1867)
WILLIAMS, JOSEPH O. TO MARTHA J. BARRATT 2-18-1865 (2-19-1865)
WILLIAMS, JOSEPH TO MARTHA N. SUMMERS 5-2-1855 (5-6-1855)
WILLIAMS, JOSHUA TO MISS JANE BATSON 3-30-1847 (3-31-1847)
WILLIAMS, JULIE A. TO WM. BROOKS
WILLIAMS, L. W. TO MARTHA RUSHING 6-13-1872
WILLIAMS, LUCINDA TO WILLIAM VANDAGRIFF
WILLIAMS, LURANEY TO JACOB A. KING
WILLIAMS, M. E. TO W. N. MARE
WILLIAMS, MARTHA C. TO H. N. HOLT
WILLIAMS, MARTHA TO ALBERT WOODS
WILLIAMS, MARY T. TO P. M. SIMPSON
WILLIAMS, MILLIA TO WILLIAM WALLACE
WILLIAMS, MILLY TO LATEN EWEL
WILLIAMS, NANCY E. TO J. R. REED
WILLIAMS, R. H. TO MISS CLARINDA MATHIS 9-8-1866 (9-11-1866)
WILLIAMS, ROXANNA TO WILLIAM THOMAS
WILLIAMS, SARAH TO MARTIN KING
WILLIAMS, SARAH TO THOMAS PARKER
WILLIAMS, SUSAN TO JOHN HERIMAN
WILLIAMS, THOMAS H. TO NANCY E. GRAY 10-13-1838 (10-18-1838)
WILLIAMS, THOMAS J. TO MISS MELVINA VANDEGRIFF 7-29-1869
WILLIAMS, THOMAS J. TO MISS NANCY VANDAGRIFF 1-3-1849 (1-4-1849)
WILLIAMS, THOS. TO ISABELLA SPRY 10-15-1872 (10-29-1872)
WILLIAMS, W. C. TO MARY HARRIS 1-10-1872
WILLIAMS, W. J. TO JEMIMA E. GRAY 12-1-1865 (12-2-1865)
WILLIAMS, WASHINGTON TO MISS SARAH MESSICK 6-10-1848 (6-11-1848)
WILLIRD, D. L. TO B. D. DAVENPORT
WILLIS, TEMPERANCE TO R. W. WOODRUFFE
WILLSEN, ANDREW TO MISS ELIZABETH ANN COOK 3-29-1855
WILLSON, B. TO J. M. BOGLE
WILLSON, ELIZABETH TO R. HALL
WILLSON, G. W. TO SARAH BARTHEN? 11-19-1852
WILLSON, LUCY TO JOHN F. BOGLE
WILLSON, LUSEY TO JOSIAH F. BOGLE
WILLSON, M. E. TO WILLIAM DEVANPORT
WILLSON, NANCY TO E. B. WHITLOCK
WILLSON, S. S. TO A. H. DEVANPORT
WILLSON, SARAH J. TO JACOB L. SUMMER
WILLSON, W. A. TO MISS MARTHA BARETT 11-10-1857 (11-11-1857)
WILMOTH, EASTER TO MADISON MERITT
WILSHER, CHARLES M. TO MISS MARY N. COX 8-25-1841 (8-26-1841)
WILSHER, MARY TO JOHN WATSON
WILSHER, WILLIAM TO EMALINE GILLEY 12-23-1846 (12-24-1846)
WILSHER, WILLIAM TO MISS NANCY J. CLOSE 5-15-1841 (5-16-1841)
WILSON, A. F. TO MISS LAVISA J. SMITHSON 2-20-1866 (NO RETURN)
WILSON, BENJAMIN JR. TO MISS THURSEY A. SEAL 1-19-1867 (1-22-1867)
WILSON, G. M. TO J. N. M. PITMAN
WILSON, H. B. TO SENA YOUNG 9-26-1863 (10-1-1863)
WILSON, H. W. TO MARY J. PELHAM 9-12-1872
WILSON, HIRAM TO MISS MARTHA CAROLINE MOON 8-10-1841 (8-15-1841)
WILSON, JAMES W. TO MISS MARTHA FRANCIS 12-5-1850 (NO RETURN)
WILSON, JEMIMA TO NATHAN GANN
WILSON, JOHN TO MISS MARY ANN ELAM 5-25-1866
WILSON, JOHN TO MISS MARY LEIGH 2-23-1850 (2-24-1850)
WILSON, L. D. H. TO MISS SARAH MUNCY 11-19-1869 (11-21-1869)
WILSON, LAURA A. TO A. J. BRANDON

WILSON, LUCIND TO W. H. SUMNAR
WILSON, M. L. TO E. D. BRYSON
WILSON, M. V. TO MARY ODOM 5-13-1863
WILSON, MARTHA TO WM. FANN
WILSON, MARY J. TO T. M. TODD
WILSON, MARY J. TO W. J. STACY
WILSON, MARY TO HENRY SCOTT
WILSON, MICHAEL TO MARTHA BRYSON 10-16-1838
WILSON, S. A. TO ALVIS BASSHAM
WILSON, SARAH E. TO CALVIN T. WINNETT
WILSON, STEPHEN TO BARTHENA BOND 10-16-1872 (10-20-1872)
WILSON, WALTER TO MARGARETT TODD 11-3-1842
WILSON, WALTER TO MISS FRANCES CRAFT 5-2-1870 (5-3-1870)
WILSON, WILLIAM TO MISS TEMPERANCE WOMACK 6-8-1848
WILY, H. A. TO MISS MARY E. SHOELFORD 8-14-1855 (RETURNS MISSING)
WIMBERLEY, ELIZABETH TO JAMES N. THOMAS
WIMBERLEY, G. W. TO ELIZABETH N. STACY 11-30-1869 (12-1-1869)
WIMBERLEY, MARGARETT TO NELSON Z? THOMAS
WIMBERLEY, MARTHA TO JOHN R. BROOKS
WIMBERLEY, POLLY TO JOHN PATTON
WIMBERLY, ELIZABETH TO PRESLEY MERRETT
WIMBERLY, J. C. TO JANE BURCH 3-10-1865
WIMBERLY, J. E. TO MISS MARTHA ANN GOFF 3-5-1868 (3-8-1868)
WIMBERLY, JONATHAN TO MARTHA BINEM 7-14-1860 (7-15-1860)
WIMBERLY, JULIAN TO G. R. LORANCE
WIMBERLY, MARRY TO JACKSON MERRITT
WIMBERLY, P. A. TO WM. B. HAWKINS
WIMBLEY, ELIZABETH TO JACOB ROBINSON
WIMBY, CAROLINE TO ROBERT GOODING
WINAHAM, ELIZABETH TO WILLIAM BOWERS
WINNETT, CALVIN T. TO MISS SARAH E. WILSON 3-20-1868 (3-21-1868)
WINNETT, CHARLOTTE TO JESSEE FOWLER
WINNETT, ELEANOR TO REZEN F. THOMAS
WINNETT, JAMES TO MISS SARAH TODD 12-21-1867 (12-22-1867)
WINNETT, NORMAN TO SUSAN TAIT 4-29-1858
WINNETT, R. J. TO WM. W. LORANCE
WINNETT, R. M. TO J. K. P. WOODS
WINNETT, SARAH E. TO JOHN S. DEVENPORT
WISER, JULIAN J. TO JAMES M. BANKSTON
WISER, WILLIAM TO MISS VIOLET PARKER 11-27-1843 (11-30-1843)
WITHERSPOON, D. TO MISS L. F. MCADOW 10-18-1853
WITHERSPOON, JOHN K. TO MISS MARGARETT A. ALEXANDER 11-21-1848 (NO RETURN)
WITHERSPOON, LEWIS? E. W. TO MISS AMANDA ROBINSON 10-29-1850
WITHERSPOON, LOUIS F. W. TO SARAH E. HARRIS 8-6-1840 (NO RETURN)
WITHERSPOON, MARY M. TO EVERT SUMMAR
WITHERSPOON, MARY S. TO WILLIAM REYNOLDS
WITHERSPOON, SEPTIMA F. TO LEONADES F. PORTERFIELD
WITHERSPOON, THURZA EMALINE TO SHANNON MCKNIGHT
WITHERSPOON, WILLIAM E. TO MISS MARY WATTS 5-21-1846
WITT, MARTIN M. TO MISS MANERVA J. BROWN 7-30-1849
WITTY, W. W. TO M. J. SHERLEY 4-22-1873
WOMACK, ABRAM TO ELIZABETH WOOD 9-10-1845 (9-11-1845)
WOMACK, BERY TO MISS BETHANY MILLER 12-26-1850 (1-19-1851)
WOMACK, J. A. N. TO P. P. WOMACK 7-12-1873
WOMACK, JAMES JASPER TO MISS JULY ANN PARKER 8-15-1850
WOMACK, JOHN N. TO JULY ANN D. SCOTT 4-6-1850 (4-7-1850)
WOMACK, LUCINDA TO RICHMOND SULLENS
WOMACK, M. A. A. TO JOHN F. BRANDON
WOMACK, MARTHA TO MUNRO BRAMATT
WOMACK, MARY E. TO T. J. DAVIS

WOMACK, P. P. TO J. A. N. WOMACK
WOMACK, TEMPERANCE TO WILLIAM WILSON
WOMACK, THOMAS J. TO MISS A. R. COLLINS 9-14-1870 (9-15-1870)
WOMACK, WILLIAM TO MISS ELEANOR ROEMINES 4-9-1847 (4-11-1847)
WOMBERLY, MARTHA J. TO CHARLES LEE
WOMMACS, MATILDA TO HOWEL MORE
WOOD, ANDREW J. TO MISS ELIZA J. PRATOR 9-25-1867 (9-26-1867)
WOOD, ANN TO BENJ. STEPHENS
WOOD, B. F. TO MISS MARY A. BAILY 11-3-1857 (11-5-1857)
WOOD, E. J. TO MISS ELIZABETH A. THOMPSON 9-7-1854
WOOD, ELIZABETH TO ABRAM WOMACK
WOOD, ELIZABETH TO JAMES MERRITT
WOOD, FANNIE TO GEORGE NEWBY
WOOD, ISAAC TO PARLEE WEBB 8-28-1865
WOOD, JAMES H. TO MISS CAROLINE SMITH 8-30-1852 (9-2-1852)
WOOD, JERRY TO JUDIE DAULES? 11-6-1873
WOOD, JESSEE TO LUCY WRIGHT 8-22-1865 (9-3-1865)
WOOD, JOHN A. TO MISS SARAH T. SANDERS 2-21-1856 (2-22-1856)
WOOD, JOSEPHINE TO SAML. FUGITT (COL)
WOOD, L. G. TO W. W. WALKER
WOOD, M. A. TO P. D. BATTON
WOOD, MARGARETT TO DANIEL GRIZZLE
WOOD, MARTHA H. TO M. E. ST. JOHN
WOOD, MARY E. TO GEO. M. SPEARS
WOOD, MARY S. TO WILLIAM MEARS
WOOD, MATTIE J. TO J. H. FREEMAN
WOOD, N. C. C. TO CAROLINE PHILLIPS 8-10-1872
WOOD, NANCY ANN TO JOHN COCK
WOOD, NANCY ANN TO WILLIAM F. ELLEDGE
WOOD, PARLEE TO PEYTON POWEL
WOOD, SARAH TO IRA HOLLANDSWORTH
WOOD, SARAH TO LEONARD ADCOCK
WOOD, TENNIE TO J. A. MCFERRIN
WOOD, THOS. O. TO MARTHA L. ALEXANDER 4-19-1864
WOOD, VIOLET TO WASHINGTON WOOD
WOOD, W. J. TO J. P. WEEDON 5-24-1860
WOOD, WASHINGTON TO VIOLET WOOD 6-11-1872
WOOD, WILLIAM T. TO MISS MARY COVINGTON 10-8-1866 (10-9-1866)
WOODALL, SARAH T. TO JAMES M. HERNDO
WOODALL, WILLIAM C. TO MISS DELIA OLIVER 2-21-1848
WOODARD, E. TO HENRY WALTON
WOODERAL, GEORGE W. TO NANCY TAYLOR 7-17-1838
WOODLEY, CLASSIE TO GEORGE WOODS
WOODROFF, WM. TO MERRY JANE MARLIN? 11-22-1851 (NO RETURN)
WOODRUFFE, R. W. TO MISS TEMPERANCE WILLIS 9-25-1843
WOODS, ALBERT TO MARTHA WILLIAMS 8-21-1865 (8-28-1865)
WOODS, BENJAMIN F. TO MARTHA PHILIPS 8-22-1855 (RETURNS MIXED UP
WOODS, G. D. TO MISS MARY J. CUMMINS 2-10-1871 (NO RETURN)
WOODS, GEORGE TO CLASSIE WOODLEY 8-20-1869
WOODS, J. K. P. TO MISS R. M. WINNET 11-8-1866 (SOLEMNIZED, NO DATE)
WOODS, M. F. TO G. D. PRATOR
WOODS, MARTHA J. TO WILLIAM T. HART
WOODS, MARY TO BRIST LILLARD
WOODS, NATHAN T. TO MISS MARGARETT PHILIPS 10-15-1857
WOODS, NATHAN TO MISS KESSIAH PRATER 11-19-1844
WOODS, SUSAN TO ROBERT ROBERSON
WOODS, THOMAS J. TO MISS C. E. EVANS 8-3-1853
WOODS?, ELIZABETH TO JOHN R. HENEBREW
WOODSIDE, MARY TO JOHN SEAL
WOODSIDE, SARAH ELIZABETH TO G. M. D. WATSON

WOOTON, J. M. TO MISS M. LOGAN 12-16-1866
WORLEY, ARTHUR TO MISS MARY UNDERWOOD 1-15-1869 (1-17-1869)
WORLEY, ARTHUR TO MISS SARAH SUMMERS 5-9-1870 (5-10-1870)
WORLEY, CLARK D. TO MISS SARAH HANEY 6-18-1870 (6-19-1870)
WORLEY, D. B. TO MISS E. A. EVANS 10-13-1870 (10-16-1870)
WORLEY, ISAAC C. TO ROXANAH JONES 7-8-1869
WORLEY, LEROY TO DIANNA THOMPSON 3-26-1864 (3-27-1864)
WORLEY, LEVISA TO WILLIAM THOMPSON
WORLEY, MARTHA TO MARK L. UNDERWOOD
WORLEY, MATILDA P. TO L. T. CUMMINS
WORLIEN, ELISABETH TO PHILLIP WEBBER
WRATHER, FARMER D. TO MISS ELIZABETH BROWN 2-15-1849
WRIGHT, ETTA TO ALLEN ARMSTRONG
WRIGHT, J. D. TO MARTHA PEOPLE 10-2-1872
WRIGHT, JOSEPH TO LOUISA MCFERRIN 8-23-1865 (9-3-1865)
WRIGHT, LUCY TO JESSE WOOD
WRIGHT, T. R. TO REBECCA A. DUNCAN 7-10-1873 (NO RETURN)
WRIGHT, WILLIAM B. TO MISS SUSAN J. MARTIN 3-1-1850 (3-3-1850)
WRON, ELIZAETH TO DAVID LAMBERTH
WYLY, NANCY S. TO OWEN DUNKIN
YEARWOOD, D. B. TO MISS NANCY A. MITCHELL 7-24-1869 (7-27-1869)
YONG, DELPHA TO JOSEPH BOWREN
YONG, JOSEPH TO MISS ADALIN CURNNAY 12-22-1852 (1-3?-1852)
YONG, MARLING TO MISS LUIZA VINSON 12-13-1853
YONG, MARRY J. TO ALFORD REID
YONG, MARTHA A. TO E. H. MITCHEL
YONG, MATILDA J. TO W. C. MCGLOTHLIN
YONG, SAMUEL TO MISS SARAH JANE MURPHY 9-10-1859 (NO RETURN)
YONG, SARAH TO BENJAMIN WHITT
YONG, SARAH TO F. THOMPSON
YONG, TILFORD M. TO MISS NANCY V. ALLEN 11-16-1859 (NO RETURN)
YONG, WM. H. TO MISS MERAN L. GAITHER 1-13-1857
YORK, ANTNEY TO MILLIA BLAIRE 7-29-1870 (NO RETURN)
YORK, ELIZA TO JONATHAN T. BLAIN
YORK, ELIZABETH TO JAMES HIGGINS
YORK, J. N. TO MARTHA A. MARKUM 12-17-1864 (NO RETURN)
YORK, JONATHAN TO MISS MARIAH LASETER 2-12-1868 (2-16-1868)
YORK, SI TO ELLEN RUSHING 5-16-1872
YORK, SYRILDA TO ISAAC FOSTER
YOUNG, ALEXANDER TO MISS MARY ASHFORD 4-6-1843 (NO RETURN)
YOUNG, C. TO JOHN ALEXANDER
YOUNG, CAROLINE TO ALLEN BOGLE
YOUNG, CHARITY TO BERRY COOPER
YOUNG, DORA TO WILLIAM CAMPBEL
YOUNG, E. J. TO JOSEPH N. CARRICK
YOUNG, E. J. TO MISS LOUISA A. MAZY 10-20-1869 (NO RETURN)
YOUNG, E. M. TO MISS A. C. BOGLE 12-14-1870
YOUNG, ELIZABETH TO JAMES PRESTON
YOUNG, ELIZABETH TO WILLIAM J. HALL
YOUNG, FELLING M. TO TERESA SUMMERS 4-19-1855 (RETURNS MISSING)
YOUNG, J. C. TO SUSAN SUMMERS 12-20-1872 (NO RETURN)
YOUNG, J. M. TO SARRAH URSERY 12-20-1855
YOUNG, JAMES H. TO MISS MARTHA E. PRESTON 8-10-1867 (8-11-1867)
YOUNG, JANE TO JOHN HAMMON
YOUNG, JANE TO THOMAS RIGSBY
YOUNG, JOHN A. TO STACY C. ELKINS 11-23-1842
YOUNG, JOHN TO MRS. JANE MULLINS 6-23-1870
YOUNG, M. A. TO J. W. WALKUP
YOUNG, MARGARET TO JAMES A. THOMPSON
YOUNG, MARGARETT J. TO W. W. MAZEY

YOUNG, MARK L. TO MISS LOCKY JANE TODD 9-20-1848
YOUNG, MARTHA E. TO JAMES B. MULLINS
YOUNG, MARTHA TO ALLEN HALEY
YOUNG, MARTHA TO BURTON L. MCFERRIN
YOUNG, MARY A. TO R. T. DANIEL
YOUNG, MARY CAROLINE TO LEROY LAFAYETTE ELKINS
YOUNG, MARY TO JAMES PRESTON
YOUNG, NANCY EMALINE TO JOHN DAVIS
YOUNG, NANCY FRANCES TO SILAS H. YOUNG
YOUNG, NANCY T. TO JOHN J. HAMMONS
YOUNG, R. A. TO J. T. BELL
YOUNG, R. E. TO J. B. MULLINS
YOUNG, RUTH TO WILLIAM H. PARTEN
YOUNG, SAMUEL TO MISS SARAH JETTON 1-13-1868 (1-14-1868)
YOUNG, SAMUEL TO SARAH MULLINS 7-22-1864 (NO RETURN)
YOUNG, SARAH A. TO WM. RIGSBY
YOUNG, SARAH F. TO T. A. CARRICK
YOUNG, SARAH TO WILLIAM FERRELL
YOUNG, SENA TO H. B. WILSON
YOUNG, SILAS H. TO MISS NANCY FRANCES YOUNG 2-5-1868 (2-13-1868)
YOUNG, W. E. TO MISS LIDY E. MORGAN 12-21-1870 (NO RETURN)
YOUNG, WILLIAM TO MARTHA BURKET 12-18-1864 (NO RETURN)
YOUNG, WILLIAM TO MISS JANE LITTRELL 10-9-1841 (10-10-1841)
YOUNG, WM. H. TO NANCY E. PRESTON 1-5-1864 (1-7-1864)
YOUNG, WM. TO SALINDA PARTON 8-31-1872 (9-1-1872)
YOUNG, YOUFFEY TO BENJAMIN F. ALLEN
YOUNGBLOOD, A. J. TO MISS ELIZABETH J. VASSER 5-21-1867
YOUNGBLOOD, ANDREW TO MISS RACHELL J. ELKINS 4-22-1857
YOUNGBLOOD, ARCHELAUS TO MISS NANCY E. HOOPER 10-5-1846 (10-6-1846)
YOUNGBLOOD, G. W. TO MISS M. E. TURNER 11-3-1870
YOUNGBLOOD, J. H. TO MISS S. A. WEST 12-21-1870 (12-22-1870)
YOUNGBLOOD, JAMES F. TO MISS N. T. HOLLANDWORTH 12-7-1859 (NO RETURN)
YOUNGBLOOD, JAMES H. TO MISS ELIZABETH C. JONES 12-21-1843 (EXECUTED SAME DAY?)
YOUNGBLOOD, JONNATHAN TO MISS MARY THOMAS 4-20-1871
YOUNGBLOOD, M. F. TO JOHN FOWLER
YOUNGBLOOD, M. J. TO R. A. YOUNGBLOOD
YOUNGBLOOD, NANCY ANNE TO WILLIAM SPIZER
YOUNGBLOOD, POLLY TO JAMES HOOPER
YOUNGBLOOD, R. A. TO M. J. YOUNGBLOOD 9-2-1860
YOUNGBLOOD, WM. TO MISS PARILEE V. THOMPSON 9-22-1870
YOUREE, G. C. TO NANCY E. LASETER 2-1-1860 (NO RETURN)
YOUREE, W. E. TO R. R. CARTER 11-13-1873
YOUREE, W. H. TO MISS M. L. HOLLIS 2-13-1860 (2-14-1860)
YOURIE, S. M. TO MISS M. F. WALKUP 1-16-1867
ZUMBRO, ELIZABETH S. TO L. M. S. BIVINS

www.ingramcontent.com/pod-product-compliance
Lightning Source LLC
Chambersburg PA
CBHW071059090426
42737CB00013B/2383